CRAFT CORPS

CRAFT CORPS

*Celebrating the Creative Community
One Story at a Time*

Vickie Howell

LARK BOOKS

A Division of Sterling Publishing Co., Inc.

New York / London

Library of Congress Cataloging-in-Publication Data

Howell, Vickie.
  Craft corps : celebrating the creative community one story at a time / Vickie Howell. -- 1st ed.
      p. cm.
    Includes index.
    ISBN 978-1-60059-468-7 (pb-pbk. with flaps : alk. paper)
    1. Handicraft--Miscellanea. 2. Artisans. I. Title.
    TT157.H694 2010
    745.5--dc22

                                    2009032650

10 9 8 7 6 5 4 3 2 1

First Edition

Published by Lark Books, A Division of
Sterling Publishing Co., Inc.
387 Park Avenue South, New York, NY 10016

Text © 2010, Vickie Howell
Interviews © 2010, Sterling Publishing Co., Inc.
Photography © 2010, Artist/Photographer as specified
Illustrations © 2010, Lark Books, a Division of
Sterling Publishing Co., Inc., unless otherwise specified

Distributed in Canada by Sterling Publishing,
c/o Canadian Manda Group, 165 Dufferin Street
Toronto, Ontario, Canada M6K 3H6

Distributed in the United Kingdom by GMC Distribution Services,
Castle Place, 166 High Street, Lewes, East Sussex,
England BN7 1XU

Distributed in Australia by Capricorn Link (Australia) Pty Ltd.,
P.O. Box 704, Windsor, NSW 2756 Australia

Every effort has been made to ensure that all the information in this book is accurate. However, due to differing conditions, tools, and individual skills, the publisher cannot be responsible for any injuries, losses, and other damages that may result from the use of the information in this book.

If you have questions or comments about this book, please contact:
Lark Books
67 Broadway
Asheville, NC 28801
828-253-0467

Manufactured in China

ISBN 13: 978-1-60059-468-7

For information about custom editions, special sales, premium and corporate purchases, please contact Sterling Special Sales Department at 800-805-5489 or specialsales@sterlingpub.com.

For information about desk and examination copies available to college and university professors, requests must be submitted to academic@larkbooks.com. Our complete policy can be found at www.larkbooks.com.

Dedication

For my wee Clover, whose creative spirit I promise to nurture forever and always. I love you, baby girl.

Senior Editor: *Valerie Shrader*

Assistant Editor: *Gavin Young*

Art Director: *Kristi Pfeffer*

Production: *Kay Stafford*

Cover Designer: *Chris Bryant*

Transcription services provided by:
Janessa Lloyd
Stephanie Tiddens
Erin Myrdahl
Sheila Yates-Vuu
Noelle Cocoran
Dawn Anderson

Contents

Introduction

I've been fortunate to make a career from crafting, and one of the greatest gifts it has given me is a sense of true community. I've been privileged to meet (either virtually or in person) thousands of fellow crafters as a result of my profession. Because of craft, I share an amazing connection with people all over the world—people of different backgrounds, religions, philosophies, and creeds. I likely would've never met or communicated with many of these folks had it not been for our common bond as creative beings and the explosion in the popularity of crafting. So I take great pride in presenting *Craft Corps*, a celebration of our unique community.

VH

This project was inspired by *StoryCorps*, the audio project heard on National Public Radio that collects and archives stories told by folks like you and me. The conversations within these pages are the result of 30 interviews I had the pleasure of conducting with some of the most influential designers in the craft industry. They include groundbreaking veterans Carol Duvall and Mary Engelbreit; knitting mavens Shannon Okey and Jessica Marshall Forbes; collage artists Traci Bautista and Claudine Hellmuth; clothing designers Mark Montano and Jay McCarroll; and indie pioneers Leah Kramer and Faythe Levine—each sharing what I call their "craftography."

The Craftographies

Every entry includes some personal history, some philosophy, and some advice; our discussions covered everything from childhood memories to favorite curse words (\$#^&!), and each offers some insight about designing and making cool things for a living. As you read through their craftographies, you'll see that

many of the interviewees have strikingly varied backgrounds. Some went to grad school and have advanced degrees; others barely made it through high school and are self-taught creatives. They were brought up on farms, in wealthy suburbs, and in busy cities.

On the flip side, though, you'll find some fascinating common threads: Sandi Genovese and Jenny Hart were accomplished artists as children; Denyse Schmidt and Cathie Filian have fond memories of creative fathers and grandfathers who made them dollhouses; Ed Roth and Travis Nichols both ran art galleries—it's gratifying to see how much commonality we all share. One of the most striking threads running through the craftographies is the notion that everyone is inherently creative, and how important the sheer act of creating *anything* is. We talked about many other things, of course, such as the rise of the DIY culture, and the importance of the Internet and social networking communities in making that happen. In the late '70s, my mom used to try to make a little extra income for our family by selling her handmade pillows door to door; think how different it could've been for her if there had been online shops like Etsy to sell her wares internationally, or social networking sites like Facebook and Twitter to promote her business. We're lucky to be a part of the exciting changes that have helped many crafters find financial freedom and fostered the amazing community I explore in this book.

The Profiles

But wait—there's more! Profiles of another 60+ recreational and under-the-radar professional crafters are sprinkled throughout, giving you a glimpse of our wonderfully diverse community that includes military men turned woodworkers, pre-teens who knit to raise money for charity, professional architects turned professional crafters, and baby-boomers who craft while caring for their elderly parents. The *Craft Corps* movement is even bigger than this book, too. I've been collecting and sharing stories on a dedicated website for over a year now. So in addition to the craftographies and profiles you'll find here, check out www.craftcorps.org for an even greater view into our crafty world. Staying connected with these people who are truly passionate about their craft, be they hobbyist or professional, inspires me on a daily basis. This community is something I value greatly, and as a voice in the creative industry I want to help nurture and sustain it for you and other crafty compadres out there.

I WANT YOU for CRAFT CORPS

The Evolution of Craft

This project is the next step in craft evolution for me. Writing it was such a great experience! I was pregnant with my daughter, Clover, during all of the six-month interviewing process. There was something so satisfying about being on the phone conducting interviews with people like *CRAFT*'s Natalie Zee Drieu, who was simultaneously running a Web magazine, answering my questions, and pacing to soothe her own baby. It just felt so uniquely...*now* to be interacting with other professionals who are juggling work and family, yet staying in touch with their creativity. We seem to be in a very interesting space where people can, in a real sense, do it all. Many of the stories you'll find here—from hobbyist and professional— certainly attest to that.

I hope that *Craft Corps* will be a jumping off point for people to relate to each other, craft together, and especially be inspired by each other. To quote Oprah, "Everyone has a story," and *Craft Corps* (both on these pages and through the website) shares some of ours with the world. I bet you'll find a little of yourself in each one of them.

Craft Corps: A book. A blog. A community. A movement. *Tell your story!* **Log on to www.craftcorps.org to fill out your own crafty profile.**

Name: Vickie Howell
Age: 35
Digs: Austin, TX
Daily Grind: designer, writer, and crafty spokesperson
Fave Crafts: knitting, crocheting, sewing, embroidery, repurposing, and general crafts
More Info: www.craftcorps.org and www.vickiehowell.com

My Craftography

Crafts have
always been
a part of my life.
Before I was born, my mother
would frequently invite all of the kids from
the block over to the house for craft sessions. She's a
teacher both by nature and profession, so this set-up worked out well
for everyone.

By the time I finally came along, my mom was primed and ready for mother-daughter craft time, so as soon as I was old enough to hold a glue stick—literally—we started making things. I remember when I was five or so, my friend Amy and I wanted to play traffic cop (which in hindsight seems a wee bit strange, but whatever). We had lollipop whistles, but needed Stop and Go signs, so mom helped us make them out of Popsicle sticks and construction paper. We lived in this sleepy little suburb of Denver that was filled with kids, so the neighborhood adults were prepared for childhood antics. They willingly stopped their cars when they saw us holding up our signs from the sidewalk, and they wouldn't accelerate until we flipped them to Go. Encouraged by this crafty success, my playtime started to always include making things, and a year or two later I moved from paper and glue to cloth and thread.

My mom used to make most of my clothes, with matching ensembles for my Rub-a-Dub-Dolly. When I was seven, I decided I wanted to give doll dressmaking a whirl myself. I remember tracing around one of Dolly's other dresses onto two pieces of seersucker, cutting them out, and then hand sewing them together. Later, I moved on to a doll quilt, made from Mom's fabric scraps and hand tied with yarn.

And so it began. Unbeknownst to either my mom or me, the groundwork was being laid for what would be my future career. We made Christmas ornaments out of bread dough, crocheted

My mom and me in 1976. She made our outfits.

blankets, punch-embroidered wall hangings, sewed pillows, painted wooden shelves, stamped cards, re-upholstered couch cushions, braided ribbon barrettes, latch-hooked rugs, embroidered shirts; you name it. If it was crafty, we did it! We crafted because we loved it, but often because we had to. We never had much money to spare so we didn't have a choice; we had to be creative. My mom encouraged me to give handmade gifts to my friends, something that I was sometimes embarrassed by as a kid but later realized the value in—those gifts made me feel special and I hope the recipients felt that way, too.

I asked all the interviewees if there was one moment that stood out for them as they grew up crafty. I'm not sure that there was any special moment for me personally, but all the hours that I spent with my mom creating things really made an impression on me. It was empowering, knowing that we could make things ourselves. It created a lasting bond.

The moment that stands out for me professionally is much more definite, however. Shooting the very first episode of the national television show I hosted for eight seasons, *Knitty Gritty*, will forever be embedded in my mind. It was so crazy! I had always wanted a craft show, but really, who gets that?! There I was, though, standing in a soundstage on a studio lot, with knitting needles in my hands and all eyes and cameras on me. It was pretty bizarre...and fantastic. That was certainly a turning moment for what crafting could be for me. Not only a vehicle of necessity, nor merely something to feed my creative soul, crafting could also be a livelihood!

My friend Jamie and me, holding clothespin reindeer we made. My mom made the barrettes in my hair and ironed my name on my hoodie. It's probably around 1982.

I should back up a bit, though. Before getting the job hosting *Knitty Gritty*, there were a few years of crafty self-discovery for me. After the birth of my oldest son I found myself a stay-at-home mom. The hard-core career I was working toward in the entertainment industry had been put on the back burner. Suddenly and purely defined as a mother, I didn't have that creative outlet and sense of professional accomplishment that was just for me. At the time there was no such thing as Etsy or these little boutiques where you could find funkier, cooler baby stuff, so I started making fun and affordable snapsuits, retro-inspired hooded towels, and leopard-print tote bags with sippy-cup pockets. I also made maternity clothes with unexpected, rock star-esque fabrics and put everything up for sale on a website, Mamarama, that my best friend's husband built for me. I didn't have much money, so my dad invested $500 and my mom bought the rest of my supplies.

Several of us were venturing into this brave new world of Internet shops. Kathy Cano-Murillo was starting Crafty Chica; Jenny Hart had begun Sublime Stitching; and Jennifer Perkins created Naughty Secretary Club. We got to know each other and also promoted our businesses through swapping links. Meeting this bunch of really creative, amazing women has proven invaluable to me. Through all of the link swapping and networking we did to promote our businesses, we met the ladies who would start the Austin Craft Mafia—a group of us crafty businesswomen who decided that united, we could be a much larger force to be reckoned with than if we were on our own. (This is another theme you'll read about in the craftographies.) Simultaneously I sought out community and camaraderie to nurture my new(ish)-found passion: knitting. I started the first Los Angeles-based Stitch 'n Bitch group, then did the same when I moved to Austin. Although these little projects of mine may have seemed like no big deal in and of themselves, they were all building blocks for what I get to do today for a living.

I created a logo for the Stitch 'n Bitch group and because of that, the *Knitty Gritty* producers where able to find me. The director of development, Alessandra Ascoli (who incidentally is engaged to crafter Dave Lowe, profiled on page 206), Googled some of the same terms I had listed in the logo's tag line and then e-mailed me. I will never forget the moment I read that e-mail. I was barefoot in the kitchen with my laptop on the counter as I was making dinner. The e-mail said that Screen Door Entertainment was looking for a young, hip knitter to host a television show, and did I know anyone who might be interested in auditioning? My heart started racing. I couldn't believe it—I mean, this was my dream job! How was it that I lived in L.A. and worked in the entertainment industry for years, but it was as a mom in Texas that this opportunity practically served itself to me on a plate?

This also happened to be the time that I had my very first knitting design—a guitar strap—published on Knitty.com. I called Alessandra and pitched myself, filling her in on my background behind the camera, telling her to pull up my design on Knitty.com so she could see what I look like and prove that I did, in fact, know how to knit. It was like everything I had done over the past three years was leading up to that moment. She asked me if I was willing to fly myself to L.A. to audition (which is a testament to how saaaad the budgets in cable programming are). I guess the stars were perfectly aligned, because I already had a ticket to be there just two days later as part of a trip I'd been planning for a year to celebrate my 30th birthday. It was unbelievable! I knew then that even if I didn't get the hosting job that something had to come out of this whole thing, because everything had just laid itself out too perfectly for it not to. Fortunately, I got the gig. Ever since, I've felt an obligation to make the absolute most of that opportunity. I was given a gift and there was no way I was going to waste it, so I immediately started working on getting book deals, speaking engagements, and developing products.

In a way, my life has come full circle, because crafting has been one of the few constants in my life. Whether I made baby blankets with my mom, plastic fork recipe holders in Girl Scouts, gifts for friends in junior high, or wore a handmade outfit to my high school graduation, crafting has helped me find balance. It allowed me to create things for my kids as my mom had for me, and provided me with a career. It kept me going during a painful divorce. It lets me work from home so that I can be here for my children. Crafting constantly evolves with me, and it has been a great source of strength for me, too.

My first quilt, made when I was about nine.

chapter one

Amy Butler

I've been a fan of Amy's

vintage-inspired fabrics for years, so I was thrilled when she accepted my request for an interview. I'd never met her before this phone conversation, but found her to be so delightful that I hope we'll keep in touch for years to come. Her laid-back Midwestern demeanor, coupled with her whip-smart business sense, makes you want to both invite her over for dinner and take a class from her. Fabric designer, author, and entrepreneur, Amy's an inspiration for all aspiring artists and crafters, because she not only followed her passion and became extraordinarily successful, she also stayed true to herself while doing it! I dig that.

VH

VH: *What's your first craft-related memory?*

AB: I have a couple of significant memories, but one that's kind of fun is that my grandma used to keep me stocked with fabric at all times. She gave me a big bag of fabric after she made halter-tops for my sister and me—I was really inspired by that. I didn't know how to sew yet, but I had glue paste in a little tub. I took the fabric she gave me, studied her halter-top, and cut out the same tops for my neighbor-friends who were on vacation that week. I glued together several snazzy outfits for them and was so proud that I left them in a cardboard box on their front porch. When they got home, they tried on the clothes and, of course, they fell apart, but my friends were really sweet. It's a really good memory. I didn't know how to sew, but I loved fabric. I was always surrounded by it.

VH: *Is there a moment from your childhood connected to craft (either directly or indirectly) that really stands out for you?*

AB: My mom and my grandmother would get together and make all kinds of stuff. I grew up in the '70s with dried flower arrangements and those little things called printer shelves (drawers that stored individual letters for letterpress printing). It was a popular collectible trend to find an old printer's shelf and make little things to put inside it—the shelves were great for displaying small kitschy items, found objects, or handmade pieces. I have all these memories of hanging out and decorating them with Mom and Grandma on rainy days. On the inside, we'd glue little dried straw flowers that Grandma grew in her garden, or we'd make miniature collages with found objects.

VH: *Did any of those survive? Are they still around?*

AB: My grandmother passed away six years ago, and my mom has a few of the little bits and pieces. I don't know who has the printer shelf, but it could be under my mom's bed. I will have to follow up with her on that, but I would love to get my hands on it.

VH: *Now, as a professional designer/crafter, is there an equally important moment for you?*

AB: It's every time I sit down and design, even with fabric and sewing patterns— it's like one of the purest moments. You're pulled in so many directions when your love of craft turns into a business. A lot of your energy shifts into being a businessperson, managing your work, or supervising the people who help you. Ironically, the hands-on craft time gets eaten away by all the other priorities. So, my favorite, strongest crafting memory as a professional is the pure, focused amount of creative time that gives me total pleasure.

VH: *Who, if anyone, do you credit for opening the crafty doors for you?*

AB: My mom and my grandma, for sure.

VH: *You mentioned making collages and working with found objects. Were other crafts done in your home?*

AB: That's the thing—they did everything. My grandmother was a prolific quilter. She also knitted, sewed garments, made curtains, pillows, and things for the house. She's kind of like a crafty MacGyver who could do anything. My mother is also artistic, and is now a quilter. So, I inherited my creativity gene from them. They also did rug hooking, macramé, flower drying, and decoupage. That was their joy and their time to have fun when they weren't raising kids and taking care of husbands.

VH: *You're most well known for your work in the sewing world, but are there other crafts you enjoy?*

AB: I love knitting, but I'm not an accomplished knitter.

VH: *I didn't know you knit!*

AB: I guess I have been knitting for six years. I'm pretty new at it. I've just graduated from scarves to hats.

VH: *Congratulations!*

AB: I have lots of good friends who love to knit, and a lot of us get together, drink wine, and chitchat. So, I really enjoy knitting, making jewelry, and beading. I do a little bit of paper crafting, too. I'm not really a scrapbooker, though. I enjoy creating scrapbook products and can appreciate it, but I don't have time in my life to really build albums.

VH: *There are so many supplies involved in scrapbooking!*

AB: It takes a lot of organization to keep all that stuff in a place where you can easily find it. I think it's cool. I just get wound up in all the little pieces. I prefer smaller projects like making cards more so than scrapbooking.

VH: *Has your card making influenced your line of stationery, or was that more directly a translation of your fabric design?*

AB: It's more directly a translation of the fabric design. I met my husband in art school, though, and we used to make cards, little artifacts, and art pieces. We would make mixed tapes for each other with elaborate handmade covers.

VH: *Although we've come leaps and bounds over the past decade, society still doesn't place much value on handicrafts, especially as related to a career. One of the many reasons I wanted to do this book was so that well-known, successful people like yourself could tell their stories in hopes of escalating that value. Please tell me a bit about how you took your passion for being creative and turned it into a business.*

AB: I've had to consolidate, but every experience is connected to the next one. I went to art school and graduated with a B.F.A., focusing on imaging and graphic design. I was hired by Hallmark Cards right out of school but was torn between two different job offers. I interviewed with Tahari Sportswear in New York City and Hallmark in Kansas. Hallmark was interested in illustrators, but they were also filling positions for a non-card-related division. My portfolio showed a lot of design work and was print intensive, and I think they saw that as a translation into their everyday occasion division of non-card products such as party goods and gift-wrap. I interviewed at both places but ended up going to Kansas City, because the New York gig was sort of a trial and error period. They wanted me to do a 90-day test run without a real salary, and they wanted me to live with a group of women that were working in the company.

> My style is very eclectic and has been inspired, for sure. My whole design vocabulary started when I was a little girl. Besides making everything, my mom and grandma were big antiquers. A great part of my childhood was spent in the rain at auctions looking at old stuff.

VH: *That's kind of creepy!*

AB: It is kind of creepy. I've never been driven by money, but I knew I had to stand up on my own two feet. My parents didn't have anything for me to fall back on. I couldn't take that risk. I grew up in a small town and thought Hallmark looked really good. I worked there for over four years, and after about two years into it, I wanted to switch to a different division.

I actually ended up in a business division with an art director role, but less hands-on. I developed products for party goods, invitations, and gift-wrap. I would translate my ideas to a studio artist, and we would create collections together. Essentially, I realized I wasn't a corporate person—there were 5,000 people on campus; it was very political; and I hardly had any creative time. It was more business-focused, but I appreciated that because I didn't get that kind of education in art school. It's come in handy ever since and was a real blessing, but I still remember having anxiety attacks and thinking, "Maybe this isn't for me."

I have been sewing all my life, even when I was working for Hallmark. On the side, I collected new and old fabrics and made bags, stuff for my house, and gifts for friends. I started a side gig where I made art-embellished bags that I sold at gift shops. Dave, my husband, was working as an art director in Kansas City at a small studio, and he encouraged me to quit my day job. We downsized, moved into a smaller place, and sold our car. I started working part-time as a receptionist at his design studio. I helped the office manager with accounts and learned about invoicing, which I started doing for us the next year with our own business. Deb Turpin, the owner there, said to take every Friday off so I could work on my business and my sewing. She explained that it's really good to do something for yourself and keep it going. Because she was so awesome, I try to do the same thing for the people that work for us. The pay-it-forward

concept was a good influence. We worked that way for a year and a half. Because our family was in Ohio, we decided to move home in 1992. We did some freelance graphic design work, and then we officially started our business, Art of the Midwest. We've been self-employed for 18 years now.

VH: *Congratulations, that's huge.*

AB: That's how it all got started. We took on any kind of freelance work we could get, and I simultaneously worked with some ex-Hallmarkers who were doing surface design. With one vehicle, I had to walk to my part-time job at an apple orchard. I picked apples during the day, painted at night, and had a couple days off during the week. Before I knew it, I was doing illustrations for Dave's graphic design jobs. Over the course of two or three years, I began illustrating full-time.

We ended up meeting some folks from *Country Living*—friends of ours had their house photographed, and they thought the editors would like to do a story about our house. *Country Living* came and photographed our place, and we hit it off with their team, creatively and editorially. We hadn't really done much story production, but they were really interested in the fact that we were artists and were always making things. They asked us to help them with stories that involved crafting or entertaining, which was right up our alley, so we became occasional contributing editors. After about two and a half years into our seven-year relationship, they found out about my fabric stash and sewing obsession. Readers of *Country Living* love to collect, and fabric is one of their main attractions. Nancy Merritt-Soriano, editor in chief at the time, wanted me to produce some stories, showing readers how to mix old fabric with new, and how to make things for the home. We thought it was important for readers to make a couple of the projects, so we ended up producing sewing patterns to sell through the magazine. I was inspired by my friend Nora Corbett, who is a cross-stitch designer and owns a company called Mirabilia Designs. She and her husband were producing and selling cross-stitch patterns, and she suggested I print up some sewing patterns to sell to the magazine. I actually licensed the *Country Living* name, which was my foray into licensing—my patterns were called Country Living Sewing Patterns by Amy Butler.

VH: *So they didn't license you—it was the other way around?*

AB: Correct, I licensed them.

VH: *Good for you. That's kind of brilliant.*

AB: They were so nice and made it very easy for me. They didn't need a minimum guarantee. I didn't have any advance money or anything. They just wanted reporting done a certain way, and they wanted me to provide updates on how things were going. I paid them my little $500 royalty payments each quarter. It lasted for a couple of years, but due to cost issues, they couldn't afford to inventory products anymore in a warehouse, so I stopped selling through the magazine. Readers kept requesting patterns, so people from *Country Living* encouraged me to sell them on the side. I had no idea on how to get it going, so I asked around at some local quilt shops and fabric stores, and they said to go to Quilt Market.

The next spring I set up my first booth at Quilt Market with a total of five sewing patterns. That was seven years ago and marks the beginning of my sewing pattern business. I met FreeSpirit Fabrics there, and a couple of other companies introduced themselves and invited me to design a fabric collection, which honestly had always been a dream of mine. Quilt Market was a real blessing, and Donna Welder, who owned FreeSpirit Fabrics, was a true visionary and was willing to take chances with different designers. Quilting was predominant at the time, and I was coming more from home décor and fashion, so my patterns were more accessory-based. I had the opportunity to do the fabric line for FreeSpirit, and that spring, my first collection, Gypsy Caravan, launched. Ever since, there's been a great connection between the fabric and the sewing patterns because one helps support the other.

VH: *Drafting patterns for sewing is definitely a skill set. Is that something that you gained from art school or kind of learned on the fly?*

AB: I kind of just winged it. I had some pattern-drafting experience, but it was more garment-focused. I didn't like technical construction sewing when I was in college, so I would scrap the pattern and just sew from scratch. I made things up as I went along, and that's how I developed the pattern. I just used common sense; I drew shapes out flat and experimented with seam allowances. I was able to get the desired effect—it comes from sewing all my life and having technical guidance in college.

VH: *What is it about fabric design, specifically, that speaks to you creatively?*

AB: I think it's a combination of pattern and color. It's the story you tell when you put all the right prints and all the right colors together. I love color, and I love print.

> I picked apples during the day, painted at night, and had a couple days off during the week. Before I knew it, I was doing illustrations for some of Dave's graphic design jobs. Over the course of two or three years, I began illustrating full-time.

VH: *Your design style has the recognizable, signature look of someone who appreciates merging the old with the new. How would you define your style, and how has it evolved since you started your first studio in the '80s?*

AB: My style is very eclectic and has been inspired, for sure. My whole design vocabulary started when I was a little girl, because of the household I lived in. I always liked a combination of modern and vintage, but I think my taste evolved over the years. I get excited about architecture and stylings from different periods. I really get excited about combining a lot of unexpected details from different eras and bringing it all together with modern color, modern scale, and the actual application of fabric. I have always been a vintage/modern kind of girl, but not 100 percent one or the other. I think *Midwest Modern*, which is the name of my book, is a good description, but it's not necessarily where you live that defines your aesthetic. I was raised in a rural environment, but I really gravitate towards beautiful designs. I guess you could call it corn-fed design!

VH: *Corn-fed contemporary.*

You've been really smart in marketing your products by encouraging shop owners to create kits from your patterns and fabrics. Has it benefited you to get retailers actively involved in the presentation of your products?

AB: It's the key ingredient. Collaboration makes everything successful. Retailers have brilliant ideas; they know how to market; and they know what their customers are looking for. I think it's important to hear about their needs. At the same time, I share my ideas with them and tell them what I have up and coming, and they give me valuable feedback. The partnership is about relationship-building, enjoying whom you collaborate with, and having open communication.

VH: *Just from a business view, it gets them invested in your product.*

AB: Oh yes, they're like kids in a candy store. Retailers never tire of new ideas, and they never stop getting excited. As long as I can keep them excited, and as long as they want to do creative things with the fabric or offer suggestions, we'll continue working together.

VH: *That is so anti-corporate and brilliant, I have to say.*

AB: I think it's a fine line. I think there are processes and things you can learn from corporations, but this is a handmade business. People working with their hands experience a process of happiness and pleasure. You can't put that into a file folder, or organize it, or categorize it—you've got to let it be its own thing; otherwise, it wouldn't be any fun. Business is necessary, along with its processes and policies, but those things can't define a craft business.

VH: *Sewing, as a trend, experienced a long dry spell in popularity. Although the*

> Retailers never tire of new ideas, and they never stop getting excited. As long as I can keep them excited, and as long as they want to do creative things with the fabric or offer suggestions, we'll continue working together.

overflowing fabric stores that were around when I was a kid are now few and far between, sewing, itself, is experiencing a resurgence. What's different, do you think, about this wave of stitchers from the last?

AB: It's interesting, and I really can't quantify this, but I don't think the spirit behind crafting is different at all. I think maybe the intensity and passion might be turned up a few notches. I think about what women's lives might have been like a long time ago. The world is a very different place now. A lot of us raising our families have a passion for craft and might even want to start a small business. That's a lot to balance. In almost every household, both partners have to work. When I was growing up, my mom and grandmother didn't work, and women crafted for the joy and pleasure of it, but it wasn't a stolen moment. Now, I think women and men who craft have even more passion for it, because it's their sole outlet; it's their stress reliever. It adds so much meaning to life and helps them define it. Crafting is not just a pastime, it's soul food.

VH: *Do you think that's why the simpler, quicker projects have become so popular? I remember my mom laying out a plaid blazer where she had to match the patterns, and it took forever. That would never happen in our lives now, but we can do a purse.*

AB: That's so true. I've watched folks' interests in patterns, and beginner patterns are the most popular. My number-one selling pattern is my easy Birdie Sling bag.

VH: *Sewing has a strong history of perpetuating community through sewing circles. Now that the days of village women spending hours together are gone, how do you see the modern-day sewing community being nourished?*

AB: I think it just gets stronger and stronger. Everybody's ability to connect through craft blogs, sewing blogs, and the Internet is phenomenal. I think sewing has exploded because people have so much access to inspiration, information, and education. If you think about it, when we were growing up in school, we had home economics, sewing, and art classes. Now girls aren't getting that. Women in their 30s possibly could have gone through a curriculum where they didn't get any sewing at all. I think it's phenomenal to see the energy flying around with people connecting and making things. It's so inspiring, and you feel even more connected because you're not alone or in an isolated world, sewing by yourself. You may not have the time to go to a meeting, but you can get on your computer at midnight and talk to people all over the world who might be trying the same pattern.

VH: *On a humanity level, it's a way to connect with people you wouldn't necessarily have anything in common with. I know through knitting and crocheting that I have dear friends all over the United States who have nothing in common with me on the surface, but once I delve in I realize this person has a similar sense of humor, and we both love this or love that—even though we have completely different styles. It's a great icebreaker, in a way.*

> What I love about women working from home who craft is that they're accomplishing three things in one. It affords them the satisfaction of making something, earns them a little extra income, and allows them to be at home with their children.

19

AB: It is an amazing unifier. It's a great symbol of how connected people are, and we don't realize it. It's such a positive connection that reinforces good stuff in everybody's lives. To be able to share that experience, whatever piece you can, just creates more good energy.

VH: *Do you actively participate in the online craft community?*

AB: I don't have time. I don't usually have the luxury of looking around and joining a chat, and things like that, but I do write blog contributions. I sometimes connect directly with people in specific sewing circles, groups, or blogs, but I don't explore much on my own or research. I wish I had more personal time to spend in blogland—the ideas are amazing.

VH: *Is there anything else you'd like to say about what crafting means to you?*

AB: It's probably the biggest gift I have in my life, because it's allowed me to live in a world of no limits. That may sound kind of hokey pokey, but craft is a creative effort, it's a creative force, a creative energy. It's always been a part of my life, but it never stays the same. Doors are always opening in different ways so that craft weaves in and around my life. It just keeps getting better. I feel blessed that I can actually make my livelihood based on the thing that means the most to me. I get to be artistic in how I make a living, and that's priceless. I can't imagine another life, and I can't imagine what it's going to be like next month, next year, or in the next two years. Unlike a corporate job where I have a specific role, I am not defined by one specific thing, and craft allows you that flexibility and satisfaction. It's the gift that keeps on giving!

For more information about Amy and her projects, go to:
www.amybutlerdesign.com

The Crafter's Studio

In the great tradition of *Inside the Actor's Studio* and James Lipton:

What craft sound or smell do you love?
I actually love the smell of fresh printing on a box of sewing patterns.

What craft sound or smell do you hate?
The sound of my sewing machine jamming up.

What career, other than quilt-world domination, would you like to try?
Master gardener.

When you break your machine or slice yourself with a rotary cutter, what is your favorite exclamation?
Sh@tballs.

Name: Jenna Lou Dauer
Age: 20
Digs: North Mankato, MN
Fave Crafts: SEWING!
More Info: jennalou.typepad.com

Words to Craft by:

Adults always ask what you want to do when you grow up. They point you in the direction of notable careers like doctor, teacher, or lawyer. Go to college. Get a degree. Work in a comfortable, secure job (usually one that entitles you to a desk and three collapsible walls). I was lucky. I was gently told these things, but I was also told to pursue my real passion, for life is nothing without passion. For the longest time, I didn't know what that was. I worked in awful jobs for awful people, until I found sewing. Being behind a sewing machine gave me the power to be someone new, to create and design, and to be free. It started as a hobby but soon turned into a full-time love affair. Then it became a way to support myself. Finding this craft has been a blessing. I want to share it with the world and show that you can unlock joy by following your dreams.

Name: Claudia Freitas
Age: 41
Digs: Rio de Janeiro, Brazil
Daily Grind: librarian
Fave Crafts: patchwork, knitting, sewing, and testing around a bit of everything
More Info: infinitadiversidade.blogspot.com

Words to Craft by:

My best friend left Brazil to marry a Dutch man, and now she has a three-year-old daughter. They were at my house visiting last January, and I took the opportunity to try making a dress for the little one. It was taking a bit more work than expected, so I stopped for us to go to a movie, and I left the pinned-up dress on the table. My little client wasn't happy; she wanted to wear the dress that day, so she picked it up from the table and ran to her mother asking to wear the dress to the movie. I was biting my nails because the dress was full of pins, and I was afraid she would hurt herself. No amount of talk would resolve this situation, so I sat at the sewing machine with the little girl standing at my side, watching my every move. Talk about pressure! I felt like I was in a *Project Runway* challenge! But I finished the dress. It gave me a very warm feeling to see something I made being so well-received and liked.

chapter two

Cathie Filian

I've known Cathie for years.

We originally met at a publishing party in Vegas, but it was our time spent together as part of the DIY Network family that really made us close. Cathie is most well-known as the Emmy-nominated co-host (alongside her crafty partner-in-crime, Steve Piacenza) of TV's *Creative Juice*, but is also a prolific designer, author, and spokesperson for Mod Podge. She's a trusted colleague, a respected businesswoman, and a great friend. Oh, and she's a redhead, so she's got to be special!

VH

VH: *What's your first craft-related memory?*

CF: Definitely sewing with my grandmother. She was a big sewer. She was the one who got me in front of a sewing machine. The first thing I made was a pair of pajamas that she helped me with. She used to go to fabric stores and always drag me along, and she traveled a lot and always brought back these crazy, exotic fabrics.

Also, maybe a little bit before that, I remember making Christmas ornaments. That was also a big thing with my grandmother.

VH: *Was there anyone else crafty in your family?*

CH: My mom was pretty crafty, and my dad was pretty crafty too, although I don't know if he would call it that. He has a lot of tools and is *super* creative. He built a dollhouse for me with this amazing yellow vinyl flooring and shag carpet. He built the kitchen with 2 x 4s, then carved lines for the refrigerator and other things. I think everyone in my family has a little bit of the crafty gene, but everyone's *little bit* compounded in me.

VH: *Do you still have the pajamas you made?*

CF: I don't have the pajamas. What I do have is Lowly Worm. When I got the measles, I went to stay with a neighbor. I was so sick and my mom was working, so this woman took care of me. We had Richard Scarry's *Busiest Day Ever* book, from which we made a felted Lowly Worm. I still have it. I remember she didn't have enough stuffing, so she stuffed it with pantyhose instead. I think that was when I realized, "Oh, you can use whatever you want." Those memories definitely stick out.

VH: *You may have already answered this, but is there a moment from your childhood connected to craft that really stands out for you?*

CF: Yes. I have a summer birthday, so we never had a birthday party during the school year growing up. Lots of times my mom would try to organize some sort of party for me that wasn't necessarily a birthday party. For several years in a row, she threw valentine-making parties. She would cover the table with butcher paper in our formal dining room. All the little kids would get together with glitter and glue flying everywhere and make these valentines. It was all the girls from my classroom—girls, no boys! I almost think of it now as an old quilting bee, or a bunch of girls sitting around having a glass of wine, but we were these little kids making valentines and giggling about boys.

VH: *I love that—that's a great memory! Do you have a memory now, as a professional designer/crafter, that's an equally important moment for you?*

CF: Wow, it's so hard to choose one. I think, probably the first day of shooting the second season of *Creative Juice*. The second time, we didn't have any other companies attached to us, so we were really on our own. For me, there was such a sense of accomplishment because of that. The craft itself was actually a television show we were making. I remember thinking that our craft always came from the entertainment industry, and we were making our craft.

VH: *Do these very different moments hold the same weight of feeling within you?*

CF: They're totally different, but hold the same weight. I feel like as a kid, it was just so special to be able to get together with friends and make stuff, and so cool that my mom thought to come up with another way we could have a party that wasn't about celebrating a birthday.

VH: *That's such a great idea! I have a son whose birthday is five days before Christmas and another one whose is 12 days after, and it's the same challenge— they're not in school and everyone is so over everything celebratory. It would be a good idea for me to implement your mom's plan.*

Who, if anyone, do you credit for opening the crafty doors for you?

> All the little kids would get together with glitter and glue flying everywhere and make these valentines. It was all the girls from my classroom— girls, no boys! I almost think of it now as an old quilting bee, but we were these little kids making valentines and giggling about boys.

CF: My grandmother. I also had a really cool woodworking teacher in high school. I don't even remember his last name. We called him Mr. Phillip. I tried to figure out who he was so I could get back in contact with him and give him a little hello, but I can't find him to save my life without knowing his last name!

VH: *Because Googling Mr. Phillip doesn't work.*

CF: Right. I went to a kind of strict school. They didn't understand the concept that I wanted to take woodworking class. They had dissolved the home economics department, which is just so sad. I wanted to do something, though, besides taking another art class. The school just didn't think it was going to be cool to have a girl in the woodworking classroom.

VH: *Another way of saying that is: the school was very sexist!*

CF: Yes—they thought I might break a nail. I really wanted to learn how to use those tools, though! Mr. Phillip took the case to the principal, laid out how ridiculous they were being, and they listened to him. I was in the class for my junior and senior years. In my senior year, two more girls enrolled. I thought it was pretty cool that we shook up the woodworking classroom.

VH: *That was your first step towards defining your own creative pathway. Please tell me a bit about how you took your passion for being creative and turned it into a livelihood for yourself—and an Emmy award nomination!*

CF: I'd been in the film industry for 10 years doing costumes.

VH: *Did you go to school for costuming?*

CF: I actually went to school for textile science. With that degree, you basically go work for a textile company and develop new fabrics, or you go work for a designer. I did the fashion industry thing for a very short time. My first job was an internship for Betsey Johnson in New York City, and it was fabulous! I actually got to work directly with Betsey.

VH: *I want to do that now!*

CF: It was pretty fantastic. People who are familiar with her know that she designs most of her own fabrics, so that's where the internship was applicable to my degree. I loved it. The fashion industry, though, is just so much about sales. I hated all of that stuff and realized that it was not for me. From there, I twisted that experience into working with costumes. It kind of fell into my lap. I made some calls and within three days I'd found a job. I was doing costumes on a television show, and that's where I met Steve Piacenza, co-host of *Creative Juice.*

> I did the fashion industry thing for a very short time. My first job was an internship for Betsey Johnson in New York City, and it was fabulous! I actually got to work directly with Betsey.

We were complaining about the lack of creativity in our jobs—I was doing costumes, and he was in the art department. It seemed like we were always telling someone else's story. After a while, you want to write the story yourself.

We decided to get out of the film business and open up a store in Los Angeles that would feature handmade items and local artists' pieces. We had no money. We barely put any money into the business, and most of the stuff was on consignment. We also made stuff to sell there. People started to take notice of us sewing things on site to sell. We decided to start doing something called Handmade Happy Hour where we'd have wine and cheese and show people how to make things. Our hope was that they'd either

purchase the materials or the finished project. Nobody ever bought the materials; they always wanted the finished goods but were fascinated by watching us make them.

Right about that time, we were getting frustrated with crafts on television. There were not many shows. I don't even think *Knitty Gritty* was on yet. This was probably eight or nine years ago. *The Carol Duvall Show* (see page 50) and *The Martha Stewart Show* were on. They were both awesome shows, but completely different than what we were looking for. We wanted to come up with a concept that was not artist-driven, but more suitable for everyday crafters.

We realized how much people enjoy watching the creative process and hoped that, along the way, they would pick up a bottle of glue or buy some glitter to make things themselves. From there, we started talking about it more seriously, and we decided to do something to get more crafting on television.

We took $3,000 and our film know-how and shot a pilot. Well, sort of—we did it all wrong and didn't follow any of the rules. What we did right was to make the pilot look like a commercial. It looked like the show had been on for a year, and we were featuring highlights from it. We were dressed in holiday clothes for some segments; we shot on location, etc. A lot of agents told us how wrong we did it, but it landed on DIY Network's desk and they loved it! Within just a few months, we were in production. It was a crazy journey. Today, it's a full-time business for us. We've done 104 episodes of *Creative Juice*; we produced our Halloween show; and have received three Emmy nominations. We took this little tiny idea, and were able to see it through.

VH: *So exciting! You're a crafty Jill-of-all-trades. Is sewing the craft that speaks to you most creatively, or is there another craft?*

CF: Sewing is the craft I started with, and I love it, but I don't sew for myself anymore. That's the sad thing.

VH: *There's your new tagline: "It's a sad thing."*

CF: It's not a "good thing," it's a "sad thing." I do love making jewelry for myself and do it a lot because I feel like I don't have to explain my choices. When I get tired of the piece, I cut it up and make something new. I love altering clothes and making jewelry.

VH: *There's got to be a level of instant gratification with those things, as well.*

CF: That's the thing. What used to be such a hobby is now business. So, if I'm making something for a project, I'm thinking things like, "Oh, don't use lilac beads because you just used lilac yesterday." It becomes much more of a science and a business, as opposed to only expression. Whereas, if I'm doing something just for myself, I feel like I can be much looser with it.

VH: *What's your favorite thing about crafting?*

CF: I think it's making something that's really mine. It's hard to explain, but you can't buy it. It's not always right. It's not always pretty—but you did it. I think it's just the idea of being able to take something from your brain and explore it

through whatever medium you're working in. When it's finished and you love it, there's no greater feeling than that! It doesn't even matter if you get compliments on it or not.

VH: *But it sure helps!*

CF: It's lovely!

VH: *Over the years I've had the opportunity to meet a variety of crafters who are also musicians, writers, actors, graphic artists, etc. I've found that if people express themselves creatively in one way, they are likely interested in multiple forms of creativity. I believe that all things creative are linked together. Do you find that to be true for yourself?*

CF: Oh yes, absolutely! Just like when you said music—for me, when I pop in a CD or listen to my iPod—it all runs together. Also like making films—we make TV shows but are constantly coming up with film ideas that have nothing to do with craft. I think it's the same for men, but they may not recognize it all the time. I think back to college—every guy in a punk garage band was my boyfriend or a good friend. We would all sit around making posters and T-shirts. Would they call that being crafty? Hell no.

VH: *No, but musicians are so crafty because they have to be!*
What role, if any, has crafting played in your own sense of community? What outlet has enriched your own community the most?

CF: I'm lucky. In Los Angeles, we have a really big craft community. It's been fun getting to know the people here. There's this funny thing that people believe because you're on TV—that your e-mail isn't real or something—it's so far from that! People think it's much more glamorous than it really is. It's not. At all. You know that!

VH: *Oh, yeah. I once read a blog post that said, "That Vickie Howell's made of money!" I thought, "Oh lady, if only you knew. We get paid like minimum wage to make our shows. We basically get paid in glitter!"*

CF: I know! If only I'd planted that money tree. Dang it!
   L.A. is filled with people who are expressing themselves through music, acting, writing, photography, crafting, or whatever. Out here, it's pretty fun. Chances are, if you go to a party, you'll stand next to someone who's pretty creative.

VH: *Is there a particular outlet, either a group or online, that's helped the most with enriching your own community?*

CF: We just went to Felt Club, run by Jenny Ryan (see page 234), and it was a huge success. I was very happy to see all the different people selling their stuff.

"

It's almost like this beast has been unleashed. There are so many places in print and online where people get their information—they're swapping not just recipes, but craft instructions!

Organizations like that are really strong parts of the community. We also have a Los Angeles Craft Mafia and lots of workshops popping up all over the place. The scrapbooking and quilting communities are really big out here. Social networking websites such as MySpace, Facebook, and Flickr have been amazing, too! You'd be surprised how many people you find through these outlets who might live in your backyard and have similar interests, but you just never knew. Even though social networking is global, it's also a great resource for finding local community.

VH: *Community doesn't necessarily involve having people over for coffee. Community's more of a feeling, don't you think?*

CF: Absolutely.

VH: *You're in the rare position of not only being a professional crafter, but also a celebrity because of it. Do you see this reality as an example of how the industry and our society are evolving, or are people just paying more attention to what's always been there because of mass-media avenues like the Internet?*

CF: I think it goes in waves. It was big in the '80s; it died down in the '90s; now it's big again. I hope it doesn't die down again. I think the involvement of big business dies down, but I think the community is *so* strong now. I believe creative people (although they may change their medium from crochet to felted beads, etc.) will always be into *something* creative. It's almost like this beast has been unleashed. There are so many places in print and online where people get their information—they're swapping not just recipes, but craft instructions! There are so many places where people get their information for free, which I think is awesome.

I do feel like craft is here to stay. I think the trick is getting big businesses to believe it: networks, publishers, and large chain retailers. Those are the people shying away. I'm so sick of the word *craft* being treated as a dirty word. It's so not! There's still this feeling that crafting is just for grandmas.

VH: *It's crazy that feeling is still out there. The fervor of fighting against that stereotype has been so high for the past decade that it's like, "Really? You're still talking about that same, tired subject?"*

CF: I actually think it's getting worse. The other day, I was working on a network pitch and wanted the logo to incorporate a pair of scissors. I second-guessed using scissors because I thought the show would be pigeonholed as craft, even though the show has absolutely nothing to do with craft. That kind of stuff is really sad to me. Especially with the economy in the state it's in [in 2009].

VH: *That's what's so interesting, because the network we worked for ended up going all home improvement with their programming. It's crazy because nobody can afford to remodel their homes. It doesn't matter though, because big* companies will still sponsor those shows. There's no money in the craft industry to sponsor them, and that's the bottom line. Advertising.

Do you feel a sense of responsibility as a feminist woman in a traditionally female community to use your voice as a forum for progression within that community and beyond?

CF: Yes. The show really came with a whole new set of responsibilities. I don't think we knew that would be an aspect of our work when we started, but it's something I feel very strongly about and embrace as much as I can. I think it's important that we all support each other as much as possible, because that's how we'll stay strong.

VH: *Is there anything else you'd like to say about crafting?*

CF: If I had to choose one thing, I think it's important for people to just try it. I think people can be crafty in so many different ways: in cooking, in making things, whatever. I think it's really important for people to make a time and space for being creative. That space doesn't have to consume rooms, either. It can be just a box of supplies. Make time, though. It's so healthy for people to have quiet time making something.

For more information about Cathie and her projects, go to:
www.cathieandsteve.com

The Crafter's Studio

In the great tradition of *Inside the Actor's Studio* and James Lipton:

What craft sound or smell do you love?
Mod Podge.

What craft sound or smell do you hate?
I hate the "eeeeeeeeh" sound that metal on metal makes.

What career, other than craft-world domination, would you like to try?
I'd like to be a film director.

When you burn yourself with a glue gun or poke yourself with a sewing needle, what is your favorite exclamation?
Sh#t, sh#t, sh#t!

Words to craft by:

I have always had a yearning to be creative and spent that creative energy drawing, painting, and writing short stories for most of my life. As much as I loved doing those things, there was still a sense of just falling short, and I could never figure out why. When my first child was born, I wanted to make her something that was unique and from my heart. I borrowed an old, clunky sewing machine, found an easy softie pattern on the Internet, and spent a few hours teaching myself how to sew. My daughter was delighted with the imperfect and wonky softie I created. Her reaction was amazing, and it instantly filled that small void I had been feeling with other creative projects. I was hooked—softie making became my passion. I have been making softies for the last two years, and I love how every little critter or doll I make ends up having its own character and personality.

Name:
Jhoanna Monte Aranez
Age: 32
Digs: Melbourne, Australia
Daily Grind: IT business analyst
Fave Crafts: softie making
More Info: www.oneredrobin.com

Words to craft by:

With six children in the family, we couldn't afford designer jeans and trendy outfits. When I needed a dress for eighth grade graduation, my mother introduced me to this wonderful thing called a thrift store. For little money, I bought vintage pieces and one-of-a-kind items that no one else in school had, and I developed an aesthetic that stayed with me. If something didn't fit, my mother showed me how to alter it, so throughout high school, my clothes were unique *and* custom made. Fashion has always been a big part of my self-expression, and it's empowering to make something with your own two hands. Knitting was another great love of mine growing up, because I was creating fabric from yarn. My mother was a meticulous knitter and would rip out eight rows to fix one dropped stitch, but I was more of a rebel with patterns. Today, that's how I create my one-of-a-kind glamspoon pieces—nothing is sketched ahead of time. I let recycled textiles inspire the design, and a couple of hours later, I have a signature piece of wearable history.

PHOTO BY
SARAH M. JAMES

Name: ## Tina Witherspoon
Age: Over 18. Well, 29. Maybe not. I don't want to talk about it.
Digs: suburb near Seattle, WA
Daily Grind: indie crafter and clothing designer
Fave Crafts: sewing
More Info: glamspoon.typepad.com/glamspoon

chapter three

Jenny Hart

Before a trip to Austin

in 2002, I contacted Jenny to see if she'd be interested in meeting to talk shop (I lived in California at the time). I was a fan of her work, but also just happy to have found someone to brainstorm with, who was also venturing into this new world of crafty Web businesses. Shortly after that, I moved to Austin, and together with eight other creative women, we founded the Austin Craft Mafia, which has since branched out into Craft Mafias across the world. Jenny's an artist, author, designer, and founder of the popular embroidery company, Sublime Stitching. Her edgy patterns, cutie-pie kits, and amazing embroidered portraits can be found in stores and galleries worldwide.

VH

VH: *What's your first craft-related memory?*

JH: I grew up drawing and doing artwork. My mom sent me to drawing classes from the time I was about five. For me, it was more about drawing than crafting. I remember making a project in school, though, where we took an egg carton and turned it into a caterpillar, which was a really cute project. I was really little, but I remember coming home and wanting to re-do the project again all by myself. That's one of my earliest crafting memories—coming home and going, "Oh, I understand how that worked, and I want to do it again without the teacher."

VH: *So you didn't want to change the way it looked, you just wanted to be able to do it independently?*

JH: I think both. I really liked taking that little bit of knowledge and going, "Look what I can do with it now!"—the independent aspect of it.

VH: *Is there a moment from your childhood connected to craft that really stands out for you and has stuck with you throughout your life?*

JH: Well, yes. Phyllis White, a British woman who went to our church, taught me how to knit when I was about 10 years old. It was something I really enjoyed. I liked having her teach me. It wasn't something that a lot of my girlfriends were doing at the time, but I remember wanting to make a scarf for my doll. After my first lesson, I was so enthusiastic to get started that I didn't realize I was adding stitches with every row, so my scarf just got bigger and bigger. It turned into a scarf that was so big, my dad used to wear it.

VH: *Now as a professional designer/crafter, is there an equally important moment for you?*

JH: To be honest, and I'm not just saying this to be wistful, there are too many to pinpoint just one. That's a really tough question. For me, personally, the experiences that have come out of learning how to embroider—what it did for me, and how I wanted to share it with other people and get them interested—has brought so many experiences that I couldn't have anticipated or imagined.

VH: *Who, if anyone, do you credit for opening the crafty doors for you?*

JH: I have always felt extremely indebted to Debbie Stoller (author of the *Stitch 'n Bitch* series of books), Laurie Henzel, and the people at *BUST Magazine*, because they were the first to publish my work. I also credit Randy Franklin at Yard Dog, an art house in Austin, who was the first person to put my work in a gallery setting. The two aspects of how I work with embroidery are as craft and as fine art, so those are the people who set my work off on those two paths. I've always been really grateful to them for that.

VH: *Even though we've come leaps and bounds over the past decade, society still doesn't place much value on handicrafts as a career. Tell me a bit about how you took your creativity and turned it into a career.*

JH: When I started working in embroidery, it was for myself. There was such an enormous response, though. People would see me embroidering and want to come talk to me about it, or they'd see the work I was doing and would get really excited about it. They'd never seen embroidery like mine before, or they hadn't seen anybody embroidering in years. I wanted to share my experience from learning it.

I didn't grow up doing needlework; I had the same attitude about it that a lot of people had. I wasn't particularly interested in it, and I didn't think it was something I'd enjoy. The way it was being used predominantly as a hobby didn't appeal to me in an aesthetic sense. When I started working with it on my own, it so surprised me—both the techniques and how much I enjoyed it. All of those

> I wanted people to stop overlooking embroidery. It was a really simple idea that I couldn't believe wasn't already being put to practice: re-introducing embroidery for a new generation with contemporary, updated designs.

myths I had in my mind vanished into thin air. I wanted to get other people to enjoy it as much as I did. I wanted people to stop overlooking embroidery. It was a really simple idea that I couldn't believe wasn't already being put to practice: re-introducing embroidery for a new generation with contemporary, updated designs. In other words, steering clear of motifs like teddy bears and bunnies, which had earned embroidery the reputation of being out of date, out of touch, and not something that a modern woman or man would do. That didn't make sense to me.

I was looking in the market for patterns like Tiki drinks, tattoos, or pin-ups, but there wasn't anything out there. I couldn't believe it! It also made a lot of sense to start a design company that offered the resources for learning that weren't available to me. Embroidery is such an oral tradition that some of the best books out there are reprints. They're great, but not geared towards beginners, because it was assumed that your mother or grandmother had already taught you. There needed to be a resource that understood this new embroiderer, so that's really how I started Sublime Stitching. Of course, the Internet and blogging, and really the Zeitgeist of crafting, was starting to take shape at that time. The people who were doing it were all really aware of it. We knew there was something going on; we were all connecting, reaching out, and getting to know each other. People were starting Web businesses and other models were being forged that didn't exist before.

VH: *We were all just faking it.*

JH: Yeah, and it was really exciting! I loved working with something that was very traditional, but then building on it in a way that hadn't been done before.

VH: *What is the biggest challenge you've faced in trying to make a living through your craft?*

JH: Keeping up with demand and growing, which we always are. I have a staff of five people. Three years ago, it was two people, and before that, it was just me and an assistant. I've been really lucky to have wonderful assistants over the years.

VH: *Was there a defining moment when you thought, "Hey, I can make a career out of my passion"?*

JH: I always felt there was a career to be made with it. Of course, I also thought it was a great idea! I was committed to it right away, and it took shape from my own motivation and enthusiasm, and the feedback I was getting from others.

VH: *So it wasn't like Jennifer Perkins (see page 57) who got featured in BUST and then quit her day job?*

JH: Well, all three of us (including Tina Sparkles, formerly of Sparkle Craft), quit our jobs within months of each other. So yes, it was like, "We're going to do this!" We could see that our businesses were going to take shape, and it was just a matter of doing it, but there are two ways about it. Right at the beginning, it just felt like, "Boom, this is all coming together. The time is now. I love it!" Then, you go through a period when you think, "Okay, how long is this going to last? Can I sustain it?" It really took about three years before I got to a place where I knew it wasn't going away—that I could sleep at night and the business wasn't going to come crashing down within a week's time. There were too many people involved and too many moving parts. It felt really good.

VH: *As you mentioned, your medium is embroidery, which spans both the craft and art worlds. As you know, both inside and outside the community, there's a big debate between the words* art *and* craft. *I'm curious to know what the difference is for you, between being an artist and a crafter.*

JH: My art is what I do first and foremost for myself. The work I do as a craft designer is first and foremost for others. It's a design platform to facilitate their creativity, whereas my artwork is an expression of my personal creativity. That isn't to say the designs I do for Sublime Stitching aren't an expression of my personal creativity—they are, but they're designed to appeal to specific sensibilities. For me, I think of the two very differently. The other way of looking at it is: If you're making something with your hands, is it art or is it craft? That's really subjective. For me, the most obvious way to think about it is that if you're using a pattern, making something purely for pleasure, and making something that's going to be used as a household object, that's crafting. I'm also reluctant to not acknowledge that personal creativity can infuse those platforms, turning them into something artistic. It's a difficult but interesting debate. What I think has happened is that art and craft have blended—that strict line is getting crossed and blurred in new ways.

VH: *You've had a large presence on the Internet and specifically on message boards over the years. Have you noticed any change in the perception of what being crafty means during that time?*

JH: Rob Walker, who wrote the book *Buying In*, has spent a lot of time talking to me and others in the DIY community. One of the things he pinpointed was that this doesn't seem to be as much a craft movement as it is a work movement. Something I notice when people talk heavily about crafting is that they discuss how they can make their living from it; they seem really motivated to use crafting as a way to become independently employed. There are more people doing it; there are more people talking about it; there are more people noticing it.

VH: *Do you think more people today believe they can make a living crafting than they did eight to 10 years ago?*

JH: I think they do. To be honest, though, I don't know how realistic that is. As soon as I started my business, just as many people were writing me about how to embroider as they were writing about how to start a business. I want to be encouraging and express that I've had a positive experience myself, but I also want to caution people that it takes an enormous amount of work. They just need to be

Jenny Hart

"

I grew up in a house where fine art and comic book art were both appreciated—like Robert Crumb or Pogo. My dad bought me *Mad Magazine* when I was eight years old on summer vacation. Reading comics by great comic artists provided as much of an education for drawing as anything.

realistic about their goals and expectations. Sublime Stitching has been a huge success, and I'm always concerned that if people are introduced to it at this point, they might not realize what my life has been like for the last seven years—how many people it takes to make that success happen and have it all come together.

VH: *How do you caution and encourage at the same time?*

JH: By doing just that. Writing a crafting business column and giving very specific advice. Just being honest with people is the best way.

VH: *I think there's also a perception out there that people who are well known in the industry must be financially successful. The two have nothing to do with each other, though especially because of the Internet. It creates a false sense of security to believe that once you get your name out, the money starts coming in. Unfortunately in this industry, that's not how it works.*

> My art is what I do first and foremost for myself. The work I do as a craft designer is first and foremost for others. It's a design platform to facilitate their creativity, whereas my artwork is an expression of my personal creativity.

JH: No. It's really exciting to have a big, glossy craft project book out there, but those are the books that probably earn the smallest amount of money for their authors and take the most amount of work—which isn't to say that I haven't loved doing them.

Sublime Stitching got buzz, international and national press quickly, and that gave the impression that money was coming in. Maybe projects and exposure were coming in, but that didn't necessarily mean money. That's why I always tell people to make sure they love what they're doing, because if the reason you're doing it is just to make money, you're going to hate it.

VH: *We're a part of the Austin Craft Mafia together, a group that has happily left an imprint on the indie craft community. Especially at the beginning, the group was one of our main sources of community, one that we based on a united we stand mentality. Will you talk about your view of what our message as a group or movement is?*

JH: Strength in numbers. Pooling resources and information. Working together in ways that complement one another. People sometimes think that because you're in business, and I'm in business, that means we have to be in competition. I like that we all do very different things, but there's something at our core that's the same and has allowed us to help each other out. The way we collaborated wasn't prescribed for us, and we weren't prescribing it for other people. I think that's why it's had such a big influence—we never promoted it as something we thought other people should do. Just by natural progression, other people saw what we were doing and thought, "We can do that, too."

VH: *I think a couple of things, at the time, made us different. One was that females in business (and I noticed this in the corporate world) have never really banded together successfully. It was always a kill-or-be-killed environment. Maybe it's rare in our industry, but we really felt that if one of us succeeded, we would all succeed. That's something I've noticed becoming true for the industry as a whole, outside of our group.*

JH: I would agree with that. I think it's because we're not working in a structure that involves a boss and climbing the corporate ladder. The people we have to answer to are our customers and each other. The way we interact with each other to make that succeed looks totally different.

VH: *Absolutely. The second thing that may have made us different is the way we marketed ourselves. You always talk about the grass-roots effort and promoting as if you were promoting your own band. Normally, people in the same industry are considered competitors and would never consider co-advertising, but joint ads were the basis for how we survived in the beginning.*

JH: Right. It allowed me to take out print ads that I wouldn't have been able to afford on my own. Then, just by extension, we had this exponential effect on our exposure for one another. I think the other thing was that we understood the importance of the way we protected one another. We're all friends, but we've also had our differences. None of that surpassed the strength of the group as a whole, and it was also not for public consumption. When we get interviewed, a staple question is, "Tell us about your cat fights." That's so disheartening.

VH: *We're not Craftzilla, people!*

JH: Exactly. People were interested in the idea that if you're a group of women working together, the fur must really fly. That was so disappointing, because I think people are just as interested in hearing about a successful group and how it works.

VH: *You know, they would've never asked us that if we were a group of men.*

JH: Nope.

VH: *You can bet there are just as many disagreements in a testosterone-filled group.*

JH: Of course. There are with any group of people. I don't want to paint a picture that we're a perfectly functioning group, though. It's hard to get us all together; we're very busy.

VH: *We're all very opinionated, and we all work in very different ways.*

JH: Right, but we're smart enough to figure out how to make that work for us.

VH: *How do you see your role in the current craft movement and community?*

JH: I hope that people see my company as a model. I hope that people continue to support it. I'd like to remain a voice of support, encouragement, and hopefully, innovation.

> We knew there was something going on; we were all connecting, reaching out, and getting to know each other. People were starting Web businesses and other models were being forged that didn't exist before.

VH: *Your designs tend to stray from the norm of mainstream embroidery artists. What inspires you and your style?*

JH: I grew up in a house where fine art and comic book art were both appreciated—like Robert Crumb or Pogo. Anything that Fantagraphics Books was putting out—I had my hands on all of it. My dad bought me *Mad Magazine* when I was eight years old on summer vacation. So, comic art has always been a really big influence. For all of the drawing classes I've taken throughout my life, reading comics by great comic artists provided as much of an education for drawing as anything.

There are also just popular themes out there that I'd like to see for embroidery. If there were designs that spoke to people's aesthetic sensibilities, that would mean they'd take interest in embroidery. Of course, once I launched the company and started putting patterns out, people started playing along and writing in with suggestions. That's so great, because we were always reading each other's minds about what should come next. Customer requests play a huge part in the creative growth of the company.

For more information about Jenny and her projects, go to: www.sublimestitching.com

The Crafter's Studio

In the great tradition of *Inside the Actor's Studio* and James Lipton:

What craft sound or smell do you love?
I love the sound of embroidering on taut fabric.

What craft sound or smell do you hate?
The smell of any chemical solvent or glues.

What career, other than craft-world domination, would you like to try?
French teacher.

When you poke yourself with a needle or mess-up one of your designs, what is your favorite exclamation?
F&*# a duck!

Name: Rachel Hobson,
a.k.a. **Average Jane Crafter**

Age: 32

Digs: Austin, TX

Daily Grind: freelance writer and Web designer

Fave Crafts: hand embroidery, sewing, collage, and mixed media

More Info: averagejanecrafter.blogspot.com

Words to Craft by:

Until a few years ago, I denied my crafty nature. I've sworn, most of my life, that I am "so not crafty." Regardless of the fact that I was decoupaging pictures of Mork and Mindy to a table in college, I saw no craftiness in my past or future. I knew that both my grandmothers were master seamstresses—one could crochet and knit like nobody's business—and that my mother, in typical '70s fashion, embroidered anything that stood still. But why did I have no desire to craft? I'm not sure. Occasionally, I'd find myself in a craft or hardware store, and that tingly sensation of standing in awe of possibility would overwhelm me. I'd pick up supplies, but lacking anyone to craft with and any guidance, I'd get frustrated with the process and swear that I was "so not crafty." I finally embraced my crafty side when my mom gave me a sewing machine a few years ago. I trolled the Internet for inspiration and stumbled upon craftster.org (see page 77). My life changed. Connecting with a craft community completely inspired me to make things and to connect with other creative people. No more denying it. I am *so very* crafty. The warm, fun, generous crafting community feeds my soul and makes me want to keep creating.

Name: Elizabeth Kalka

Age: (cough) 41

Digs: San Antonio, TX

Daily Grind: Etsy shop owner and WAHM of four boys

Fave Crafts: crocheting and cross-stitching

More Info: lavenderlizard.blogspot.com

Words to Craft by:

Every Christmas since my oldest son (now 12) was born, I have made ornaments for each of my boys. Usually they are cross-stitched, but sometimes they are crafted or crocheted. Some of them are personalized. My wish for them is that when they leave home, they will each be able to take a boxful of their own handmade ornaments for their first Christmas away from home.

chapter four

Ed Roth

I sometimes joke that Ed and his stencils are the gateway drugs that bring guys over to the crafty dark side. The design choices are butch enough that any dude would wear the images spray-painted on a T-shirt, and once they take that step—the one that pushes them into a craft supply store—we've got 'em! Part urban with just a drop of kitsch; I love Ed's style. He's brilliantly discovered how to mix nostalgia with art in a commercial way, but it still feels like an underground secret. I spoke to him from his place in Brooklyn, New York, about how he went from being a psychology major to an art entrepreneur.

VH

VH: *What's your first craft-related memory?*

ER: My parents were into different arts and crafts. There was a store in our town where you could paint little figurines, so I took classes there and remember my mom would paint things there as well; she got me into that. I just wanted to paint these little dog figurines all the time—that was kind of my thing. I collected dogs, and my brother collected cats. My dad would create things around the house a lot. He painted a mural on the garage wall with extra house paint that was lying around, and he built a funny sculpture in the garden. So really, suburban crafts were how I started.

VH: *Was your dad an artist by profession, or was it just a hobby?*

ER: I'd ask mom, "What does dad do?" and she would tell me, "Oh, he's a jack of all trades." He did different jobs all the time. He repaired trucks at a truck facility, and then he did maintenance at an apartment building. He could build anything—a carpenter/mechanic kind of guy.

VH: *I can't wait to tell my youngest son that you got started by painting dogs, because he just went on a ski trip with his dad's family and (he's totally my child), he opted out of the Colorado slopes to take a pottery class instead. He painted a cat that he named Dennis. It's nice to hear that's where it starts. It just made me so happy to hear he did that.*

Is there a moment from your childhood connected to craft that really stands out for you?

ER: I don't know. It was always one hobby after the next, but that was a pastime. I was always painting color by numbers, or painting those porcelain figures, or later I got into macramé. I got really into macramé in the '70s! It got sort of ridiculous, like 14-foot macramé plant holders.

VH: *Oh, you were serious!*

ER: Oh yeah—my friend and I would put wooden beads on them and yeah! In seventh grade, you'd think kids would be going outside and being crazy, but we were making macramé.

VH: *You should bring that back and spray-paint stencils over them for a modern touch. That would actually be really cool.*

ER: I bet I can remember how to do it all too, because, you know, when that's all you do for a year.... I also made latch hook rugs, anything like that. So I guess it just continues. It's why I'm a designer now.

VH: *Do you have a memory as a professional artist that will always stick with you?*

ER: For a year, I ran an art gallery here in Brooklyn with a friend. Patrick and I had a storefront that we rented as a design office, and we wondered what else we could do with the space. It was ground-level and a mess of a store, really. We had to fix it up, but it was pretty sad looking. Anyway, we made it into a gallery for one year called Who Do We Appreciate. It was all street art—affordable, up and coming graffiti artists. Basically, the whole theme was art that you could buy for under $100.

Since I have a Web design background, we built a website for each exhibit and would sell the art online as well. We always sold out of the art, whether it was during opening night of the gallery, or on the website. That impacted me or pushed me into doing a stencil design company, because we had so many stencils. I was buying a lot of graffiti design books and was surrounded by those artists, which inspired me to start this design line.

VH: *Did you go to art school or are you self-taught?*

ER: I have a degree in psychology.

VH: *Oh, that makes sense. So does Jennifer Perkins (see page 57). That's so funny!*

> I got really into macramé in the '70s! It got sort of ridiculous, like 14-foot macramé plant holders.

41

ER: And then after college, I landed a graphic design job. A friend was leaving a position and they trained me. Then I went back to school for computer classes that I just wanted to learn. I went to New York University; I went to the Academy of Arts; I take classes anywhere I live just to keep up. I'm taking a class next Saturday in editing. So, I have somewhat formal training, but it didn't happen until after I got my psychology degree.

VH: *Do you credit anyone in particular for opening the professional crafty doors for you?*

ER: I have influential teachers, but for business, not really. I had some great art teachers after college who inspired me to dream big and do whatever I wanted. I think what pushed me the most was going into all these corporate jobs and wanting to rebuild from all that and do my own thing. I was craving not to be directed so much.

> I was buying a lot of graffiti design books and was surrounded by those artists, which inspired me to start this design line.

VH: *One of the reasons I'm doing this book is to help elevate the way society looks at handicrafts and people who make a living through them. I don't know about you, and maybe it's different being a guy, but I get patted on the head a lot (not literally) when I tell people what I do. I think a lot of that is because people still have a misconception that you have to be over 70 and probably female to be interested in anything crafty, even if it is a bit more urban and subversive, like your stuff is. So if you wouldn't mind, I would love for you to tell me how you took your passion for being creative and turned it into your livelihood.*

ER: I guess I'm lucky that I had a few tricks up my sleeve. I could design a website, which a lot of people can do now with so many programs, but I had a Web design background and a graphic design background. I also constantly fed myself pop culture, read design books, and looked at T-shirt design, graffiti design, and things I just gravitated towards. I think there are some things I love and some things I hate, and then other things I relate to—you take what you like, and that's what your job should be. I'm lucky to focus on imagery and designs I like, and that's what inspires me every day. I made stencil drawings of the stuff I was interested in, and then figured it out on the Internet.

I approached publishers because my idea was to make and sell a design book with stencils in it. I had seen a lot of books about stencil graffiti, but I hadn't ever seen one with a stencil inside. I knew what I wanted, so I approached publishers in 2004, and they were saying, "We've never done something like that; we don't even know how to do that." So I found somebody who would cut individual stencils out of my designs, and I could sell them individually.

It was all about little steps; okay, the publisher said no, so what next? Well, actually, it might be easier to cut the stencils and package them, so I started doing that out of my house. I had to learn the formula. I'm not trained as a businessman, so I had to learn about pricing and building a website with products. Years later, after proving that my formula worked, a friend at Chronicle Books said, "Why don't we do a book together!?"

VH: *And Chronicle's such a perfect fit for you!*

ER: I love them. They're great to work with. They lay out my books and art beautifully, and I just can't say enough good things about them. So I think if you like what you're making, chances are, some other people will like it too. Figuring out a way to sell what you're making is a lot easier now than it used to be. If you see it selling well, then it will probably grow.

VH: *Does most of your inspiration come from the same street art that you used to celebrate at your gallery?*

ER: I would say that a lot of my work is graffiti-inspired imagery, but I'm also a nature freak, so that really got infused in my work as well. Then, as a graphic designer, I study patterns, so my whole new line is related to that. Of course, some of it is based on what will sell. At first, I think about what images I would want to put on a T-shirt or a wall, because that's where most people use my stencils. But then I think, "Well, I like bird imagery, and lots of other people like bird imagery, so why don't I make some beautiful birds, and people can make what they want with them." That's what I like seeing—what people make with my creations.

VH: *I had a bib-making party for my baby shower, and one of the guys combined two of your stencils to make what I would call a* mird; *he took a monkey head from one and a bird body from another. It has this twisted Wizard of Oz look, and I really love it. It's one of my favorites. So people are definitely using your stuff as a jumping board and not just as is, which I always think is so cool, because that means you're inspiring people.*

ER: When we do an event or when people send me imagery, I'm always surprised by the layout, the overlay, and the colors they choose. Everyone is going to do it differently. People have sent me images where they've painted the back of their toilet with stencils using porcelain paint. They do plates, UGG boots, and so much more. I love that, because I never would have thought of it, you know?

VH: *What is the biggest challenge you've faced trying to make a living through your craft?*

ER: I guess, because I have the designer brain, learning the *not fun* stuff, as I call it, is a challenge—billing people and learning business formulas. Now I have a distributor, a manufacturer, and a shipping place. It's challenging to put all the pieces together, and I have to realize that a lot of it is trial and error. I do all this myself, so when I try something that doesn't work, I kill it and try another thing. Growing pains are the hardest.

VH: *Was there a defining moment when you thought, "Hey, I can make a career out of my passion"?*

ER: Probably when I started getting press. It was nice that somebody wanted to write about my work. Right away, the *New York Times* wrote about my book, and I thought it was cool that they considered it to be worth a story. Then, we were on *Martha Stewart*, which was a nice pat on the back, and it was interesting to watch Martha Stewart make a skull T-shirt—kind of crazy.

VH: *Did she choose that? She didn't go for one of your nature ones?*

> When we do an event or when people send me imagery, I'm always surprised by the layout, the overlay, and the colors they choose. People have sent me images where they've painted the back of their toilet with stencils using porcelain paint.

ER: It was a Halloween gig, so she and Cynthia Nixon did Frankenstein and skulls. It was surreal.

VH: *It must have been!*

Your main medium is stencil painting, which technically spans both the craft and art worlds. For you, what's the difference between art and craft?

ER: I don't know if there's a difference, but I know there is a stigma to the word *craft*. I always look at things like one person's art and one person's craft are the same thing, but they call them different names. I know guys who make graffiti flip books with black sketchbooks, while another girl makes a scrapbook of writings, drawings, and collage, but they're naming their projects differently. Never would a guy say, "I'm scrapbooking." I don't know—when I think crafts, I think knitting, but I've gone to art galleries and seen sculptures made of knitted things strewn across the whole gallery. So that's a very good question. I tend to use the word *art* more, but girls I know tend to use the word *craft* more. I think the concepts are very similar and there are just stigmas to the words. Some people are uncomfortable saying, "I'm an artist," and some people are uncomfortable saying, "I do crafts."

VH: *What is it? I'm not sure if it's a male/female thing, or if it's that art has always been more respected than craft, but something's going on. My brother, who obviously was raised by my mom and me (two crafters), avoids that word at all costs. But he bought your book,*

> I know guys who make graffiti flip books with black sketchbooks, while another girl makes a scrapbook of writings, drawings, and collage, but they're naming their projects differently. Never would a guy say, "I'm scrapbooking."

and he's a 31-year-old firefighter. He refuses to believe that he's crafty, although he totally is. I think there's just something about the word. Do you think in the male community (not to make you speak for all of mankind) but, in this sort of hipster male community, is there a reluctance to use the word craft?

ER: I think there is. I think it makes you think of an older woman doing something crafty, doing something creative. It makes you think of traditional grandma crafts or something. It makes you think of older women knitting. We (guys and girls, now) have taken that craft to a whole new level, and we're making kitsch, modern, and retro work with a tongue-in-cheek look to it—or just plain cute stuff. But, I think guys definitely don't like to say, "I'm crafty" or "I do crafts." I don't; I'm in the craft community, but I like to say, "I'm painting." I call myself a designer first.

VH: *That's totally the new word for crafter, though.*

ER: Yes.

VH: *That's what crafters who make money crafting call themselves now, and I think it's for the very reason we're discussing—because there's not much respect behind the word craft. Which I think we all need to change, but that's a different conversation.*

ER: Maybe we should spell it differently, I don't know.

VH: *With a K! It would be a whole different approach if we spelled it with a K!*

Over the years I've had the opportunity to meet a variety of crafters who are also musicians, writers, actors, graphic artists, etc. I've found that if people express themselves creatively in one way, they more than likely are interested in multiple forms of creativity. I believe that all things creative are linked together—do you find that to be true?

ER: I do find it true about myself, and I was nodding my head as you were saying that. I do motion graphics for broadcast, and I do Web design, and I do stencil lines, and, when I can, I do other art projects. I've taken welding classes, and played with collage, and decoupage, and all that. I do think it's common that if you're interested in creativity and creating things, that you want to work on a lot of stuff. Somebody asked me, since I do all of that, if I would just want to do the stencil lines? Would I want that to be my whole livelihood? I mean, they're not asking me if I want the company to get bigger, because I do, but....

VH: *No, they're just asking if you would be satisfied doing only that one thing.*

ER: Right, and I wouldn't be. I remember reading about a person who was designing the shapes of bottles for perfumes, but he was also a graphic designer. He had his hands in so much stuff. That's what I want to do, and that's what's nice about my company—at least I can say, "Okay, I need to design packages for my paints; okay, well now I'm a bottle designer." When you're working alone, you do have multiple jobs. So basically, I want to do a lot of stuff.

VH: *Are there non-handicraft creative aspects to your life—writing, or music, or poetry?*

ER: I guess my non-handicraft things would be doing motion graphics on the computer and editing. Those are definitely my other creative outlets.

VH: *What do you specialize in when you're working in graphics?*

ER: Broadcast—a lot of typography and effects. I work in a program called After Effects, so I do a lot of TV graphics.

VH: *Your book* Stencil 101 *was met with great success by the craft community. How have you been treated within that community? Do you find that you're treated any differently because you're a man?*

ER: I don't know if I'm treated differently. I've met so many nice people in that world. I do notice that people in the craft community speak about it as if it is a women's community, so I'm always saying, "I like being a part of this club too." I think it's funny when I hear women defining it as *their* community.

VH: *Well, shame on us. That kind of thing makes me so upset, because I have two sons and want them to see the craft community as a world they could completely be a part of.*

ER: I saw *Handmade Nation* (see page 257), and a lot of the interviewees define themselves and their community by saying things like, "This is a place where women can come together." I'm thinking, "Okay, not invited." But, I've been asked to take part at the Craft & Hobby Association convention this year doing demos on indie crafts; I'm defined as indie craft, so I was like, "Okay!"

VH: *Yes, we all are.*

ER: So that was nice that they knew of the company, and asked me to demo there and show people what I do.

VH: *As a mother, I'm really conscious of informing young boys of non-traditional, creative career paths. As someone who's followed that path, do you have any advice for kids who may not be aware of their options?*

ER: Sure. As I get older, I feel more responsible for encouraging kids. If a child studies a creative path he is drawn to, teachers should encourage him to apply that art in other studies as well. I always look at Flash design and programming: 90 percent of the beautiful creations you make also involve math. Patterns are also about math. I guess there are lines of study that meld different subjects.

> I do notice that people in the craft community speak about it as if it is a women's community, so I'm always saying, "I like being a part of this club too."

VH: *If that had been presented to me, I would have had a completely different journey. If somebody had taught me geometry within the context of quilting, or algebra within the context of knitwear design, maybe I wouldn't have struggled so much in math.*

ER: Thank you. You totally just put it into the words I was looking for. Think about all the patterns and shapes in geometry and knitting. Exactly! But it's kind of like sneaking healthy ingredients into treats.

VH: *Well, that's just a big statement about where our educational system is in this country. But something that simple and that fundamental absolutely would have changed my educational path.*

ER: Sure.

VH: *Is there anything else you'd like to say about what crafting means to you or has given you?*

ER: It's given me a lot of confidence and a reason to be creative all the time. I'm so glad that I got fired a few years ago from one job, because I was like, "What can I do with this time right now?" I'm grateful to have a position where I can be creative every day.

For more information about Ed and his projects, go to:
www.stencil1.com

The Crafter's Studio

In the great tradition of *Inside the Actor's Studio* and James Lipton:

What craft sound or smell do you love?
I love the smell of spray paint.

What craft sound or smell do you hate?
The sound of pump sprays clogging.

What career, other than craft- and art-world domination, would you like to try?
Motion graphics, which I'm already trying, and psychology, which I have a degree in.

When you rip a stencil or spill paint all over the floor, what is your favorite exclamation?
Eureka!

Words to Craft by:

I have always been first and foremost an artist—too scatterbrained for math, too inconsistent for science. When I went to art school, I thought I'd be a printmaking teacher. When I needed spending money, my boyfriend and I started making T-shirts for bands and selling them at rock shows. We would sneak into the studio at 2 a.m. and print entire runs of album covers without anyone knowing except the band. Seeing kids around the city wearing our shirts was a great feeling. I liked that T-shirts are so utilitarian and affordable. Five years later, I make my living selling my own designs, and I married that boyfriend. We have our own studio and no longer have to break in to print (though, every once in a while, you *can* find us printing at 2 a.m.). I pack and ship orders every day and send them all over the world, and still, when I spot someone wearing one of our shirts, my stomach does cartwheels. I call my husband and act as if I've won the lottery.

Name: **Rachel Bone**

Age: 26

Digs: Baltimore, MD

Daily Grind: owner of Red Prairie Press (apparel screen-printing and design)

Fave Crafts: screen-printing!

More Info:
redprairiepress.blogspot.com

Words to Craft by:

I've always had an appreciation for beautiful wood-crafted items, whether they are large furniture pieces or small, lathe-turned, exotic wood items like pens. Since retiring, I have rediscovered the spiritual nature of woodturning, and it has become a hobby run amuck—but in a good way. I guess all crafters know the good feeling that comes from taking raw material and turning it into something beautiful.

Name: **David Lindquist**

Age: too old to rock and roll, too young to die (53)

Digs: Austin, TX

Daily Grind: retired military

Fave Crafts: woodturning

I got in the knitting world when my wife saw a picture of a nostepinne and said, "Can you make me one of these?" I said, "You betcha." I did, and she liked it, so I made a few more. Now they're in all the knitting shops in Austin. I have also become the undisputed Etsy king of nostepinnes (still waiting for official recognition—a crown, a plaque, something). Then came knitting needles, niddy-noddies, drop spindles, needle cases. Woodturning is my attempt to leave a positive imprint. Hopefully when I'm gone, beautiful heirlooms will remind people of that crazy guy who was always in his garage turning perfectly good wood into chips and dust.

chapter five

Carol Duvall

As the original face of crafting and one of the first women on live television, Carol Duvall laid the creative groundwork for many of the people featured in this book, and most who will read it. Her ability to relate to her audience while helping them understand the value of making things made *The Carol Duvall Show* an iconic success. I had the privilege of meeting her several years ago at a craft convention and have seen her a handful of times since. She's always been exceptionally kind to me—from introducing *Knitty Gritty* to her fans, to agreeing to be a part of *Craft Corps*—and I try to pay that attitude forward as often as possible. With a career spanning over 50 years, she remains a force to be reckoned with. Carol's a pioneer, an inspiration, and one helluva woman! I want to be just like her when I grow up.

VH

VH: *What's your first craft-related memory?*

CD: Oh, good grief. Well, we didn't call them crafts at the time; we just called it making things. I was in the fourth grade. I remember one of my classmates and I would get together and set up a card table in the little hallway to my bedroom. We made yarn dolls. They were little four-inch things—we wrapped yarn around a piece of cardboard the same way you would start to make pompoms. We made little skirts for girls and divided and tied two sections for boys' pants. We joined some dolls together with strings and made them in school colors. I remember having plans to sell them, but whether we ever actually got anybody to buy them or not, I don't remember. I do know we agreed to sell the girls for two cents and the boys for three. It would have been smart to charge four cents for the pair, but obviously, math and merchandising weren't my long suits.

VH: *Is there a moment from your childhood connected to craft that really stands out for you?*

CD: There was one project my father taught me, and I still mystify kids with it today. I always called it a *magic trick*, though I later learned that it's named Jacob's Ladder. My father brought me little pieces of wood and some kind of material that was used to connect the pieces. I remember making the tricks with four blocks of wood so you could flip them, and he showed me how to do a magic trick where you put a dime inside and make it disappear. I made a lot of those, and I remember selling them for a dime. That was when my dad would go to the gas station on Saturdays to get his car checked out, and I would go along to sell my wares at the station. I also sold some door to door. I paid for half of my two-wheeler that way. In my book *Paper Crafting*, I featured a magic photo frame with invisible hinges. It's really just another version of Jacob's Ladder.

VH: *Were either of your parents crafty?*

CD: Not really. My father was an engineer and my mother knit some. It was my grandmother who was the hard-core knitter in the family. She taught me to both knit and crochet when I was in grade school.

VH: *Now, as a professional designer/crafter, is there an equally important moment for you?*

CD: I never thought of myself as being a designer, much less a professional designer. I remember being asked to speak at Hobby Industries Association (HIA) one time—as a designer, to the designers. I didn't know where I fit in. I didn't realize that what I was making up and doing on the air made me a designer.

VH: *Is there a memory that stays with you?*

CD: I suppose it's more of a group memory of the many things that went wrong along the way. Because I was doing everything live and learning as I went, there were a lot of goofy things that happened—like trying to demonstrate how easy and clever this new wraparound quick-sew dress was, and not being able to get out of it while we were still on the air. I knocked over an entire glass full of green dye on my project while demonstrating. That's when I learned to say, "Get over it. It's only television."—a lot!

VH: *Who, if anyone, do you credit for opening the professional craft doors for you?*

CD: That would be Woody Fraser, the producer of ABC's *The Home Show*. It was Woody who decided that crafts should be a regular feature on the show. He was really responsible for bringing crafts and me to network television.

VH: *Will you explain how you were able to turn your passion for being creative into a high-profile career that's spanned over 50 years? And, you began during a time when it was difficult for a woman to get a job in TV!*

"

Because I was doing everything live and learning as I went, there were a lot of goofy things that happened—like trying to demonstrate how easy and clever this new wraparound quick-sew dress was, and not being able to get out of it while we were still on the air.

CD: That's a tough question to answer. Keep in mind that it was a different world when I started. There was no television. I actually did the very first television program ever produced in western Michigan, and much of that was pure luck and being in the right place with the right idea at the right time. I had the advantage of being in this brand new medium that fascinated people. I could have read the phone book and they would have watched, but I think a good part of what kept them with me over the years was that I was enthusiastic about what I was doing. I wanted to share whatever it was with them.

Quality mattered, and my staff used to tease me because I kept insisting that neatness counts, no matter how simple and basic a project might be. This carried over into the guests we presented as well. The viewers were always number one in my mind, because they gave their time to me and our show, and it was up to us to make it worth their while. In this changing world where the Internet seems to be rapidly replacing television as our source for learning, the same rules apply. Just because the screen is smaller does not give you permission to cheat on the small stuff.

VH: *So how did you end up getting your own show,* The Carol Duvall Show?

CD: That was another stroke of luck. The original host of *The Home Show* was Robb Weller. After leaving *Home*, Robb had joined forces with TV writer Gary Grossman and formed a television production company. The two men had been pitching ideas to a brand new network, Home and Garden Television (HGTV), and when Robb learned that *The Home Show* was about to go off the air, he contacted me.

He thought a craft show with me as the host was exactly what the new network needed. I thought he was crazy and really resisted the idea. "Five days a week of Duvall? No way." Obviously, TV programming was not one of my long suits either. And of course, Robb eventually convinced me that he knew better—and how grateful I will always be that he proved me wrong. *The Home Show* ended its run on April 9, 1994, and we started taping the first 75 shows for HGTV in June. The shows, well over 1,000, and their many re-runs finally came to an end in January of 2009!

VH: *Had there ever been a show solely focused on crafts?*

CD: Not to my knowledge. Even the network was a bit dubious, and on the first batch of shows, they insisted that we have a number of known TV personalities co-host with me. They didn't have to know about crafts; they just had to have a familiar name to help get the audience. It was ridiculous. Even though every star we had was delightful, it certainly didn't help the viewers learn any more about the projects we were trying to teach. Fortunately, they let the network know and we didn't do that again.

VH: *What was your main goal with* The Carol Duvall Show *in terms of how crafting and being creative was perceived by the public?*

> I had the advantage of being in this brand new medium that fascinated people. I could have read the phone book and they would have watched, but I think a good part of what kept them with me over the years was that I was enthusiastic about what I was doing.

CD: I don't remember having such lofty ideas about public perception when we started. I think the goal was simply to put on an interesting and worthwhile show that a lot of folks would enjoy watching. HGTV helped by giving us the goal of their network: "To inform and entertain." I don't know that I gave much thought about how being creative was perceived by the public. I just hoped they liked it.

VH: *What changes have you seen in the craft industry over the years?*

CD: If I had to say it in one word, it would be *growth*. When I was first doing my craft shows in the early '60s, my main materials were milk cartons, bleach bottles, egg cartons, etc. This was not just by choice, but necessity. There were only two craft stores in all of Detroit that I knew of, and their staples were things like Styrofoam balls, chenille stems, bump chenille, and sequins—lots of sequins. The incredible growth in the amount of tools and materials available has made it possible for almost anyone who has the desire to craft to make things that are truly items to be proud of. It used to be that if folks thought they were not artistic, they couldn't craft. That is not the case anymore.

VH: *Is there one craft that speaks more to you creatively than others?*

CD: Not necessarily one craft, but one craft material speaks to me. It's paper. It's what I started with and what I still prefer, although the choices these days are much greater and certainly more wonderful. The possibilities for creating are endless.

VH: *I think one of the reasons crafting has become popular again is because it nurtures a sense of community that we've missed out on since the days of quilting bees and knitting circles. What role, if any, has crafting played in your own sense of community? What outlet has enriched your own community the most?*

CD: I really can't answer that question, because most of my crafting has been either in front of a television camera, or conducting workshops, or demonstrating at some event or another. Other than a few occasions at a yarn shop, I don't recall crafting in a group.

VH: *So you never had time to be part of any kind of crafting group or knitting circle?*

CD: I never was. When I wasn't working, I was either with my family or doing other things.

VH: *Did you craft with your kids?*

CD: No, not my sons. My grandsons, though, always looked forward to crafting at Grandma's.

VH: *Are you conscious of the community that you helped perpetuate just doing your job?*

CD: Yes, when I look at my mail or meet people on the street, it makes me realize that, and it makes me feel good. It also makes me appreciative of my good fortune.

VH: *Now that you're semi-retired, do you still have any desire to be creative, or are you crafted out?*

CD: No, I'm not crafted out, though I discovered that I don't have all the time I thought I would have. First of all, everything takes longer because I don't have deadlines. I'm having a very difficult time accomplishing anything. There is always tomorrow or later today, which is not conducive to accomplishing anything of value. I'm still doing a little bit of knitting, but not a lot. I made German paper stars in the fall while I was watching a lot of television. Even though it's something I've been making since the '70s, I had to keep my hands busy.

VH: *I fully believe that if it weren't for you and your work, people like me wouldn't have the jobs we have today. What advice do you have for us craft TV hosts during a time when lifestyle television seems to have waned?*

> It used to be that if folks thought they were not artistic, they couldn't craft. That is not the case anymore.

CD: It thrills me to the core when folks tell me that I've made a positive influence on their lives, whether on a personal or business level. And I am grateful for that. As for the advice, I suppose it's the old, "Go with the flow." Television is like everything else—it goes in cycles, and God help you if you happen to be in the wrong cycle. Trying to make your own cycle is not that easy. But some of what I said in answer to the question about how I managed to hang in there for over 50 years would be my response. Whether you craft on television or the Internet, quality in what you do and caring about your audience matters.

VH: *Is there anything else you'd like to say about what crafting means to you or has given you?*

CD: In addition to giving me a very fine living doing what I enjoy, crafting has given me a great sense of satisfaction when something turns out as I had hoped. It has allowed me to meet hundreds of wonderful and talented people I might never have met before, and it has allowed me to watch television without feeling guilty about wasting time.

For more information about Carol, go to:
www.diynetwork.com/carol-duvall-bio

The Crafter's Studio

In the great tradition of *Inside the Actor's Studio* and James Lipton:

What craft sound or smell do you love?
I love the sound of knitting needles in use—especially wooden ones.

What craft sound or smell do you hate?
The sound of the guillotine paper cutter cutting paper.

What career, other than your own, would you like to try?
The theatre; the stage. I decided that when I was in grade school.

When you burn yourself with a glue gun or poke yourself with a sewing needle, what is your favorite exclamation?
Oh crap! Although, I do say damn a lot.

Name: Libby Bailey,
a.k.a. Vickie's mom

Age: 64

Digs: Lakewood, CA

Daily Grind: high school special education teacher

Fave Crafts: knitting, without a doubt

Words to Craft by:

All of my life, the most important thing to me was becoming a mother, in the true sense of the word—not just one who gave birth. When my kids were little, my focus was to be the kind of mother that mine wasn't. Back then, in my mind, one way to do this was to craft at home. Knitting made the first connection when I made my brand new daughter a pretty, pink Scandinavian sweater and put it on her little body saying, "Mommy made this just for you." After that, every year, I repeated the sweater in a different color and size. When her brother joined us, every year, there were two sweaters knitted by their mother's hands. As my children grew, we did many crafts together as a family—with mommy's hands teaching little hands. And now, decades later, the grown-up little girl teaches her mother the advanced intricacies of knitting. The circle is complete.

Name: Shannon Delanoy

Age: 32

Digs: Baltimore, MD

Daily Grind: jeweler and seamstress

Fave Crafts: sewing

More Info: sweetpepitaclothing.blogspot.com and www.baltimorecraft.com

Words to Craft by:

It was parent day at elementary school, and I was in first or second grade. In my mind, everyone else's mother was there except mine. My mama worked a lot, and had to. I know this now, but at the time, I felt so, so sad. I began to cry this kind of trying-hard-not-to-but-can't-help-it cry, and Miss Fran, a friend's mom, noticed. She said, "Oh, Shannon, did your mom make you that vest? It's so pretty!" And I stood up, still crying, with snot starting to run down my face. I modeled the vest for my peers and their (probably horrified) parents and announced, "It's (hiccup) re-ver-si-ble." One day, if for some reason I cannot be by my daughter's side, I can at least make sure she's wearing something I made. Just for her.

chapter six

Jennifer Perkins

Jennifer's one of my closest compadres in craftiness. We've known each other since 2001 when Jenny Hart of Sublime Stitching (see page 31) brought both Jennifer and Tina Sparkles, of Sparkle Craft, to a drinks meeting—I was visiting Austin before I moved here. Since then, Jennifer and I have been through marriages, divorce, babies, travel, a blizzard, co-hosting a TV series and two specials, co-founding a group, collaborating on various projects, and starting a consulting business together. We live a mile apart in South Austin, so hers is the one interview in this book that I got to do in person, from her couch while crocheting. Not only do I love her as a friend, but I truly respect her as both an artist and businesswoman. She's one smart cookie, that Jennifer Perkins! One smart cookie.

VH

VH: *What's your first craft-related memory?*

JP: I don't know why this always comes to mind, but I made a macaroni wreath for my mom. I don't know if it was in kindergarten or preschool. We took a little paper plate and made it into a circle, and then glued macaroni to it and spray painted it green. It was on top of our Christmas tree for forever and ever. Then about 10 years ago it wasn't—you know how moms go through that phase, when they decide they don't need family ornaments anymore and they just want pretty ones?

VH: *Well, your mom goes through that stage.*

JP: I know! Now our Christmas tree is just fancy glass ornaments. It's like, "Where are all the family ornaments?" There aren't any handmade ones anymore, like she's too good for them. Anyway, maybe five years ago, I asked where the macaroni wreath was. I was all bent out of shape about it. She said, "Well, the rats got to it in the attic, and it got all eaten up." So, I made my mom a new one for Christmas. It made one appearance on the tree, but it has never been back, even though I tried really hard to recreate the original macaroni wreath. Nope, it's back to the fancy ornaments. It looks like she doesn't even have children! Who has a Christmas tree with just Christopher Radko ornaments? That's her.

VH: *Is there a moment from your childhood connected to craft that really stands out for you?*

JP: There are a lot of moments that have stuck with me. I remember when I'd go visit my dad's family that my grandma and great aunt were always crocheting. Then my mom—she was always crafting something or making clothes for my sister Hope and me. My maternal grandmother was always sewing, painting, or working on ceramics. Crafting is just something I was always around, always exposed to. It wasn't forced on me or anything, but crafting is how we spent time together. If you wanted to talk to my mom, then you'd have to do it while watching her make a stiffy bow or decoupage.

VH: *Now as a professional designer/crafter, is there an equally important moment for you?*

JP: I guess there's been a culmination of things: getting television shows, or having people e-mail me for advice, or when they quit their jobs to follow their dreams. It took several of those things for me to go, "Wow, I'm a full-time crafter. That's what I do." I thought I was going to be a shrink. That's what I went to school for.

VH: *When was the point—because you generally describe yourself as a jewelry designer—that you went from considering yourself a professional crafter to being a jewelry designer? Was there a pinnacle moment when that happened?*

JP: If anything, it was switched more the other way. I thought of myself as a jewelry designer, and then I felt like I got switched to a craft person. My original job as professional designer was doing jewelry stuff with my online site Naughty Secretary Club. From there, I guess it transitioned when *Styleicious* and *Craft Lab* came along and changed my public perception as more of a general crafter. I was no longer pigeonholed as a jewelry designer—I think that can be hard for anybody who's a crafter.

VH: *Yeah, we have these great jobs, but also don't want to be put into one creative box.*

JP: When you're a crafter, I think people want to pigeonhole you: Vickie knits, Jennifer makes jewelry, Kathy Cano-Murillo uses glitter, and Jenny Hart embroiders. All of us do a myriad of things. I mean, I'm sitting here

> It wasn't forced on me or anything, but crafting is how my mom and I spent time together. If you wanted to talk to my mom, then you'd have to do it while watching her make a stiffy bow or decoupage.

crocheting now, and I just got done making cupcake-toppers out of decoupage.

VH: *Who, if anyone, do you credit for opening the crafty doors for you?*

JP: As far as when I was kid, it's definitely my mom, since she was always crafting. My little sister Hope too—she loves to craft even more than I do! She was always making stuff and tearing stuff up. When you went into her room, you'd always find stuff she painted with puffy paint. So the two of them opened the doors for me—just being around them—I didn't have much of a choice at my house.

As an adult, it was probably meeting my friends with the Austin Craft Mafia, especially Tina Sparkles and Jenny Hart. Meeting with them in the early days was pretty significant for me, and talking to them about being crafters as full-time jobs—wondering, "Is this possible?" It really helped to have the two of them with me at the exact same time I was going through my own growing pains and starting my business; they were starting Sublime Stitching and Sparkle Craft. It's easier to do those kinds of things with a support team. When one of us quit our job, it was like, if she can do it, I can do it!

VH: *That was the point that I met all of you. I think you had recently quit your job, and Tina had literally just given her notice that day.*

JP: It was weird, because it was also right at the same time Jenny got laid off from the University of Texas. We were all done with our day jobs within a few months from each other. Jenny worked in the university's art department, but had already started Sublime Stitching. It happened for all of us, randomly, at the same time. It has all worked out. I'm not saying that it's not scary—but I haven't had to go back and answer phones or flip burgers.

VH: *Although we've come far over the past decade, society still seems to frown on handicrafts, as related to a career. Please share how you turned your passion for being creative into a livelihood.*

JP: You know, it was luck more than anything, but it wasn't *just* luck. I hate to give luck all the credit. I like making crafts, and I like making jewelry. The way the jewelry took off was just one of those things that happened organically; people wanted to buy it. *BUST Magazine* did a feature on it. Then I got to quit my day job. But I guess you are asking more about the perceived value of craft. After I quit my job, people were still like, "Oh, you make crafts. That's cute!" Literally, I've been doing it full time for years, and my dad just quit sending me things about graduate school and jobs. I've had other adults make comments like, "This isn't going to last forever," especially in the early days.

People don't give me a hard time about it as much now. I think they weren't sure I could make money from it. They didn't realize (even I didn't realize) that there were things like the Craft & Hobby Association or endorsement deals. In the beginning, I just made jewelry and put it on my website hoping someone would pay $15 for it. I would hope to make enough to pay my mortgage that month. I didn't realize there were so many tentacles to the business.

VH: *Well, at the time you got started, I had also started a little business online, and there weren't a lot of us out there, so we didn't know much. I had no idea that there were numerous jobs in the craft industry other than just being an artist. Growing up, I thought that in order to go to art school, you had to paint. I had no idea that there were all these other art forms—or that knitting could be considered an art form, or jewelry sculpting was considered an art form. There are even jobs at major companies where all you do is make crafts that go into magazines or go to conventions. There are so many things that I didn't know existed.*

JP: Well, you know, honestly, it's not even about going to art school, for me—I wish I had gone to school for business. If you want to make a living from your craft business, or if you already know how to craft, then maybe you should get a degree in business because the two go hand in hand. If you can make amazing stuff, but you don't know how to sell it, a business or marketing background can help you greatly.

VH: *If I had to go back to school and it wasn't art school (because I would love to go to art school, in theory), it would definitely be for public relations.*

JP: For sure.

VH: *You're possibly most well known for Naughty Secretary Club. Will you explain the philosophy and inspiration behind the name and its kitschy, signature style?*

JP: The inspiration behind the name is just that I literally was a secretary. I was an administrative assistant for a business and did government relations at a telecom company here in Austin. They never really gave me anything to do. I wasn't just bored; it irritated me that I had a college degree and was just sitting there, and no one utilized me. I even begged for stuff to do after my own business started becoming successful, and I talked to the higher-ups about it. I was getting all this press; I knew how to market things. I asked them if I could help out the marketing team, and they said no. They had a whole marketing team full of people who had no clue about what they were doing. I was like, this is your website, and it's kind of sad. I got disenchanted with the company that way.

The Naughty Secretary Club name came about when I started making my jewelry at work. I was like, if you guys are not going to give me anything to do, then I'm going to bring my jewelry up here. I learned how to do some marketing on the computer and get on the posting boards. I met a lot of people that way and just learned the ins and outs of the Internet. That's where the name came from, because I was a naughty secretary working up there.

VH: *And the style? You have a very distinct kitschy, vintage-inspired style.*

JP: I have had weird taste since I was a kid. When I was in fourth grade, I would wear a derby to school. I had two pairs of pajamas with giant neon numbers on them, because I thought I was Boy George in my color-by-numbers outfits. There was never any jewelry that I wanted to buy, so I just got into making my own. I would always go to flea markets and thrift stores and stuff with my parents. I was always buying weird things as a kid, and making them into something different, and I think that has transferred over into my jewelry. Nothing is safe around me if it sits still long enough—I'll end up looking at it somehow. Right now, I'm sitting here looking at the Fisher-Price apple, thinking it's big, but it could be a necklace.

VH: *I've personally had to tell you to step away from a tea saucer—it's too big for a charm!*

JP: I'm thinking that if Flavor Flav has necklaces that are bigger than that, than why can't I wear that dinky apple?

VH: *I'm going to sit you down with Flavor Flav for 30 minutes and not say a word, and you will know exactly why.*

JP: I know, I know, but you know what I mean. That's where my taste comes from. There has never been jewelry big enough, or tacky enough, or colorful enough for me. Plus, I was that kid—you know how it is when you're a teenager—I was that kid who would say, "I love that band," and then when the band gets played on the

> After I quit my job, people were still like, "Oh, you make crafts. That's cute!" Literally, I've been doing it full time for years, and my dad just quit sending me things about graduate school and jobs.

radio, you're like, "I don't like that band anymore." It's the same with clothes; I didn't want anything that anybody else had. I should be getting over that attitude, now that I'm in my thirties. It's the same way with jewelry. I just want to have different stuff.

VH: *I want to backtrack for a second, because I've never asked you this. You've talked in other interviews about how your jewelry got featured in BUST Magazine, and you were able to quit your day job, but I feel like a part of the story is missing that people might want to know. How much business did it have to bring you in order for you to quit your job? Was it that you suddenly got five orders and had a bunch of money saved, so you thought you could do it?*

JP: I should clarify that, because it's not like I mystically got so many orders from *BUST* and had thousands and thousands of dollars and could quit my job. Before the *BUST* thing happened, I was already walking that fine line of whether or not to quit my job—I just didn't know. *BUST* pushed me over the edge, because even before that, I was waking up early to pour resin before I went to work, and on my lunch break, I'd drive to the post office to mail packages. When I got home from work, I was immediately in my garage drilling and pouring resin and putting together orders for the next day's mail. I was probably making as much money on my jewelry business as I was being a secretary, at that time. The two were working hand and hand. I think a lot of people want to just quit. You can't just quit.

> If you want to make a living from your craft business, or if you already know how to craft, then maybe you should get a degree in business because the two go hand in hand.

VH: *Or be discouraged if you can't. That's the real reason why I wanted to clarify the situation—so people wouldn't feel discouraged.*

JP: I got so many orders from *BUST* that there just wasn't enough time before and after work to fill them. I would have had to write people back and tell them I was sorry, but I couldn't do it—or I had to tell my job that I was quitting. And at that point, they didn't even know I was there. I could have stayed at home and poured resin. They would have never known. I just figured I would quit because there are plenty of other secretary jobs. It was just a $10 an hour job, and that was 10 years ago. I could always find another job if I needed to.

VH: *So it was a little leap of faith, but you had done a lot of groundwork to get there?*

JP: Exactly!

VH: *Is there a craft that you've always wanted to try, but just haven't had the chance to yet?*

JP: There are lots of crafts that I've wanted to try, especially in the needle arts, since you've been coaching me with my crochet. I would like to get more into that. I wish I knew more about crocheting, and how to knit and quilt. Quilting interests me some, but I'm not the best seamstress. It's hard to be good at all those things or find the time for all of them. I hate when I look at a craft and have no idea of where to start making it.

VH: *Do you feel like, because you teach so many classes, that people expect you not to take classes? I know for myself, there are so many classes I'd love to take, but I feel a little strange about taking them because of people's perception of what I should already know.*

JP: It's funny that you should say that. A few years ago, I went to Art Unraveled in Phoenix to take jewelry classes with Susan Lenart Kazmer. People knew me from *Craft Lab* and television, and stuff like that. They were like, "Wow, you're taking jewelry classes?" I never said I know every single thing about jewelry. I never said I was the all-knowing seer of the western jewelry world. Everybody can stand to learn more.

VH: *Do you ever feel frivolous taking classes, even though, technically, it can benefit your business by opening up a new world? At the same time, it's not physically making you money. Or, am I the only one who's neurotic?*

JP: You're not neurotic! I don't feel that way with a jewelry class because I know I'm going to utilize what I learn—and I have utilized it. I ended up using the skills I learned from Susan in my book. I've always had a hard time reading a fiction book, because I feel like it's wasting my time. I feel like I should be reading a business book or a how-to book.

VH: *Do you think part of that is because you are working from home, and even though you're in bed, it's part of your office?*

JP: Partly, but it's partly because of my dad, too. He watches a lot of TV, but he rationalizes it because it's CNN or PBS. I've never seen my dad read fiction. He reads about stock markets or psychology. My dad would pay Hope and me on the weekends to watch the *Wall Street Week in Review* or *Nova*. I would get paid in high school if I would read hard-core philosophy and psychology books. I had a convertible Mustang in high school, but before I could get it, I had to write a report on skin cancer and the benefits of sunscreen. If I ever got caught without sunscreen in my car, I would lose my car for six weeks. My dad was king of the reports. I'm afraid I'm going to do that to my kids.

VH: *Of course you are, only you will make them do a collage, or explain something via diorama.*

JP: "I want an art journal explaining what this means!"

VH: *What role, if any, has crafting played in your own sense of community?*

JP: Honestly, it has played a huge role with the Craft Mafia and you. Ninety percent of my close friends are crafters. You know what I mean; it wasn't always that way. I tell my husband, Chris, we're going out to dinner with Vickie and Dave. He's like, "Great, are we going to have to sit there and listen to you guys talk about crafting all night?" All my friends are that way. I have about two friends who don't craft. It just naturally progressed that way. Here in town, a big part of my community involves the Austin Craft Mafia, Babes in Business, and Stitch Fashion Show.

VH: *What role do you think our group Austin Craft Mafia has played in perpetuating community?*

JP: I think it's done a big thing. There are about 40 groups worldwide now. Even though the Austin Craft Mafia has become self-sustaining, we don't necessarily get together and have a meeting and take notes anymore; we're all still friends who get together, hang out, and like to know what each other is doing.

VH: *And genuinely respect each other's opinions and go to each other if we need to bounce ideas off someone.*

JP: You need community; you need a moral support group. I like to think the Craft Mafia has helped girls in other towns, and that it's formed bonds and business relationships. There's power in numbers.

VH: *How do you see your role in the current craft movement and the community around it?*

JP: What's my role? That's such a hard question to answer about yourself. I think people consider me to be a person who not only does jewelry, but is known for marketing and business. I think a lot of girls who are artists have a hard time being marketing savvy or business savvy. I would like to think I've helped people with that, and that I've perpetuated the idea that the two are both important.

As far as my style goes, I would like to think it had some influence in making the other kitschy, weirdo people in the world feel okay—that it's okay to make kitschy weird things and wear them. I'm not saying that I'm the first person in the world to do it, and I'm not saying other people do it because of me. I've just never caved.

VH: *I definitely agree that your role has been getting the word out about how to promote and market yourself. Going back to what you just said, I think you've also played a big role in making alternative and indie things much more accessible. I remember going to Tennessee to shoot a TV special. Before that, the network thought tattoos were big and scary and only a certain type of person had them. They spent the weekend with us, and it's like all of a sudden, their eyes were open. "Oh, she's a relatable, relatively normal person who happens to display artwork on her body." You could literally see it on their faces—they realized we weren't going to pass out in our hotel room with a bottle of bourbon and a cigarette. We were professionals.*

You're a professional crafter, but also a celebrity because of it. Do you see that as an example of how the industry and our society are evolving, or are people just paying more attention to what's always been there because of mass-media avenues like the Internet?

JP: First of all, I've never used the term *celebrity* for myself. It just feels awkward. I think that, with you and me, people are paying more attention because of the

Internet. Also, our faces are on the Internet through our own websites, our blogs, and Twitter and Facebook. Plus, there's the DIY network. I think you and I have more recognizable faces because we've had the help of the Internet, as opposed to people who did it 10 years ago. They might not be as well known on the street as us. I think the Internet has helped our businesses get our brand names out there. What would we do without it—make phone calls?

VH: *So it's not necessarily a shift in society's perception; it's just a difference in the tools we have.*

JP: I think so, even if it was 1974, and we were on PBS doing a craft show, people would know us. I just think we've had the benefit of the Internet to help us.

VH: *You and I were on DIY's* Stylelicious *together. Making that series was a big challenge in many ways, but it was also a lot of fun. What was the best thing you took away from that experience?*

JP: In high school, I had this traumatic public speaking event—you know, you have that one time that scars you for life—and I never wanted to do it again. I mean, I dropped out of college classes if I had to speak in class. I had one professor in college who would call on people and ask them questions in class, so I would go to the professors and tell them that if they called on me, I would drop out. I don't talk in class. Don't call on me. I don't want to speak. I had another class where I lost 10 points off my final grade because I didn't want to do the oral presentation.

VH: *You must have had a really traumatic experience.*

JP: I just got choked up reading some stupid thing. It wasn't like it was sentimental. I ended up going to speech class, and my dad had to send me relaxation tapes. It was so bad. Doing *Stylelicious* made me neurotic and upset. It was very traumatic; I did not want to do it at all. I would get up every morning and practice for about two hours before going on, and then I'd come home every day and read, because I was really nervous about speaking publicly. That helped me get over my fear, and now I'm not afraid to teach. But even after *Stylelicious*, they asked if we wanted to host another show—not knowing it was *Craft Lab*, I said no. I sent an e-mail saying no thanks, because I was still traumatized.

VH: *Ironically, you were on the short list of who they hoped would say yes, because on camera, you seemed fine.*

JP: Little did people know that I was dying on the inside. It was like, "Oh my God, this is killing me." Otherwise, though, it was so much fun! I got to be in California with my friends. The main thing I really walked away with was a renewed sense of self-confidence.

For more information about Jennifer and her projects, go to:
www.naughtysecretaryclub.com

> As far as my style goes, I would like to think it had some influence in making the other kitschy, weirdo people in the world feel okay— that it's okay to make kitschy weird things and wear them.

The Crafter's Studio

In the great tradition of *Inside the Actor's Studio* and James Lipton:

What craft sound or smell do you love?
I really can't think of one.

What craft sound or smell do you hate?
I hate it when my fingers get all balled up with decoupage.

What career, other than craft-world domination, would you like to try?
I would definitely do marketing or public relations.

When you burn yourself with a glue gun or spill that resin all over the floor, what is your favorite exclamation?
Fu#@ity f#ck sticks.

Words to Craft by:

I wanted to be a hair-dresser and drive a Trans Am. That was my first childhood dream. After receiving a set of Fashion Plates for my 10th birthday, I changed my mind and wanted to be a fashion de-signer. That dream stuck with me until a very mean high school teacher informed me that I had no artistic talent. I ended up getting an M.B.A. and owning a human resources firm instead. In 2004, I had a surprise pregnancy and my life completely changed. At 35, I was forced to take a hard look at what I was doing with my life and re-alized that I still wanted to do something artistic. I worked through the damage that was done by my wicked art teacher (and my own misconceptions about my capabilities) and have been painting and crafting ever since. I've been published in several magazines, sell my artwork online and in retail stores, and have won awards for my artwork, which is collected worldwide. Since I am an artist with an M.B.A., I also publish a free, monthly electronic newsletter geared towards helping others make money from their work.

Name: Laura Bray
Age: 38
Digs: Aliso Viejo, CA
Daily Grind: artist
Fave Crafts: painting and paper crafting
More Info: katydiddys.blogspot.com

Words to Craft by:

I have always made things, since I was a tiny girl who couldn't have a Polly Pocket. I made one from a sweet tin and a card, and now it's saving my life. I got sick eight years ago at university. In the following months, I watched every dream shatter, and moved home to be taken care of. The only things I had were family who loved me and the ideas inside me. I nurtured them until I was well enough to craft, grabbing moments to string beads on wire or paint wooden plaques. When I couldn't move physically, I could dream of designs. I'm now much more physically able, but that fire burns brighter than ever. I have so many ideas, and I try to get as much done as possible when I have moments of energy. I learned how to knit two years ago, and its influence has been so much more than fun. It taught me how to pace myself, because I had tangible evidence how burning out affected me. These days, crafts save me and let me believe I still have value, even if I can't work. Crafts give me hope for the future, beauty in life, and the ability to say, "I made that."

Name: Fiona Brechin
Age: 27
Digs: Aberdeen, Scotland
Daily Grind: disabled and unable to work; starting up a yarn-dyeing business
Fave Crafts: knitting, crocheting, spinning, beading, card making, glass painting, bookmaking, and much more
More Info: thewildatheartkeptincages.blogspot.com

67

chapter seven

Kathy Cano-Murillo,
a.k.a. the Crafty Chica

Kathy and I met virtually, swapping links in 2001 to help promote her still-thriving website and my long-lost business, Mamarama. In those days, there weren't many crafty entrepreneurs taking advantage of the Web, so we made sure to keep in touch with others like us. Since then, Kathy has taken her passion for crafting and spun it into the Crafty Chica brand. She continues to inspire the masses with her Latina-infused books, colorful projects, and delightfully sparkly craft supply line. We eventually met in person and, over the years, have become good friends and trusted colleagues. She's truly one of my favorite people in the industry, embodying both the vibrancy of creativity and the spirit of community. Ms. Kathy and all of her endeavors deliver what her website's tagline promises: crafts, drama, and a whole lotta glitter!

VH

VH: *What's your first craft-related memory?*

KCM: This is going to be a good memory. I always save the bad memories of art class and not getting my pictures on the wall, but I do have a good memory with my Aunt Linda. She was a major crafter—she used to draw on denim shirts with a pen and then embroider the heck out of 'em with our names and all the different things we liked. So, she taught me how to do embroidery, and one of my first memories was creating a shirt following my aunt's style.

My other memory is from second grade—feeling empowered and going crazy with my artwork and then not getting it displayed on the wall. I guess the two memories balance each other out.

VH: *It's funny, I've been talking to a lot of crafters during the process of this book, and I'm really surprised at how many of them were affected by elementary or junior high teachers who didn't appreciate their work or straight-out told them they'd never be artists. Because of that, these people didn't pick up any sort of creative outlet again until they were in their thirties or forties. That's so upsetting!*

KCM: It is, but the good thing is that they come back with a rebel attitude ready to prove everyone wrong.

VH: *But it's 20 years later, which is craziness! I just want to put the message out there that adults have more power to shape these young minds than they know. Instead of saying, "You'll never be an artist," why not say, "How about exploring a different avenue? Let's try a different creative medium."*

KCM: You know what it is? Growing up, they would give us exact formulas of what the project was supposed to look like or be.

VH: *Then mark you down if you colored outside the lines or made something an unorthodox color.*

KCM: Yes! They'd say, "That's not realistic," or "That's not what the original model looked like." In my high school crafts class I always got Cs because I'd make my own patterns instead of using the ones that were given to us. I didn't care—I just wanted cool stuff to hang in my bedroom, but now that I look back, that was a good thing I was doing!

VH: *It's interesting how early that oppression starts. I had to have a talk with one of my son's first-grade teachers after she marked him down for coloring a person green instead of the appropriate peach or brown. You know, she was shaping my son's artistic integrity by judging him in that way. I've since made sure to counterbalance that with as much encouragement to think outside the box as possible.*

Wait, you had a craft class in high school?

KCM: I did—it was so much fun! I did latch hook, resin, pottery, etc. All the stoners were in that class, but I just did it because I thought it'd be really cool. This was 1980, so Foreigner, Heart, Queen, and Foghat were playing in the background. I loved that class! I made latch hook rugs of all of my favorite band logos. I was such a nerd but got to hang out with the stoners and rocker chicks; they totally accepted and took care of me. I want so badly to find that teacher Mr. Schlenker and say, "Thank you for that class!"

VH: *And also maybe send him a press release with a note saying, "Maybe you should've given me an A."*

KCM: Totally. After that I thought maybe I shouldn't waste time on art and craft, but I was the marker girl—I loved markers! With every office job I had, I'd use all the markers from the supply cabinet to color and doodle. You know, you cannot hide your passion to create. It's going to come up at one point or another. If you're meant to be creative, you just have to give into it, and eventually, it takes over.

VH: *You mentioned learning how to embroider from your aunt. Is your entire family creative?*

KCM: My dad is very creative. I could show you an article I just found about how he used to design model cars. He'd sketch them, make them in clay, carve them out of wood, then hammer all the metal. He won all kinds of awards. He also made jewelry and did many other crafts. My Nana, his mom, was a master seamstress and a crocheter and knitter. My dad told me that the reason he doesn't like knitting or crocheting is because all of his life, growing up, he saw his mother work so hard on these big, elaborate crochet doilies, which she'd finish and show people who'd just say, "Oh, that's nice." He said to me, "There's no payoff for it, so I'm not going to put my time into that." I think that's so heartbreaking!

VH: *Ironically, even though craft still isn't valued that much today, I think people are more appreciative than they used to be, because there aren't as many people doing it—it seems more unattainable.*

KCM: I *so* appreciate it! It makes me feel guilty that I didn't take care of the things Nana made for me. I always had that stigma of, "Oh my gosh, she should have bought me something instead." Or, "She must not have any money." It's horrible! Now as an adult, I'm motivated to use what she taught me and inspire others with craft.

VH: *Is there a moment as a professional designer/crafter that really stands out for you?*

KCM: I think my most validating moment as a professional was when I had a producer from *The Martha Stewart Show* call me and say, "We love your website. Can you give us some ideas for possibly having you on as a guest?" Granted, I haven't been on the show yet, but just the fact that the Martha Stewart people looked at what I did and thought it was good enough to be considered made me feel really good. I had always thought, "Martha's so perfect and polished. I'm nothing like that. I see all the people who emulate her style, and I just can't do it." So, the fact that they appreciated my style for what it is and found value in it was a really cool moment for me.

The other moment that stands out for me is before I crafted professionally. It was when I made jewelry to sell at flea markets. The first time someone bought something from me and wanted more, I felt like a singer performing on stage for the first time. I got goosebumps. I knew then that somehow, some way, I wanted to make a living out of this. Now I call it the *crafty hustle*—making things to sell, writing books, coming up with product and project ideas. There are so many aspects to it.

VH: *You're a crafty Jill-of-all-trades, but is there one craft that speaks more to you creatively than others?*

KCM: Assemblage. I love making shrines. I'm very passionate about the things I love, so I like to have visual manifestations of them. I make shrines for everything, from little shrines, to big shrines, to suitcase shrines. I feel like if I see

My most shameful crafty secret is my art room because it's such a mess. At the same time, it adds an element of fun to the creative process, because I'm always finding things I didn't know I had.

it, I can make it happen. I really love the art of gluing in layers—old school collage. Give me a glue stick, some paper, some glitter, and some foam core, and I'll go to town!

VH: *What's your favorite thing about crafting?*

KCM: It's a way to express things that I'm happy about. Because I'm so passionate, I have a lot of highs and lows—crafting is such a strong outlet to release all of that in a visual way. I love making people happy with things I craft, and using bright colors to surprise people and cheer them up. I love that I can make a living from crafting, and that it requires coming up with different things

and staying a step ahead of what everyone else is doing. Even the time it takes to sit and make something is special. Granted, not everything turns out perfect, but that's the fun of it. When something turns out the way you want it to, you appreciate it more.

VH: *When do you still find time to make things that you're not getting paid for?*

KCM: During any break that I have. Usually about once a week (on Sundays, when things have calmed down), I just know it's time. I have to clean the whole art room because by the end of the week it's a mess. So, I clean it and start from scratch. I look at what I have, fiddle around, and make stuff with it. I try to keep a record of everything by taking pictures. Creativity is nothing that I have to force—something clicks in me, and I need that outlet to go in the art room and try something different.

VH: *Is it imperative that you have an isolated craft space?*

KCM: It is, just for the ease of things, because everything's right there. My most shameful crafty secret is my art room because it's such a mess. It's horrible, and I would be embarrassed for anyone to see it. At the same time, it adds an element of fun to the creative process, because I'm always finding things I didn't know I had.

VH: *It's like your own scavenger hunt every week.*

KCM: Exactly! Every time I say I'm going to clean the whole space to make it look super beautiful I decide, "You know what, I'd rather be making something." I leave it alone and start crafting instead.

I feel like all of us need to take time to create, but we must learn to recognize it. It's so easy to suppress, but that turns us into grumpy people down the road.

VH: *As a parent, what do you hope your children gain by being raised by two artists?*

KCM: I'm already starting to see the benefits of it. I've noticed that my children have very open minds to world culture, and they appreciate different types of art and techniques. By having artists as parents, if they really want to do something they love—as long as they work hard and find the right resources—they can make it happen. There are no excuses in this house for saying, "I can't do that." They've seen us work every which way to make our dreams reality. We've always had the bills paid. We've always had food on the table. They've always had clothes. Now one of them is in college. We've made all of that happen by doing what we love to do: making art, music, and writing.

The kids are more respectful of having artistic parents now; whereas, when they were little, we got a lot of, "Why can't you guys just be regular people? You know, like work at a bank or something." We explained that we're doing something different, and not everyone has to work at a bank. Now they have business skills and understand marketing at ages 15 and 18! They know what a press release is. They know how to give a pitch. They know how to talk to customers about art.

VH: *That's a big gift that you've given them.*

KCM: When they apply for jobs, they can write resumes including all the things they've achieved by helping with our business. My daughter isn't a hard-core crafter, but she knows how to make a necklace, what jump rings are, the basics of a sewing machine. In sixth grade, she had her own little business selling handmade fuzzy animals. She collected the money, then decided she didn't want to make them anymore, so she's been through the whole business cycle herself.

VH: *Your artwork and craft line are heavily rooted in your Hispanic heritage. Can you talk a bit about the tie between culture and craft?*

KCM: On a personal level, it comes because I didn't embrace my culture growing up. I hadn't even eaten rice or enchiladas—none of that. I grew up in a school with mostly Anglo kids. I was kind of stuck in the middle—frustrated as I tried to feather my hair, and mad that it didn't work.

When it came to art, I made jewelry to sell at concerts. It started with an African style: red is for the blood of the land; green is for the land itself; yellow is for the sun. Those are still my favorite colors. One day a black girl said, "I love your work, but I have a question. Why don't you make Mexican jewelry?" I thought about it and didn't really know how to respond, but I said, "You've got a good point!"

After that, I told my husband, Patrick, I was going to start making Mexican art, and I got a Flamenco dancer, which he told me wasn't Mexican at all—she's from Spain! I just had to catch up on everything. Patrick pulled out his high school notebook filled with Aztec calendars and goddesses, and I connected to the strong sense of pop culture I saw. It became the missing link to who I am and what I had missed out on. As time went by, I got tired of seeing items in stores like piñatas, the sleeping sombrero guy, or the drunk guy on the side of a shot glass. I thought there was so much more to our culture than that.

On the opposite end of the spectrum was really high-end Mexican art like intricately carved wood pieces from Oaxaca. There was nothing in the middle for mainstream chicas like me. That's how we started making Mexican-inspired art for ourselves, and low and behold, other people wanted it too. We sold so much of it, because not many other people were making it then. We couldn't even keep up with our 300 store accounts!

It's kind of weird to think how many people are making Mexican-inspired art now. I was at a fiesta recently, and a guy said, "This stuff looks like so-and-so's art. He's been doing it for about four or five years." I'm like, "We've been doing it for 20 years." I told Patrick we need to put up a sign that says, "Since 1990," because we haven't copied people—they've copied us. There are some people who know our work well and tell us how they bought Day of the Dead stuff from us in 1993, but now there's all of this Ed Hardy stuff.

As long as we can keep making a living at what we're doing, we're okay. There are a lot of different reasons why incorporating culture is so important to me—not just on a personal note, but also to break stereotypes and combine my love for American and Mexican pop culture.

> There are no excuses in this house for saying, "I can't do that." They've seen us work every which way to make our dreams reality.

VH: *Let's switch gears now and talk about community, which is the focal point of Craft Corps. What role, if any, has crafting played in your own sense of community?*

KCM: The people I love to work with are those who have never crafted. I've tried to reach out to people who already have a sense of community, especially in the Latino culture of hanging out together. Workshops for networking and empowerment already exist, so I've tried to add crafting to that cycle as a way of encouraging visual manifestation and releasing creative energy. The main message is really to connect with all different types of communities, because we all feed off each other and inspire each other. We correct each other when we need to be corrected and help each other out. It's really crucial. Otherwise, you're just living in a bubble. You have to take time to connect with people, which is why I encourage people to join some kind of craft group. It's fun to step out of your normal routine and join a diverse group to share ideas and projects. It's a stress reliever. Community is everything!

VH: *Do you feel any sense of responsibility as a feminist woman in a traditionally female community to use your voice as a forum for progression within that community and beyond?*

KCM: Definitely. As far as feminism goes, yes—on so many different levels. Whether you're a mom, or work in an office, or whatever you do, it's important to get your message out there anyway you can. For me, I do it through crafting, even if I'm sitting in a meeting with people at a newspaper, it's my job to get crafting recognized. Any way I can get that creative voice out there, I do it.

VH: *You're a celebrity because you're a professional crafter. Do you see this as an example of how the industry and our society are evolving, or are people just paying more attention to what's always been there because of avenues like the Internet?*

KCM: I site the Internet as my main launching point of success just because I'm so active on it. Instead of thinking on a local level, the Internet allows me to think big. I didn't have a lot of money and the Internet's free, so I found affordable ways to promote my art. If you use it to your best ability, find the resources you need, have a good product, and want to put yourself out there wholeheartedly, I think anyone can have a successful career. The Internet is definitely a *huge* part of that. I happen to use it for crafting, but no matter what industry you choose, it's all about marketing and staying true to your identity.

For more information about Kathy and her projects, check out: www.craftychica.com

> There are a lot of different reasons why incorporating culture is so important to me—not just on a personal note, but also to break stereotypes and combine my love for American and Mexican pop culture.

The Crafter's Studio

In the great tradition of *Inside the Actor's Studio* and James Lipton:

What craft sound or smell do you love?
It's not really a sound or smell, but I love dipping a big brush in paint and putting it over raw wood. There's something about the wet going on the dry—I get goosebumps from that! I also love blowing glitter off a project I've made, because once you've blown off the excess glitter, the shape underneath takes form—it's the big reveal! Oh, and I still love (and want to eat) the minty paste from kindergarten. Of course, now you could never eat glue, but back then, it was all gritty and sugary.

What craft sound or smell do you hate?
I hate the smell of varnish when I think it should already be aired out. I *hate* the smell of anything moldy, like wet wood. Oh, and I *hate* when I spill unmixed resin, because it never cures—it stays sticky forever. It's like getting syrup on your skin.

What career, other than craft-world domination, would you like to try?
Fiction writing. That is my dream and something that I've always loved to do.

When you burn yourself with a glue gun or spill resin all over the floor, what is your favorite exclamation?
Definitely the F-word. People always say, "Oh, you're so nice. Do you ever get mad?" I'm like, "Oh, hell yes." Like when I get glitter in my teeth—I hate that—it doesn't come out for weeks.

Words to Craft by:

Name: **Susan Barclay**

Age: 38

Digs: Chilliwack, BC

Daily Grind: family support worker

Fave Crafts: sewing, creating bath and body products, bookbinding, paper crafting, knitting, crocheting, shrinky-dink jewelry making, and fabric stenciling

I must seem like a dilettante, flitting from craft to craft, but if I'm going to keep the kids interested, I have to learn everything I can! I created a free youth craft group in partnership with my local library. I offer all the supplies for free, so no one is left out, and I challenge the kids to get out of their comfort zones and try something new. I can't express how wonderful it feels to have a girl show you the book she made for her best friend based on our bookbinding class, or see a homeless street kid take pleasure in decorating a cookie. I've had low-income mothers thank me for showing their girls how to make inexpensive gifts, like bath salts, for the holidays, and I've had parents thank me for offering them a fun way to spend time with their teenagers. I think of our craft groups like a quilting bee—come for the sewing, stay for the conversation. When the topic turns to the differences between love and lust, I know we're doing something right!

Words to Craft by:

Name: **Alison Reeve**

Age: 32

Digs: Sydney, Australia

Daily Grind: director of policy at a government department

Fave Crafts: sewing, knitting, embroidery, and woodwork

More Info: machenmachen.wordpress.com

Last year I designed and made a bag. I wasn't completely happy with how it turned out, but I put a picture of it on my blog anyway. Everyone else thought it was great, so I wrote up the pattern and posted that too. Twenty-four thousand downloads later, I'm glad I made the Wasp Bag, and especially glad that it's free to download. I hope that by helping people make something beautiful, I'm helping them re-engage with what makes them human—the ability to create something from nothing. I was always going to get famous by writing a Booker-winning novel or, failing that, negotiating the next Kyoto protocol. Instead, I'm famous in the most dynamic and varied community in the world for making a bag. Funny how things work out.

chapter eight

Leah Kramer

Leah is at the very soul of
the grass roots, indie craft movement. As the founder of Craftster (www.craftster. org), one of the first social networking sites for hipster crafters, she's connected hundreds of thousands of alterna-crafters across the world. Through this online community, a subculture emerged of the crafty masses, who thrive more than ever today. I spoke to Leah from Craftster's home base in Boston, about her love of kitsch, the craft community, and turning her passion into a viable business.

VH

VH: *What's your first craft-related memory?*

LK: I remember when my mom taught me how to sew a pillow when I was a kid. It was the most exciting thing in the world to take two pieces of fabric, stitch them inside out, and stuff it. It doesn't matter how sloppy your stitching is, when you turn it inside out and stuff it, it looks like a real pillow. It was so exciting that with my own two hands, I could create something that looks like it should look when it's done. I had a lot of fun going into my mom's sewing basket and cutting up things I wasn't supposed to cut up with her good scissors. That's always a fond memory.

VH: *Did you keep that pillow?*

LK: You know, I don't think I have that one pillow, but I do have a lot of stuff from when I was a kid. I have too much stuff! I have a lot of clothing that I used to sew for my dolls and stuffed animals. Looking back on it, they are so awful with their raw edges and buttonholes that are just slits cut in fabric.

VH: *That's great, though—it's uninhibited. It's so funny, making doll clothes out of scraps as children seems to be a common theme among people I'm interviewing.*

LK: We weren't happy with the clothes "as is." We needed to do more.

VH: *I think it also seemed accessible.*

LK: Yes, definitely.

VH: *I did the same thing. I traced around a doll dress onto fabric and basically just cut out two pieces, hand sewed them together, and called it a day! I wasn't a fan of using patterns.*

Is there a moment from your childhood connected to craft that really stands out for you?

LK: I just always loved, loved making stuff. I remember in school, whenever we had projects that were arts and crafts related, like making a valentine to take home, or whatever, I would always go way above and beyond. Mine would have crazy pop-up elements, cutouts, windows, and this and that. My teachers would give me extra kudos for doing extra creative things. I think it was a nice shot in the arm, because that's the one thing I used to get recognition for when I was a kid. I wasn't the best student, otherwise. I always did extra creative things whenever we made hands-on stuff in school.

VH: *Crafting sort of equaled positive reinforcement for you.*

LK: Definitely. I was not so much into gym class, doing sports, and all that, but when it was time for arts and crafts, I was like, "YES!!"

VH: *Who, if anyone, are your crafty influences (past and present)?*

LK: I think it will probably be easier to say who I really love, crafting-wise, in the present. I tend to love really bright, kitschy crafts that incorporate existing items or pay homage to the '50s and '60s. There's a woman named Hannah—her website is www.madewithlovebyhannah.com. She has this really cute, kitschy style that often incorporates Germanic woodland creatures and gingerbread elements that I really love.

I also love Heidi Kenney's site www.mypapercrane.com. It's definitely cutesy, wacky stuff that comes out of this special place in her brain that no one would ever be able to replicate.

There's also Danielle Thompson, who does gorgeous photography, often of kitschy plastic toys and things like that. She has a line of digital scrapbooking elements, which is not something I necessarily do, but they're called Kitschy Digitals. They are beautiful photographs of yarn, flowers, tacky lace in bright colors, pompoms, and this and that, but you can use these elements to make digital scrapbooking layouts.

VH: *Oh, I love that! What about your family, was there anyone else in your family who was crafty?*

LK: My mom, when we were kids, was definitely crafty. She used to make us dresses, and she went through the whole macramé thing in the '70s. I can clearly remember all the owl wall hangings, so that was good.

VH: *Don't you want one of those now, to spray paint hot pink or something?*

LK: I know! That would totally make it perfect.

VH: *Who do you craft with now, or do you have time to craft at this point?*

LK: Actually, I don't have a lot of time to craft. I craft when I have to, like when someone has given me a project to do for a book, or whatever. I spend all my time in front of my computer looking at other people's crafts and wishing I could.

VH: *Tell me a bit about how you took your passion for being creative, melded it with your background as a computer programmer, and turned it into a livelihood.*

LK: I've always been crafty, and I've always loved computers. I know it's kind of geeky, but they have always been on par for me. When I was 10 years old, my family got an Apple 2E with a color screen—I used to write my own little programs in Basic and show them to my parents. It was always so exciting to create things on the computer, as well as to create things with my hands.

I remember the first thing I did to really meld the two was in college. I wrote a program—I was really into beading then, and I created a program you can use with Windows that charted out your design before you beaded it. I actually wrote a few more programs like that, over the years, as I was learning different computer languages. I'd think, "Oh, I'll write a program that has to do with crafting." That way I could learn how to do the computer language and also apply it to something fun.

Whenever I was working my regular day job as a programmer, I just always thought how I would love to do my own thing for a living, and I would love if it had something to do with crafts. I didn't know what it would be, but I thought about it constantly. At first I thought—like a lot of people do—that I would make stuff and sell it.

VH: *And then we all learn the hard way!*

LK: It's hard when you run the numbers. And then, for me (and I know this isn't true for everyone), I don't enjoy making the same thing a hundred times.

VH: *Me too!*

LK: Some people really love it. They have no problem with it. They love the Zen of doing the same thing over again, but I get bored. After making something 10 times, I want to try something else. You really need to be able to make the same thing a hundred times if you want to sell.

VH: *Right, or else you can't make money at it. Unless it's that rare thing where you happen to have the right thing at the right time and can charge a gazillion dollars for it, because it takes hours and hours to make.*

LK: And that's especially hard. The people who are making it out there have gotten to a point where they can have other people make things for them. So, it's tough. I think selling crafts is great as a side business, and a lot of people are able to do it for extra income, but it's really tough to make that your thing.

When I figured out it wasn't going to work for me, I thought about creating the website Craftster. Actually, I didn't think that it would become my job. I was like, "Oh, it will just be a side project like everything craft related." I remember spending five bucks a month on Web hosting and thinking, "Sixty bucks a year—that's expensive!" It just grew and grew. After keeping my job and doing the safe thing for awhile (I needed realistic things like health insurance), and doing the website on the side, it just became apparent that it could potentially be a viable business.

There was a long period of time where I was living like a starving artist, trying to make it work, after I decided to quit my job and give it a go. I think it's important for people who are going to turn crafting into their job to allow themselves to try it. There are a lot of people on the outside who will look in at you, and say, "That's not a real job, you can't do crafts for a living," even when you know it's more work than anyone does at their regular jobs. You need to tell yourself that it's okay to do something you love as a living, as long as you can make it work—and it's going to be a lot of work.

VH: *Do you think people's conception changes when you say, "I'm making a living as an artist" versus, "I'm making a living as a crafter"? I have been talking a lot with the people I'm interviewing about the difference between the words art and craft. I wonder if the stigma of one word over the other affects how people respond to what you're doing.*

LK: Good question. I know there are probably a lot of people who think of crafts as a superfluous, useless part of life. People are used to going to craft fairs and seeing little dishtowels with crocheted tops, and the little scrubbies that the older ladies make. They're cute, and they're good little gifty items, but they're not important to society; whereas, people perceive art as something that is more important.

The fact of the matter is: people love to incorporate fun, unique, one-of-a-kind things into their lives, and crafting is a way you can affordably buy something really unique that makes you happy. Hopefully people's perceptions have changed, but I do see what you're saying—people who aren't fully entrenched in it don't understand that it's like tiny little wearable pieces of art. Hopefully that's changing more and more, especially as sites like Etsy are on the tips of everyone's tongues these days.

VH: *Is there one craft that speaks more to you creatively than others?*

LK: I guess I'm really drawn to cleverly reusing old things and making them into new things. I love that kind of craft because it can keep crafting really cheap—like if you go to a thrift store to buy a bunch of old bed sheets, and you make something out of them. It can also be environmentally friendly, which I love. I also love how there's an extra challenge involved. I see something cool looking, or an old thing on the side of the road or in a thrift store, and I hem and haw over what can I make out of this thing, and it eventually clicks.

One of my favorite projects on Craftster a few years ago was made by this woman who had an old eight-track player, like the kind you have in your house, not in your car. She made a lamp out of it. The base was the eight-track player, and the neck of the lamp was all the eight-tracks stacked up.

VH: *Cute!*

LK: I just love that she pondered over this thing that she could have thrown away, but instead, she has this clever idea and a great conversation piece. I am really drawn into that kind of craft.

VH: *What's your favorite thing about crafting?*

LK: I really love how it makes you think, and that you have to figure out what you are going to do. I love figuring stuff out. I like how having patience pays off. You add one little thing at a time, and it eventually turns into something else. I always say I love do-it-yourselfers because they're not afraid to think and figure stuff out. I like hanging around people who like to think of creative things, because usually, that translates to other elements of life. They like to figure out how the economy works, how the refrigerator works. So, I love that mode of thinking.

VH: *The focus of this book is community, and your site Craftster has been at the forefront of nurturing community on the Web since the beginning of this craft enthusiasm wave. What were your hopes for your site when you started it in 2003?*

LK: I started to think about crafting a couple of years before I started the site, as something that I wanted to do as an extension of my personality and my own style. All my life I have been crafty, and I started to get to a point, right around

> I like hanging around people who like to think of creative things, because usually, that translates to other elements of life. They like to figure out how the economy works, how the refrigerator works. So, I love that mode of thinking.

the time I started Craftster, where I would go into a craft fair or a book store and look at the craft magazines, and my heart started to sink a little bit about what I was seeing. Those cross-stitched home-sweet-home plaques weren't doing it for me, personally. I really wanted to make stuff, but I wanted it to be my own style and my own personality. My idea of Craftster came about because a lot of other people think of crafting that way, and I wanted us all to get together and inspire each other, and redefine the idea of crafting.

VH: *Can you talk about Craftster's role in perpetuating that community and future goals to continue doing so?*

LK: The thing that's really neat about Craftster is that you may have only a couple of people in your own little neighborhood, in your school, or in your friendship circles that are crafty, or you might not even know anybody that's crafty, but here, you can get into this community and meet people all over the world who think like you—which is really great. It really helps fuel each other's fire, and you can resonate with a group of people that you wouldn't have been able to communicate with otherwise. They don't live near you necessarily, but real life friendships are made. Sometimes people meet someone they happen to live near, but I always hear people saying, "I am going to England for a vacation, and I met up with this person I met on Craftster who's going to show me around." I love the real life connections people make with people they never knew about. That's been really cool.

For the future direction of Craftster, it will pretty much be on the same track of allowing people to easily share ideas with each other and allowing people to gain inspiration. We hear a lot of people tell us they didn't even know they had a crafty bone in their body, and then they came to Craftster and saw these ideas, and they were tempted to try them. We just want to keep making that easy for people to do.

VH: *Do you think that people don't know they're creative because there is this little box of what people think being creative is?*

LK: Definitely. I was talking about being a kid and doing hands-on artsy-crafty things in school, but then high school or junior high came along and you start doing fine arts, for a lack of better words. You learn how to sketch, you learn how to draw, learn how to paint, maybe you learn to do pottery, but not crafts. If you're not good at drawing, painting, and the kind of stuff you learn in the upper years of school, then maybe you think you're not creative.

Acceptable creative outlets at that level are probably music, painting, and drawing, but crafting is still not a big part of the high school art program, sadly. A lot of people think they are not creative, but it is so important to have a creative outlet in life. It's great that crafting has been exposed as something people can get into at so many different levels and can express in so many different styles. I think people are opening their minds to the fact that crafting can be a really cool creative outlet.

> We hear a lot of people tell us they didn't even know they had a crafty bone in their body, and then they came to Craftster and saw these ideas, and they were tempted to try them.

VH: *What role, if any, has crafting played in your own personal sense of community?*

LK: For me, it's mostly online, although I have been involved in the Bazaar Bizarre craft fair in Boston for years, so that's real people getting together. That's been really cool. Then, for four years, I was the owner of Magpie. I'm actually not an owner anymore, but I still call myself a founder of the store. I decided to trim back the amount of projects I have going on so that I have more time for life. I'm sure you know how that is! It was always really cool to have real live interaction with people, to be at the store, working the register and have people come in and see the reactions on their faces when they looked at the crafts. So, probably the Bazaar Bizarre and the Magpie are the real live interactions I've had.

VH: *What does the indie craft movement mean to you, and how do you think it's changed over the past few years?*

LK: Sometimes I think about where, and when, and why it started. It seems to me—this is just my experience—that in order for any kind of movement to take off, there has to be people at the very center of it who have social capital.

That indie core of people—they were like renegades in their time. They were maybe art school students who were bucking the system and sewing in addition to painting and drawing. Or they had their regular jobs but were also in a band, and they decided to branch out even more and get into making stuff.

At the core of it, they were doing something really unexpected; they were almost crafting because it was unexpected of that particular kind of person, if that makes sense. When I think about the very first Bazaar Bizarre that happened in Boston in 2001, there were about 20 vendors, that's it. They were all people who knew about each other from being in each other's bands and this and that, and the stuff they made was just so wacky and off-the-wall awesome.

There was this one guy who probably never crafted a thing in his life. He decided to make record-album cover re-creations that were all different colored pieces of macaroni glued onto cardboard. I think it started there and people gravitated towards it. I guess now, there's just a lot more people participating. Everyone's taking what they personally love in life and translating that into a craft. On Craftster, we see a lot of pop culture-related crafts—people who love old school Super Mario games and translate that into their work.

> I really wanted to make stuff, but I wanted it to be my own style and my own personality. My idea of Craftster came about because a lot of other people think of crafting that way, and I wanted us all to get together and inspire each other, and redefine the idea of crafting.

VH: *I designed wrist warmers with the Mario mushrooms on them!*

LK: Those are so cute! There's a wider audience of people, but they are still holding true to the idea that it's unexpected of them to craft, so they're going to craft. Maybe it's less unexpected now, but people definitely take what they love in life and translate that into crafts.

VH: *There's been an influx of indie craft fairs across the nation, one of which, Bazaar Bizarre, you were behind for years. What role do you think those fairs play, not only in our sense of crafty community, but also in shattering some of the still prevalent stereotypes about who crafters are?*

LK: I think they have been so important. It's amazing to me. A craft fair is like a happy marriage of the people who just want to make stuff and show it off to the world, and the people who love to buy stuff. We are floored by the attendance we get every year at the Bazaar Bizarre. In fact, we can't even find a venue big enough for the event without getting into trade centers, which are crazy to work with.

I think people who love to make stuff also enjoy showing it just as much, and getting feedback from people. Some artists I know are happy to paint in their room all day long and never show anyone what they make. Then, there are a lot of people, especially in the craft world, who get as much satisfaction out of making things as they do from the feedback. A craft fair is a great place where someone walks up and says, "Oh my God, this is really clever," or "This is really beautiful," and it works out for both parties involved.

VH: *Do you think that's also why so many crafters are also gift makers? There's some sense of validation when you make someone a gift and they truly appreciate it.*

LK: I think that's definitely true. I hadn't really thought of that aspect of it. There's something so satisfying about giving something to somebody. You know they're going to appreciate it an extra amount, because you spent time and thought about that person while you were making it.

VH: *What's the most exciting change you've seen in the craft world over the last five years? What do you see as our community's biggest challenge?*

LK: Maybe I have already said this too many times, but I think it's exciting that people are looking at crafts in a whole new way and thinking of them as a socially cool, acceptable creative outlet. I know that's kind of broad. My first thought was that maybe the crafting industry doesn't understand this community, and maybe they should, but that's not really a problem. People in the indie craft movement don't really want the craft industry to start making products for them. They will always use materials in their own way. The most important thing in the world is that they can do whatever the heck they want with the material at hand. I do hear a lot of people struggling and wanting to make a better living at their crafts. That does seem to be a challenge for a lot of people. What is the solution to that? I don't know.

VH: *Well, part of it is escalating the value, which we are trying to do. We have to be able to value ourselves before anyone else will.*

LK: Definitely. There's one challenge I face on Craftster that doesn't really apply to the indie crafters who try to sell their stuff—this is a different kind of challenge. I was talking about the crafting industry and how we don't really want them to create products for any crafters, but it would be nice if they understood how big the movement of indie crafting is and maybe lent a little more support to it. On Craftster, for example, we try to reach out to a lot of advertisers in the crafting industry because that's how we pay our employees. They are happy to drop lots and lots of money on a mainstream crafting magazine, but they don't quite understand the indie craft movement and how most of it happens online. That's where they need to reach people, and that has been a problem for us.

VH: *There's a big shift in that happening right now. So many magazines are going under because of that very thing—people are finally starting to realize, for better or for worse, that they can get more bang for their buck on the Web, and people can click through to purchase something right there.*

LK: We see a lot of companies that probably want to be online and reach this audience, but don't know how yet. We are not seeing as much of a relationship with these organizations as we would like to. I think that will definitely change. It's like anything, like when television first came about, people said, "I don't understand advertising on television. What are you talking about?"

VH: *As a feminist woman in a traditionally female community, do you feel any responsibility to use your voice as a forum for progression within that community and beyond?*

LK: We try to keep politics out of Craftster, but there are lots of days when I hear something in the news and think, "Wow, Craftster has a huge audience, and

I would love to write something about this." I always wanted to push Obama onto Craftster, but we try not to because we have people from all walks of life. Whenever any kind of political discussion comes up, it just turns into a crazy drama, so we try to avoid anything to do with religion or politics on Craftster.

Feminism is more acceptable on Craftster, and people do post a lot of girl power context. I think it's great that there is never any drama surrounding it. I think the concept of taking back crafts, in general, is a cool twist in the feminist movement. There was a time when you were expected to craft if you were a woman—like mending your husband's socks. Now you can craft just because you want to. There is no stigma anymore. You are doing it because you want to, and not because you should.

VH: *Do you try and perpetuate that belief?*

LK: I don't know if we purposely try to perpetuate it, but we are 96 percent female, and we're all very supportive of one another. It's such a hugely supportive community. I think it's just perpetuated in a more organic way.

For more information about Leah and her projects, go to:
www.craftster.org

The Crafter's Studio

In the great tradition of *Inside the Actor's Studio* and James Lipton:

What craft sound or smell do you love?
The smell of wood craft, unfinished wood, and wood shavings—it's really nice.

What craft sound or smell do you hate?
I hate E6000, even though it's the most awesome glue ever.

What career, other than craft-world domination, would you like to try?
I really love researching things to death, and sometimes I think I'd love to be a researcher.

When you burn yourself with a glue gun or or cut yourself with with a craft knife, what is your favorite exclamation?
The F-word.

Words to Craft by:

A few months back, I put together an art fair featuring over 30 local artists in Chicago. I am fortunate to be friends with such great artists who collaborated on a poster design, silk-screened and distributed posters, and made a website. I spent so much time trying to promote the event and make it successful for the participating artists. I've found that sometimes artists have a hard time promoting their own work, and I wanted to create a venue to help them. The event was a success! I couldn't believe the outpouring of gratitude I received for putting the fair together. The media was very receptive to the handmade cause; Etsy even came on board as a sponsor. It was a boost of confidence, and although it was a lot of work and stressful at times, it was so worth it!

Name:
Stephanie Keller
Age: 28
Digs: Chicago, IL
Daily Grind: retail extraordinaire
Fave Crafts: Gocco'd greeting cards

Words to Craft by:

My first batch of soap was made in my tiny kitchen on 8th Street in Brooklyn, circa 2000, so the name 8th Street Soap Kitchen was accurate. But these days, I make it in my basement on Taylor Street in a different city altogether. Never expecting my soap to get into the hands of anyone but friends and family, I wasn't concerned about the longevity of the name. The biggest compliment I've ever gotten was from my neighbor's daughter. She lives across the alley and knows my house isn't on 8th Street. Turns out, she's been operating on the assumption that every morning when I leave my house, I'm going off to my big soap factory somewhere on 8th Street (where I employ scores of Oompa-Loompas). She looked so disappointed when she saw the real factory—the cluttered corner of my basement lit by Christmas lights, filled with bottles, pails, and soaps in mid-cure—and discovered I have a day job that has nothing to do with soap. People sometimes ask me if I've thought about quitting my job and doing soap full-time, but the beauty of making soap is that it isn't a job. If I *had* to do it, it wouldn't be as fun. It would become, well, a job.

Name: **Jenny Isaacs**
Age: 38
Digs: Washington, DC
Daily Grind: advertising art director
Fave Crafts: soap!
More Info: See www.8thstreetsoap.com under "the soaps." I joke that some people write blogs; I make soap.

chapter nine

Shannon Okey

Shannon Okey is a force

to be reckoned with. She's a teacher, editor, designer, and author of a whopping 12 craft-related books. In addition, she owns Knitgrrl Studio, a learning center for all things fiber, and founded the indie pattern distributor Stitch Cooperative. Although I've been in contact with Shannon since 2002, it wasn't until a couple of years later when she was a guest on *Knitty Gritty* that we actually met in person. I find Shannon to be a powerhouse in our field, and she's someone I trust and respect. Because of the way we both work, we are, in a sense, co-workers sharing virtual cubicle space in the industry. For this interview, I met her at the water cooler via phone from her place in Cleveland, Ohio.

VH

VH: *What's your first craft-related memory?*

SO: That's a good one. Probably sewing Halloween costumes with my mom—I went through this *Clash of the Titans* stage. I was Athena for Halloween one year. My mom went to art school, so not only can she sew, but she can do tons of other things. In addition to sewing the robe for the costume, she made me a papier-mâché helmet in the backyard; you know, where you blow up the balloon and put the papier-mâché over it and pop it. I remember watching her and sort of micromanaging and art directing, "No, no, no, it should be this way." That's probably some of the first stuff I can remember in terms of actually helping and being presented with something.

VH: *How old were you?*

SO: I was probably six, if I had to take a guess.

VH: *What did your dad do?*

SO: He is a carpenter and a musician, so he builds things and plays music.

VH: *Your mom—you said she was an artist, but what kind?*

SO: She's a photographer and watercolorist; those are her primary things. There are a lot of painters in my family.

VH: *Is there a crafty moment from your childhood that will always stick with you?*

SO: I picked up embroidery before I picked up knitting. My mother doesn't have the patience for knitting, and she is also left-handed and perhaps slightly dyslexic. Even though she can knit, she has no interest in it, so I came to knitting really late. I came to embroidery on my own—got the materials from somewhere. You have to understand, my mother is a big thrift store/garage sale person, and we always had stuff sitting around. It was just a question of picking it up and doing something with it.

It's not like my mom gave me the pre-printed pattern and said, "Here you go." My experience was more focused on watching my mom, who is really into antiques, doing these little antique-style samplers. I'd think, "That's kind of boring. I'm going to make my own." I remember watching her make colonial samplers and thinking, "Ha, I don't have to do this boring colonial one that you're doing. I can do whatever I want." That strikes me as one of the first moments when I really went, "I don't have to follow along; I can do whatever it is I want to do."

VH: *That's a big deal, especially to get that feeling so young, because I think you come across people who are really intimidated by going off-pattern, no matter what the craft genre is.*

SO: It's amazing. I have to fight constantly inside the Yarn Forward group on Ravelry.

"Oh, could I do this?"

"Yeah, sure do it."

"Yeah, but, but, but can I do this?"

"Yeah, sure do it."

"Well, but..."

You'd think you were telling them to stomp on a kitten or something. The very thought of deviating from a pattern in any way is terrifying for people. When I'm teaching, I say, "Listen, nothing is going to blow up. If you have to rip it back out, that's cool. Don't worry about it."

VH: *Where do you think that fear comes from?*

SO: I don't know. I talk to my test knitter a lot, who is from the United Kingdom, because I need to ask her if I'm saying it wrong to them. How are they not getting this? She says they are trained from a very early age to follow the pattern at all costs. I guess there's the fear of ruining the materials or not doing it right. Name one thing you did perfectly the first time you ever did it. That's just sort of freakish, if you can.

VH: *I recently interviewed Diva Zappa for my Knit.1 column. She was telling me how it bums her out that she doesn't make a lot of mistakes anymore. She felt like her mistakes were the only thing that made her pieces stand out from something you buy at the Gap.*

SO: She also comes from a musician family background and sees her parent practicing, practicing, and practicing all the time. Maybe it's drummed into us that it's okay to practice; it's okay to not always do something perfectly. You can just sit there and fiddle around. I used to get dragged to gigs and band practice all the time. I know you don't just suddenly play the song. It's a little more involved than that. Maybe people who don't come from artistic backgrounds think they should be able to do it perfectly the first time, or don't bother. That's something we need to correct—it's something people should realize.

VH: *Who, if anyone, helped open the professional crafty doors for you?*

SO: Obviously, I had the childhood experiences, in terms of getting primed. But the two people I give big credit to are Lucy Lee, who owns Mind's Eye Yarns in Cambridge, Massachusetts, and Kathy Cano-Murillo (see page 68). When I moved to Boston, I started knitting at Lucy's store. She taught me how to knit better and how to spin. Then, Kathy—this is back when knit blogging was really new and there weren't that many—Kathy said, "Well, my publisher wants to do a knitting book, and I know you write and knit. Are you interested?" She introduced me to my first publisher. So between the two of them, they really got me going professionally.

VH: *How did you become a career crafter?*

SO: I was always a writer; I got out of school and went to work for a software company doing international software rollouts. While I was there, I got a job to freelance a traveling book. I was traveling around and writing about six European cities in the course of about two weeks. So, I had experience writing lengthy things, and I had always written, in general. But being able to turn that around and do a how-to book with descriptive text is a different ball game, as you know.

My first knitting book, *Knitgrrl*, was adopted by some adults because it had full-color photos instead of blind drawings, because my mother is a photographer. I was able to sit down and say, "Okay, I need you to do these photos for me, and this is what we need to show." I worked through how to communicate what I needed to express. I mean, if you're sitting here next to me, it's very easy for me to show you what to do. In a photo, you have to break everything down into component steps, and know what each step is trying to achieve.

The best photographer I've ever worked with on any of my books wasn't even a full-time photographer. He was a construction guy who did photography part-time, but because he was a construction guy, he understood that things are made up of different steps, and you have to show each step clearly, or it will not come across to the reader. So what he would do—instead of just take a pretty shot, like

> I have been in a real free-form mode lately, where I draw a little sketch for myself and think about what I want to do. Then I cast it on and go for it. I think I've really stepped back and retrenched—I have my mojo back, as it were.

a lot of photographers—is say, "Okay, what are we trying to show here?" That's the question you have to continually ask yourself. Whether it's something you are writing, designing, or trying to communicate, you ask, "What I am trying to show here?" If you can answer that question clearly and provide materials so audiences get the point, you're much better off than somebody who went to school to do illustration books or some other career path.

VH: *So you got your book deal, and from there, sort of turned it into a career?*

SO: Yes. I did the first two books because I had moved back home from Boston and got the contracts for them back-to-back—they were tied together. I finished those books and then sent out an e-mail to my mailing list saying I'm interested in alternative fibers. Back then, it was pretty much hemp and soy; I was playing with them and said I'd really like to do a book on this subject. All these publishers were not interested working with me. That's when someone from Interweave raised their head and said, "What?" They ended up giving me the next two books.

I think you have to continually communicate with your network of people and other people who are interested in what you do. That is how each successive deal has come about. The crochet book came about because another writer I know said she didn't have time to do it, and she asked if I would be interested in it. With my book *Alt Fiber*, I had shopped all over the place and finally Ten Speed said, "Oh yeah, that fits into what we are doing." *The Pillow Book* with Chronicle came about because I quite literally kept in touch with the editors and kept saying, "I want to do this." They'd turn me down, so I'd say, "Okay, what do you want to do?" They said, "We would like to do a book of pillows." All right, no skin off my nose.

VH: *It's like George Clooney who says he does "one movie for them and one for me." You agree to do a pillow book, if you can do another book later.*

SO: That's exactly it. You see it in the submissions world too. Rather than someone not submit anything at all, I would much rather get an e-mail saying, "Hey, I'm

trying to design this thing for the magazine. What do you think?" Because chances are good I'm going to have an opinion about it. I might tell the person we've just done 18 cardigans in the last issue, so would you do a pullover instead? I think book editors are the same way. They are human; you have to ask what they want. They are looking to fill specific spots in the same way that you are looking to push your fabulous idea.

With the book I'm currently negotiating, I tweaked the concept because the publisher said they would rather do it more like a technique book. I think people who get too attached to their initial idea are just going to be frustrated. If you are willing to be flexible and are willing to change, it is much better for everybody in the long run, and you'll get more work.

VH: *There's a way to do it without compromising your own artistic integrity, too.*

SO: Sure there is. It all comes down to communication, because we're essentially in the business of doing that. We are communicating about crafts, and with how-to books you must get your message across. Turning it into a career means that you also have to continue to get your message across to the people who are going to give you work.

VH: *You mentioned sewing, crocheting, and obviously knitting—are there any other crafts that you really enjoy? Or, are there some crafts that you have no interest in at all?*

SO: Spinning and felting, and anything related to raw fiber are my big three. In terms of things that I'm not really interested in—I'm not a big jewelry person. I just don't generally wear it a lot, so making it isn't interesting to me.

VH: *One of the focuses of this book is to nurture the community that we are a part of. You have fought so hard when it comes to fair trade for designers. Talk about why you started the Stitch Cooperative and what you hope it achieves.*

SO: I was actually looking this up the other day. The history of the Stitch Co-op started about six or seven months before the winter trade show of the National NeedleArts Association (TNNA) in 2007. I was seeing people start to publish their own stuff and independent patterns. Knitty (www.knitty.com), an online knitting publication, was one sort of magazine-style source, but I was not seeing other ways people could get patterns into yarn stores. So, I started playing around with different ideas of how you could best do that. Obviously, I am a big technophile. I love technology. I looked at some ideas of doing CD quarterlies for yarn stores and experimented with other super ideas.

What ended up happening was that there was a meeting at TNNA about possibly starting a union for designers. It never got off the ground, though. A bunch of designers had dinner and decided, the heck with this, let's just do it. *If we are going to put things out, if we are going to publish them, let's join together.* It's the same way your Craft Mafia happened. People started realizing that there's good strength in numbers, and we can help promote each other. I think that's the organic way of starting something, and it makes sense to people who have our skill sets. We can't always be in one place at the same time, and we can't all keep up with 800 things, but if we band together, we have a greater power.

So, we saw a lot of companies and service providers who were getting patterns into the end-user's hand, but nobody was targeting the yarn store market. The thing about running a store is that you don't want to deal with invoices from 40 different designers. That would drive you nuts. So, we offered one-stop shopping where people could get designs from all these different designers in one place, with one invoice and one ordering form.

At TNNA shows or similar events, we could band together and afford a decent booth that we might not be able to get alone. Going to TNNA since 2005, I noticed many designers who took out their own table—it was inevitably a really small table—and people walked by them like, what could they possibly have? But when you're all there together in a big group, you can have a big booth full of stuff. People want to stop and look. Having all of us in one place makes it easier for a yarn company to approach us about doing a design booklet or other work. They don't have to contact 80 people to get five responses. So, really, it was just about joining together and doing good things for ourselves and for other parts of the industry we interact with.

> The very thought of deviating from a pattern in any way is terrifying for people. When I'm teaching, I say, "Listen, nothing is going to blow up. If you have to rip it back out, that's cool. Don't worry about it."

VH: *How do you approach the current dilemma of selling patterns during a time when there is so much available for free online?*

SO: That's true, there have always been free patterns out there; there will always be free patterns. I think there is an expectation, though, that more work goes into a paid pattern; it's not just somebody who has thrown it out there. I'm not saying Knitty or other reliable sites do that, but the vast majority of free patterns have not been tested or tech edited. If you pay for a pattern, you should expect better service. You should expect it to be fully tech edited, have really good charts, and have really good imagery. I think I do fairly well selling individual patterns because customers who bought from me in the past, or who have heard about my patterns, know that I'm going to e-mail them back if they have a question. I'm going to address a question if it comes up multiple times, and I'll post answers on the website. That responsiveness trumps what the knitting magazines are often able to do. They couldn't handle questions from 10,000 people all at once; that would be crazy. I think there will always be a market for patterns that you buy, because you can expect better service.

VH: *What role, if any, has crafting played in your own sense of community?*

SO: When I think about it, my community is who I speak to on a daily basis, and who I interact with on a daily basis—they are pretty much doing the same things I do. There are other designers and other craft people to mingle with. They are my water cooler of the day.

VH: *That's how I consider Twitter and Facebook, for sure.*

SO: Twitter's also great if you have a question. You throw it out there, and 50 people will write back with a response right away. It has made working from home much easier.

VH: *It really has; it's not as isolating.*

SO: You don't think, "Oh, it's only me today, having a horrible day."

VH: *You are also the editor of* Yarn Forward Magazine *out of the United Kingdom. Do you find a difference in how knitting is perceived overseas as opposed to the United States?*

SO: Yes, I think there is a difference. Besides being a little less daring in the United Kingdom, I think they tend to learn younger than we do, which is something to their advantage. My test knitter, who is from Yorkshire, learned at the age of four. She has a good 20+ years of knitting time on me. It's nice because I can rely on some of her experience to take care of things I don't know about. But in terms of audiences, we like the same sort of patterns, the same sort of challenges. They are really hungry for information, because the typical United Kingdom knitting magazine is a lot more like a women's magazine than a craft magazine. So the details, how-to's, and technical articles aren't really good. Otherwise, it's pretty much the same. We are all knitters, and we all want something fun to knit.

"

A bunch of designers had dinner and decided, the heck with this, let's just do it. If we are going to put things out, if we are going to publish them, let's join together.

VH: *That's interesting, since it seems like there are a lot more knitters overseas.*

SO: It is much more common.

VH: *They teach it in more schools, you know. It's very common there, but here it seems to be trendier. Trendiness is always linked to media attention, so maybe that's the big difference.*

SO: There's also that age difference thing. You get more of us who were getting married and having kids in the '70s. A lot of us were raised in non-crafty households—obviously, some of us were—but the majority of us were not. Elsewhere in the world, it's much more common to grow up knowing how to do a variety of crafts.

VH: *For aspiring designers who might be reading this chapter, what tips can you offer for getting their design submissions noticed by an editor?*

SO: Completeness; paying attention to any calls they see. For example, if we post a call for submissions, I'll be very specific and explain that I want certain things e-mailed. People write me asking where to mail it. Well, you don't mail it; that's not going to work. You have to pay attention, and you have to be very complete and thorough, and take tips from whatever the call is telling you. Don't make publishers do the work. I think the more work you make an editor or publisher do, the less likely they'll take time to do it. You'd have to be really amazing for them to say, "Oh yes, I will invest 20 minutes to figure out what you are talking about."

The best designers, who get things accepted almost immediately, present a swatch, a sketch, and describe exactly what they're thinking. If you are open and responsive, and stay on top of your e-mail, your work will get accepted. Also, be professional. I see a lot of budding designers on Ravelry who throw a fit and say, "They wanted me to knit it in a different yarn." Well, that is often the case. It's kind of like saying, "I took a job as a car mechanic and they wanted me to fix Hondas, but I only want to work on Porches." That happens, that's part of the job. If you don't understand that, then maybe it's not the right job for you.

VH: *Is there anything else you want to say about what crafting means to you or has given you?*

SO: I love watching something shape up on the needles. I have been in a real free-form mode lately, where I draw a little sketch for myself and think about what I want to do. Then I cast it on and go for it. I've been getting the greatest results, and I'm knitting faster than I've knitted in ages. I think I've really stepped back and retrenched—I have my mojo back, as it were. I think sometimes you need to reevaluate your own working style.

VH: *You get in knitting slumps; that happens to me all the time.*

SO: You sit there going, "Oh God, I don't want to write this pattern out and then knit it." Why not start knitting it, and then write it, and change it up a little bit. Changing it up really makes a difference.

For more information about Shannon and her projects, go to:
www.knitgrrl.com

The Crafter's Studio

In the great tradition of *Inside the Actor's Studio* and James Lipton:

What craft sound or smell do you love?
Buffy the Vampire Slayer going on TV while I'm knitting.

What craft sound or smell do you hate?
Hot glue.

What career, other than knitting-world domination, would you like to try?
Writer of more general topics.

When you drop a stitch or make one sleeve longer than the other, what is your favorite exclamation?
The F-word.

Words to Craft by:

I have been crafting all of my life. My most amazing experience was when I proposed a knitting class to my executive director at the day program where I teach (Hope University in Anaheim, CA, a fine arts program for adults with developmental disabilities). I was allowed one class to see if our students would be able to knit. My first student learned after just a few hours of one-on-one; I must admit that I cried when this woman who had been told her entire life that she was not capable of learning how to knit actually knitted on her own. She and several other students of mine are now happily knitting, crocheting, purling, and even reading patterns! I found that my autistic students who could not verbally contribute to other classes will engage in conversation within knitting groups. I now teach three to four knitting classes a week. It has been an amazing experience to bring craft to this population, to see them succeed, and to build their confidence. I am so proud of them.

Name: Sandra D. Carter
Age: 48
Digs: Long Beach, CA
Daily Grind: special education instructor, horticultural therapist, knitting teacher, and yarn shop employee
Fave Crafts: knitting, crocheting, nalbinding, sewing, and sculptural work
More Info: yarnivore.blogspot.com and www.hestiashands.com

Words to Craft by:

Knitting has enriched my life in many dimensions: community, mindfulness, creativity, and pure tactile pleasure. But when I really think about it, its most profound gift is *omnipotentiality*. I picked up this concept from a book that describes how growing up means coming to terms with the fact that we're not omnipotential, that we can't always do or be whatever we want. Real life has constraints. This has been a theme of my twenties, as I've made choices and commitments and, in the process, closed some doors. I'm not angsty or unhappy about this; it's just the way things are in life. But knitting has none of those constraints or closed doors. It can be challenging or meditative, summery or wintry, glamorous or rustic, generous or self-indulgent. In my hands, yarn becomes whatever I want or need it to be. My embrace of omnipotentiality definitely shapes the kind of knitter I am. I often have projects on the needles to suit every mood and season. It means I exuberantly experiment and don't feel bad about abandoning things that don't work. It means I don't feel burdened by my stash, because I see it as a store of fantasies rather than just yarn accumulation.

Name: Hanna Breetz
Age: 29
Digs: Phoenix, AZ
Daily Grind: Ph.D. student in environmental policy
Fave Crafts: knitting, spinning, and natural dyeing
More Info: evergreenknits.blogspot.com and www.greenknitter.com

Photo by Alisa Breetz

chapter ten

Christina Batch-Lee

The first time I met Christina, she was a guest on my show, *Knitty Gritty*. At the time, she was editor of the beloved magazine *Adorn* that encouraged readers to embellish items with various crafts, including knitting. Through ups and downs in our industry, I've gotten to know Christina better, and have had the pleasure of keeping in contact with her since she accepted her position at the groundbreaking Web phenomenon, Etsy. She's a smart, creative lady who's full of ideas and fun to be around. I called her at the Etsy Labs in Brooklyn, where we talked about elevating the value of craft, promoting community, and Christina's journey from traditional fine arts to the world of crafty goodness.

VH

VH: *What's your first craft-related memory?*

CBL: My nursery school was really crafty. I remember making butter, hand-painted plates, and things like that. I just loved it.

VH: *You're the first person I've talked to who recalls making butter as their first craft memory!*

CBL: That's what popped into my head when you asked that. I remember being blown away like, "Wait, you can make butter?!" It just completely stuck with me. I think I've always been a non-traditional learner, too, so it always spoke to me when I could get my hands into things.

VH: *Is there another moment from your childhood connected to craft that really stands out for you?*

CBL: Sure. I think it's when I first discovered that I could make clothes for my own dolls and get exactly what I wanted—at least as much as my skills would allow.

VH: *How did you discover that?*

CBL: My mom had some scrap fabric and lace lying around. I was so drawn to it and wondered what I could do with it. I was maybe five or six years old. My mom sewed a little bit but wasn't super involved because she worked. She said, "Why don't you make something out of it," so I made a little tube dress for my Barbie doll out of blue corduroy and white lace. It was really simple, but I loved it! I also made her a matching hat. Just being able to create something from scratch was really mind-blowing to me.

VH: *Do you still have that dress?*

CBL: Somewhere. I still have all of my Barbies. There's a suitcase in my parents' attic with my whole collection. About five years ago, my mom actually loaned them to our neighbors who have young grandkids, and I was like, "What? You let my Barbies go?!" I'm still attached.

VH: *Now, as a professional designer/crafter, is there an equally important moment for you?*

CBL: What I love about being involved with crafts professionally is that every day is so different. The people I meet and the collaborations I become involved with keep it so interesting and engaging. The first time I realized that I could do this for a living was really exciting. I had studied fine arts and painting but always looked at crafts as my outlet and release from more serious studies. My first job in the industry was being an assistant editor at the Jo-Ann magazine. I just helped out with photo shoots and made samples, like this seashell wreath that ended up on the cover of the magazine—I was completely blown away by that! There really is a way to do what you love and get paid for it. That will stay with me. Even though I've changed roles a lot in my career, it's that ability to be in touch with things that speak to me, personally, that's so amazing.

VH: *What's the difference for you between art and craft?*

CBL: This is definitely my personal experience, but I took art a little too seriously for my own good. It's what I wanted to do and what I studied. Craft was a release where I could do whatever I wanted—it was freedom. Ultimately, I don't think there's very much difference, though. You can create craft from the perspective of an artist using whatever tools are at your disposal. On the flip side, you can create art like a craftsperson and really get into the materials and the technique, while creating something that's traditionally considered an art medium.

VH: *Why do you think the perception between the two are so different?*

CBL: Traditionally, there has not been a high perception of value for things women do as a part of their daily survival. I think that's changing, but still lingers. Traditionally, I think women ran their households and created things out of necessity, whether it was to recycle feed sacks for quilts or dresses, or whatever they needed for their family's well-being. Yes, there's art and beauty in that, but it wasn't a means to create wealth; whereas, art developed along a different line and had more to do with pursuing and supporting the desires of the wealthy.

VH: *Obviously, it's changed leaps and bounds since the '50s, but there's still a stigma with craft, even amongst people who are making money from it. Do you feel any sense of responsibility as a leader in the industry to work on changing that even more?*

CBL: Definitely! My involvement with Etsy has been mind-blowing because it's flipped that stigma on its head. Every day I hear stories about people finding an audience for their very particular creation. They're able to sell and make a living. If there's anything we can do to help promote that, we want to. It's definitely a priority. As far as the perception of craft goes, within the craft community itself there's a divide between old and new craft. For example, people recognize whether someone has had guild training or not.

VH: *The other one that's even more recent, and I'm definitely not guilt-free on this one, is the divide between stereotypical grandma crafts and what the current wave of the craft movement represents. For years, you were seeing the phrase, "Not your grandma's..." attached to new statements surrounding craft. In fact, we did that with Knitty Gritty until I had a grandmother write me saying, "I am a grandma, but I still like your show." I had the network take that tagline off all the spots after that, because that was not where I wanted to go with our message.*

Your colleague Adina Klein of Vogue Knitting *actually brought that up to me, too. She said, "Grandmas are awesome. Grandmas have orgasms. We can't say they're so different."*

> The art school's version of creating was so narrow. Craft is wide open—anything goes when it comes to creating and inspiring people.

CBL: Totally! I mean, I understand where the desire comes from. The indie crafters, let's say, were just getting their footing, and there was a need to stand out and differentiate themselves from things they, perhaps, didn't want to be associated with. It's true, though, that it is your grandmother's craft, and we need to own that tradition and learn from history. I think it's important to indentify craft beyond the concept of trend.

   I want to do my work forever, and I want others to be able to do it forever; society needs to perceive the value in that and provide outlets to support craft. I want it to sustain itself. Although we may be coming from different backgrounds or perceptions about what we feel craft is, it's important to learn from each other. You may not want to make the same thing as someone else (a grandmother or whomever), but that doesn't mean that what they're doing isn't just as creative in its own right, and that they're not also seeking beauty.

VH: *In doing these interviews, I've asked so many people about their childhoods, and nine times out of 10, their love for craft seems to come from a mother or a grandmother. You have to embrace that—to know where you come from.*

CBL: Completely. My grandmother actually supported her family through the Depression and put all of her siblings through college by running the notions department at Macy's, back in the '40s. The sad thing about it, though, was that because my grandma was working all the time, she didn't really get to participate in the making of things.

VH: *You've pretty much covered the crafty gamut of jobs in the biz—you've taught painting, been a photo stylist, editor in chief of* Adorn *magazine, and you now work for Etsy. Is there a part of the industry that speaks most to your passions?*

CBL: Coming from an art school background, where my professors were telling the whole class, "Maybe one out of 500 of you will become professional artists," it's been so inspiring to see how many different jobs out there involve being creative. The art school's version of creating was so narrow. Craft is wide open—anything goes when it comes to creating and inspiring people. For me, it has a very accessible and exciting feeling to it.

VH: *Do you have a favorite craft?*

CBL: I definitely like to learn all the different crafts, and then as a project comes to mind, choose what I think the best materials are for it. I still paint and knit. Lately, I've been doing more sewing. I just took an awesome pattern and dressmaking class here at Etsy with designer Cal Patch. At first, it was really intimidating because I didn't know how to operate the machines, but it's been great to get more comfortable with them and add sewing to my crafty vocabulary—I feel freer to make things just for the sake of making things.

VH: *Have you done that yet?*

CBL: Yes, I made a dress for my best friend for her birthday. I also made a skirt. I always have lots of ideas; it's another thing to sit down and take time to do them.

I think what was so fun about *Adorn* magazine was that I got to play with so many different materials. I've always had a good sense of what I like and what works best for me, so the more I learn about what I can make myself, the happier I am, because I can live out those fantasies. I don't have to settle for only what I find in stores.

VH: *I've found that if people express themselves creatively in one way, they are more than likely interested in multiple forms of creativity. I believe that all things creative are linked together—do you find that to be true? Are there non-handicraft creative aspects to your life?*

CBL: Definitely. I think they're all interrelated. There are so many aspects of ourselves that aren't honored in the day-to-day grind, so wherever we can find that creative outlet is rewarding. I started in traditional painting and photography, and I still do them. When I got involved in publishing, writing proved to be an interesting learning experience. It was something I never thought I was good at. I still don't consider myself a writer, but I like the challenge of it. I think it gets my juices flowing in a way that's different, but helps all of my other creative outlets. It's a different kind of muscle but can inform other things you do with your hands. I also like to cook a lot and invent recipes—some turn out better than others.

VH: *The same thing can be said about crafts, though. We've all had craftastrophes!*

CBL: Like that pile of gifts that'll never be given.

VH: *Yes, banished to the Island of Misfit Crafts.*

Since you've worked in both print and Web, how would you say possibilities have changed for crafters since newer forms of media have become available?

CBL: It's a great time to do anything creative. Just the fact that you can publish anything you want to publish on the Web and find an audience for it really opens doors that didn't exist before. The Web has created a level playing field. In the past, if you wanted to submit your work, you'd write up a whole press release and proposal. That's still a valid way of doing things, but now you can send a quick e-mail saying, "Hey, check out my Flickr page. Check out my Etsy shop. Check out my blog." It's created a window into people's creative lives—what they're working on, and what they're about.

That said, it's a changing time right now. There's definitely a learning curve for print going into Web, but I see real opportunities there. As crafters, we love to get things for free, and we love to share information. That's all good, but we have to value people's work that goes into creating projects and quality instructions. That's my two cents as a former magazine editor.

VH: *You unfortunately had the experience of watching a really great magazine go under because so many things are available for free, and advertising's cheaper on the Web. Do you think once we get past this tipping point that there will be a place for both print and Web?*

CBL: Yes, for sure. However, until traditional print advertisers can discover creative ways to monetize the Web, there's going to be a lag where some things will get weeded out. I think it's great to be able to share information, but there's also huge value in gaining *quality* information, and sometimes we have to pay for that. We need to realize it's not some nameless, faceless company behind things, but a real person who might be a mom with a small business editing instructions as a freelancer. We forget that people are behind all of these things.

> As crafters, we love to get things for free, and we love to share information. That's all good, but we have to value people's work that goes into creating projects and quality instructions. That's my two cents as a former magazine editor.

VH: *We have to figure out how to get people to place value on that. You know as well as I do that rates for designers working with magazines haven't really gone up significantly since the '80s. This is especially true for knitwear publications. It's crazy. I mean, some garments take 40, 60, or even 80 hours of work, and then they're bought for pennies on the dollar. That's another challenge we're dealing with right now.*

CBL: Yes, but I think it's great that if that same nameless, faceless knitwear designer creates a successful blog, Etsy shop, or Flickr page and markets herself, there's an opportunity to create her own persona. You have to set your value high. If that's your calling card, then you can come back to whoever's trying to underprice you and say, "No, I've got my own community of readers, and this is what I'm worth." It goes both ways. It's easy to say there isn't enough value placed on small businesses and individual artists, but at the same time, the individual has to create his or her value.

VH: *The focus of this book is community, which Etsy has single-handedly taken to a whole new level. Can you talk about Etsy's role in continuing to perpetuate that community and its future goals?*

CBL: Sure. We feel super fortunate that we've had this amazing role and ability to help small businesses get started. We love being part of the community and definitely want to continue that going forward. Especially as we grow larger, we realize that we wouldn't be anything if it weren't for all the small businesses that continue to work with us. We want to keep supporting them by thinking of creative tools and ways to help them grow, while making the site as valuable as possible. At the same time, we need to leverage that value into the craft community and raise the water line, if you will, of the whole industry so we can help expose it to a larger audience and remain a viable, alternative economy. We're much bigger together than we are as individuals.

VH: *Right. Which is sort of a unique philosophy for our industry. We've all realized that it's united we stand, instead of stepping on each other as we try to claw our way to the top.*

CBL: Yes. There's so much strength and possibility in that unity!

VH: *What's the most exciting change you've seen in the craft world over the last five years? What do you see as our community's biggest challenge?*

CBL: The most exciting thing is simply the emergence of this young, really vibrant voice of indie craft—individuals taking hold of the tools that are out there and exposing themselves to a wider audience. Whether people are born crafty or not, I believe everyone has it in them to be creative, and it's really exciting to be able watch people make their mark.

For more information about Etsy, go to:
www.etsy.com

> We [at Etsy] feel super fortunate that we've had this amazing role and ability to help small businesses get started. We love being part of the community and definitely want to continue that going forward.

Photo by Elizabeth Weinberg (www.elizabethweinberg.com)

Christina Batch-Lee

The Crafter's Studio

In the great tradition of *Inside the Actor's Studio* and James Lipton:

What craft sound or smell do you love?
I love when the sewing machine is full-tilt, and there's that humming going on.

What craft sound or smell do you hate?
I really hate the sound of dropping a box of beads and watching them go everywhere.

What career, other than craft-world domination, would you like to try?
I could see getting really into hairdressing or being a make-up artist.

When you burn yourself with a glue gun or spill those beads all over the floor, what is your favorite exclamation?
F@#k! My mom's is: f@#k me!

Words to Craft by:

Hat making is by far the most fun craft. If people would only make and wear more hats (the fashionable variety—caps don't count as hats), the world would be a happier and more peaceful kingdom. In the meantime, I do what I can to help ordinary folks learn all about millinery (not to be confused with

Name: Mary Beth Klatt

Age: Do I really have to?

Digs: Chicago, IL

Daily Grind: writer, designer, and milliner

Fave Crafts: millinery! sewing! knitting! crocheting!

More Info:
thelazymilliner.blogspot.com

military). My favorite story is about milliner Linda Campisano's vintage hat block collection. She owns thousands of old, highly coveted wood blocks. A while ago, her garage was vandalized. Thieves swiped dry-cleaning, a cell phone, two bikes, hockey equipment, and a weed eater. Oddly enough, the criminals missed some of the more valuable things in that garage: 3 to 4 boxes, each full of 20 antique hat blocks, each worth nearly $1,000. The irony isn't lost on Campisano, who uses the sculptured wood pieces to fashion chapeaux for the likes of Helena Bonham Carter, Bette Midler, Bill and Hillary Clinton, Andie MacDowell, Oprah Winfrey, and Michael Jordan. One day I hope to be like Linda with great clients, wonderful hat blocks, and beautiful hats. It's going to happen!

Words to Craft by:

My work is very cerebral. I read sheaves of paper every day describing procedures that will be conducted during clinical trials. My job is to make sure that each procedure and questionnaire is safe, ethical, and pre-serves the dignity of the trial volunteer. While I love my work, there are days when it seems

Name: Faith Landsman

Age: 37

Digs: Los Angeles, CA

Daily Grind: HIV researcher

Fave Crafts: crocheting, knitting, and sewing

More Info:
soqueer.blogspot.com

like the sheaves of paper won't end, and there is often little creativity involved.

In 2003, I showed up to the Santa Monica Stitch 'n Bitch, and it was like I had come home. Here were eight or nine women of various ages, with a myriad of stitching implements, moving at speeds from sluggish to breakneck. Within crafting, I can design, make enormous and embarrassing mistakes, rip it out and start all over again, and again, and again, without feeling a pang of guilt. I can work on five or six projects at once (currently, four bags, a blanket, and a top for my niece) without feeling like I have to finish any of them, but eventually, I'll likely finish them all. Crafting is both a recess and an employment unto itself. Today, one is necessary for me to be able to do the other.

chapter eleven

Mark Montano

Photo by Auxy Espinoza

As an artist, author, and TV host, Mark is probably most well known as a designer on TLC's hit show *While You Were Out*. That, however, is only a thimble-worth of what he's accomplished. Mark's a syndicated columnist, has co-hosted multiple television shows, owns a New York boutique, and his book, *Big Ass Book of Crafts*, has been wildly successful in the craft community. He's a veritable powerhouse in the worlds of art, fashion, and design. I called him at his place in Los Angeles to talk about growing up crafty, living creatively, and having the business know-how to avoid being a starving artist.

VH

VH: *What's your first craft-related memory?*

MM: Probably my mother allowing us to color on the walls in her studio when we were growing up.

VH: *Really?*

MM: Yes, she would paint, and she would just let us draw wherever.

VH: *Your mother was an artist, I'm assuming?*

MM: Yes, she was an artist and a poet. We always had pen in hand.

VH: *Was there anyone else in your family who was creative?*

MM: All of my family is totally creative. All my uncles are sculptors and cabinet makers; my grandfather was a carpenter; my mom painted; and my dad studied architecture and was a master mechanic—so these were all people that worked with their hands.

VH: *So you had a fantastic foundation, it sounds like.*

MM: Yes, so my first real memory was wanting to be like my mom, painting and drawing.

VH: *Is there a moment from your childhood connected to craft that really stands out for you?*

MM: I guess when I made my first loom. You know when you take two combs, set them up on a piece of wood, and then thread beads back and forth? That really got me excited.

VH: *Under what circumstances were you given that opportunity? Because that's not something you hear a lot of, especially from young guys.*

MM: Well, I was a member of a group called the Koshare Indian Dancers. As part of this group, we were required to make an authentic Indian costume. Sometimes people worked on their costumes for years! You joined when you were very young, and you learned all the dances and songs. You basically got together and learned to do leatherwork and beading. We would build and bead our kilts, make our headdresses, brush plates, and things like that. We would even cut our own abalone shells.

VH: *You never had a crafty chance did you?*

MM: I never had a crafty chance!

VH: *There was nowhere else to go!*

MM: Yeah, so my first memory was making my loom. Then, when I was about to start beading the band that goes around my feathered headpiece, I was like, "This is so cool!" I got seriously into beading at a very young age.

VH: *Do you still have that costume?*

MM: Yes, I actually do have some pieces of it. My favorite, favorite kind of beading was peyote beadwork, where you bead on a tube in a circle, and I can still do that. I don't do it very much anymore, but every once in a while I still like to.

VH: *Now as a professional designer/crafter is there an equally important moment for you?*

MM: I think it's when I was on my first episode of *While You Were Out*. I had to come up with projects to decorate the room, and I thought, "You know, I want this show to be fun, and I want my episodes to reflect who I am." So I decided to make a rococo mirror out of macaroni and pasta.

> I was a member of a group called the Koshare Indian Dancers. As part of this group, we were required to make an authentic Indian costume. Sometimes people worked on their costumes for years!

VH: *How was that received?*

MM: I got a lot of flak for it.

VH: *I bet! You definitely made your mark and showed that you didn't follow the same designer guidelines as most.*

MM: Definitely not. I mean, I'd always been a huge fan of Tony Duquette, and I loved that he was forever spending thousands of dollars at the dollar store. So I thought, here was a man who was very respected in the design world—he's more of a crafter than anything, and I'm going to use macaroni. Screw everybody.

VH: *Who, if anyone, do you credit for opening the professional crafty doors for you?*

MM: Opening the professional crafty doors? I think those are doors that you have to open yourself. I don't think anybody says, "Come on in to our crafty club, you're welcome." You do your work, and if it's good, and if you put yourself out there, you become more recognized by people. I don't want to say the word *accepted*, because that's not why I do anything. I don't care about being accepted; I care about having a crafty, creative life. I care that I get up in the morning and make something, or bead something, or paint something. That's what I care about. I think sometimes we spend too much time worrying about what other people think of us, and you know, my mommy loves me—that's enough for me.

VH: *Society still doesn't place much value on handicrafts, especially as related to a career. Please tell me a bit about how you took your passion for being creative and turned it into a livelihood.*

MM: Well, I think it's interesting. I remember, I always sewed. My aunts sewed their own clothes; my grandmother always had a sewing machine out; and there was always hemming going on or a dress being made. My mom had 11 brothers and sisters, so there was always sewing to be done, and I remember helping with that, either sewing on buttons or something similar. My mother also painted these beautiful Spanish women with castanets and terrific dresses; that was one of her subjects. She was really terrific at painting women, so of course, I followed suit and would always draw women. I remember thinking I wanted to be a fashion designer. It sort of encompasses everything that I really love: the sewing machine, needle and thread, fabric, and dress design.

VH: *About what age was this?*

MM: When I was 14, I decided that I would move to New York as soon as I could and become a famous fashion designer.

VH: *Well, that makes sense. Did your parents let you go at 14?*

MM: No, that's when I made the decision. At that age, I figured out how I was

> What are those things in your home that give you safety and warmth? Well, things like your grandmother's handmade quilt, maybe drawings by kids in your family that are stuck to the refrigerator, things like that.

going to make it happen, so that was the turning point. And that's what I did—I went to college for business and fashion design. I moved to New York City and worked for Oscar de la Renta and then started my own collection. I was a fashion designer in New York and showed during the collections for many, many years.

VH: *I want to talk about the fact that you have a degree in business, which is pretty rare for an artist. I'm just curious how that education helps you in a career that thrives on how you can sell yourself and your art.*

MM: Huh. Well, I think it was more because of my dad who said, "I understand that you're talented, and this is a career that you want to have; however, no one is ever successful in business without knowing how to run a business. So if I'm going to help you with college, you're going to go to business school first, and then you can follow your dreams. You can get a foundation and then do whatever you want, because you'll always know how to run it."

I think that with crafting and art in general, you have this image of the starving artist. I never wanted to be that; I'm not interested in being a starving artist. I'm interested in being a comfortable person who gets to create art every day.

VH: *Here, here, my friend!*

Photo by Auxy Espinoza

MM: And I know how to manage my money, and I'm really glad I have that background.

VH: *Was it frustrating at whatever age, 18 or 19, that you had to go that route? Even though in retrospect, it was probably a huge gift that your dad gave you? I imagine it must have been frustrating not being able to just jump right into your dream.*

MM: I think I understood; it can be a little daunting to choose a career that looks like a pipe dream. I want to be a fashion designer in New York City! Okay, but what small-town boy really says that and sets the wheels in motion? School gave me a sense of self. I felt safe knowing that I was studying something that could be applied to anything I wanted to do. I still sewed, and I made all my money in college hemming people's pants and fixing buttons. I had my sewing machine set up in my dorm room and made a decent amount of money doing that, so I was still creative.

VH: *You got a masters from the Fashion Institute of Technology; you have a background in fashion; and in your book* Big Ass Book of Crafts, *you cover the gamut of crafty genres. Is there one craft, though, that speaks more to you creatively than others?*

MM: No, there really isn't. I think that as creative people, we keep exploring whatever it is that pulls our gown down for the time being. For a long time, I felt very pinned down as a fashion designer because my only medium was fabric. It was great, and I think I made my mark in fashion doing different things with fabric because I had an artistic background—I'd make dresses out of canvas that I'd painted on, things like that. So when I finally busted out of fashion, it felt like, "Wow, I've done this, and it's time to do other things." I never wanted to be pinned down to anything, and I still don't.

VH: *What do you think the difference is between an artist and a crafter, or do you think those lines exist?*

MM: I don't think there is a difference—and all the artists in the world are going to hate me for saying that.

VH: *No, this is a common theme. I've asked a lot of people in the book about this, because there's such a huge debate within the community. It always amazes me how many of my colleagues are making their living through craft but refuse to identify themselves as crafters because of the stigma attached to the word. I'm just interested to see what people think in this day and age—if the lines have completely blurred.*

MM: I think crafting is more of a verb, sort of doing it, but you're still an artisan.

VH: *Your show* While You Were Out *focuses on making over spaces affordably within the home. It seems, now more than ever, the craft and home décor worlds have collided. Can you talk about that?*

MM: I think that happened when people got tired of mid-century modern, thank God! No more sleek, manufactured, steel, uncomfortable pieces of furniture! We realized that things made by hand actually have a comfort level and fit into the home much more logically. Your home is where you want to be comfortable, where you feel safe and warm. So what are those things that give you that safety and warmth? Well, things like your grandmother's handmade quilt, maybe drawings by kids in your family that are stuck to the refrigerator, things like that. Things that are touched by the human hand and actually make a home feel like a home. So I think it's natural that in home décor, we head toward handmade things that make our home feel touched, rather than shot out of an assembly line.

VH: *What role, if any, has crafting played in your own sense of community?*

MM: It's allowed me to spend very quality time with people who love doing things that I love. Everybody wants to get involved, everybody wants to embellish their shirt, or sculpt a sculpture, or paint a painting, or fix something, or create something. So instead of getting together and watching a movie, or doing something like that, crafting created a great life for me and my friends and family—we do meaningful things together. It's sort of like the modern quilting bee, but without the bee and without quilting. It's nice to have real quality time of human interaction, which things like the Internet, television, and video games have sort of taken away from society and culture.

VH: *One could argue that, more than ever, there is a reachable community in the craft world because of the Internet—you can connect with people on sites like Craftster, Ravelry, or Facebook.*

MM: Yes, it's certainly great for information and a little hi, hello, how are you? Or, what kind of glue should I use? That's great! But, I don't want my life to be about

> I remember thinking I wanted to be a fashion designer. It sort of encompasses everything that I really love: the sewing machine, needle and thread, fabric, and dress design.

111

Photo by Auxy Espinoza

> I think crafting is more of a verb, sort of doing it, but you're still an artisan.

sitting in front of a computer. I want my life to be about human interaction. I'm put on this earth with people, and I want to interact with those people.

VH: *As a guy who grew up being creative and has a voice in the industry, how important is it for you to encourage young boys to embrace their creative side?*

MM: I mostly have nephews, and they know that when they come visit me, they only get about half an hour of television a day. They love it! The first day they go into withdrawal saying, "Oh, come on Uncle Mark, let us watch this show." And then about two days later, they don't even remember there's a television in my house—they're so busy creating and making a mess, having a good time, laughing, painting, making papier-mâché, or whatever it is we're doing at the time. I start with my family and my nephews first.

VH: *Do you feel like there's still a bit of social stigma against boys crafting, as there was when we were kids?*

MM: No, not at all! Think about it: boys make models; we made models growing up. We had cool train sets; we would make little houses and little trees out of sponges, and that's crafting—that's making something.

VH: *Still, there are categories. For instance, I have boys too, and I make a living—a lot of what I do is knitting. And people still consider that women's work, and it's not at this point. There are boys everywhere creating knitting groups and creating great sculptural pieces by knitting, but there's still that stigma on it. I guess my point is—is there a stigma for things that were traditionally considered women's work, or do you think that we're working away from that?*

MM: Oh, I think we're working away from that. I mean, we have young pop stars who wear eye makeup and who are known as knitters and crafters. I think we're sort of getting away from that whole thing. I don't think anyone really cares anymore.

VH: *You're a professional crafter and a celebrity because of it. Do you see that as an example of how the industry and our society are evolving, or are people just more aware because of mass-media avenues like the Internet?*

MM: No, I think it's something that is happening culturally. I think people are sick of playing video games and watching television. Although, I have to say that I just read something recently that said people on average are watching five and a half hours of television a day.

VH: *Wow!*

MM: Which is pretty awful when you think about it. It's definitely how things are evolving. I think people are realizing, "Wow! I can do that, I can make that, and I'm going to!" They're going to make that pillow. They look at things and say, "I can make those paper flowers; I can sew those pillows—that's easy." So yes, certainly the media has had a play in it, but it's caused a revolution, a crafting revolution. Because of TV shows like *While You Were Out*, people realize they can make a really easy frame out of rulers, or they think, "I can make these curtains; you know what, I'm not even going to hem them. I'm just going to leave the selvage edge, and fold down the top, and hot glue some ribbon to the bottom— and look, they're couture."

VH: *Those are accessible projects.*

MM: People are realizing, "I can do that. I can do that." And they're doing it! They're realizing they can spend $400 on new drapes for their living room, or they can spend $30 and have something they really want.

VH: *Is there anything else you'd like to say about what crafting means to you or has given you?*

MM: I think that being creative is a gift, and I think everyone has it, everyone! We should use it.

For more information about Mark and his projects, go to: www.markmontano.com.

Photo by Auxy Espinoza

The Crafter's Studio

In the great tradition of *Inside the Actor's Studio* and James Lipton:

What craft sound or smell do you love?
I love the smell of E6000 glue.

What craft sound or smell do you hate?
I hate the sound when a sewing machine needle breaks.

What career, other than designer-world domination, would you like to try?
I would love to be a singer. But I have a terrible voice.

When you break that sewing needle or spill seed beads all over the floor, what is your favorite exclamation?
PHUCK (spelled with a "PH").

Words to Craft by:

Name: Erin Stoy (La Chapina Huipil Crafts)
Age: 31
Digs: La Antigua, Guatemala
Daily Grind: former marketing analyst
Fave Crafts: hand sewing, but I just bought my first machine!
More Info: huipil-crafts.blogspot.com and lachapina.etsy.com

My husband and I moved to Guatemala in March 2007 to care for the daughter we're adopting. In August of that year, a local orphanage was raided in Guatemala, and political tensions surrounding international adoption were running very high. Agencies suggested that foster parents stay inside with their children until things calmed down. So, for close to two months, I only left the apartment with our little girl a handful of times. Being confined to apartment grounds with a toddler for that long was challenging.

Eager for something to do while she napped or played, I started looking at craft blogs for inspiration. I hand-sewed about 20 stuffed animals out of Azucena's outgrown baby clothes. It was a fun diversion from the stressful reality of our situation. Soon after, I came across scraps from *huipiles*—traditional hand-woven blouses worn by indigenous women in Guatemala—and began using the fabric to sew things like Christmas ornaments, baby dolls, mosaics, and fabric collages. After learning the origins of different textiles, the methods of making them became a new passion for me. I'm also thrilled that I have the opportunity to earn money to help pay for expenses we're incurring with households in both the U.S. and Guatemala.

Words to Craft by:

Name: Lisa Filion, a.k.a. Upstatelisa
Age: 46
Digs: Queensburg, NY
Daily Grind: SAHM, landlord, jack-of-all-trades, and a speech-language pathologist in my former life
Fave Crafts: first passion is quilting, but I sew, knit, scrap, and stamp
More Info: upstatelisa.blogspot.com

When I was 13, my grandmother gave me $100 to buy my first sewing machine. She did this for all five of her granddaughters. The new machine sparked something in me, so my mother registered me for sewing lessons (Mom would later be a sewing class drop out, but she knits a mean pair of socks). I was hooked! My first project was a sun dress with a ruffled skirt (aw, the '70s). Then I took home economics and family studies in school and sewed mostly clothing.

After I married, I took a quilting class that opened a whole new world for me! I had three children and my productivity was cut way down. But now, I have a sewing room, a supportive husband, three (usually) great kids, and a lot of fabric. On Thanksgiving, 2005, my six year-old daughter was diagnosed with type 1 diabetes. I was shocked and sad but soon learned that we could deal with this chronic disease. I'm involved in raising funds for research to cure diabetes, and quilting has allowed me to make a contribution. I've made two quilts that raised $3,600 and $1,700. Thanks to my wonderful grandmother, who provided the materials to start creating.

chapter twelve

Traci Bautista

I met Traci a few years back through a friend at the Craft & Hobby Association convention. What immediately struck me was how her look and attitude exuded a funky but approachable confidence. Her artistic style truly represents the bridge between traditional art and urban craft. She's a smart, capable businesswoman, a talented mixed-media artist, and a respected teacher and author. I can always count on her to trade tips, cross-promote, or just generally be supportive. In the craft biz, there are no other more valuable qualities in a colleague.

VH

VH: *What's your first craft-related memory?*

TB: It's probably when I was five or six and used to make clothes for my Barbies.

VH: *Just out of scraps of cloth?*

TB: Yes. I would tie ribbon around scraps, because I didn't know how to sew. When I was seven or eight, though, I started making buttons and artwork with the Badge-a-Minute machine. I sold things at the craft fairs at our church. I also used to make those barrettes—you take ribbons, weave them in-and-out, and put pony beads on them. Jennifer Perkins (see page 57) and I were talking about doing this whole craft revival of all of those things we made as kids.

115

VH: *Remember hanging feathers on the roach clips that everyone used to wear in their hair?*

TB: Yes! I remember later, my grandparents and parents buying me latch-hooking kits—I loved making those!

VH: *Do you still latch hook?*

TB: Yes, actually. I created a journal for my book *Collage Unleashed* with a spine that's all latch hooked. Sometimes I'll also use latch hook as parts for a purse.

VH: *Is there a moment from your childhood connected to craft that really stands out for you?*

TB: I remember growing up, going over to my grandparents' house in Monterey, California. My grandma was always doing ceramics and painting, so I saw that from a young age. Watching her is a memory that's always stuck with me.

VH: *Now as a professional designer/crafter do you have a memory that stands out as much?*

TB: Hmmm, there are so many! That's a good question, but it's hard to choose one.

Probably being a guest on *Craft Lab*, a show formerly produced for the DIY network. Actually, doing my artwork in front of TV cameras and then seeing myself on TV—that was a big one for me.

VH: *Was that your first time being on TV?*

TB: No. I was on TV as an XFL cheerleader for the San Francisco Demons, but that was a totally different experience. I danced around on a field in front of millions of people—it was so much fun!

VH: *Do the memories from childhood and as a professional hold the same weight for you?*

TB: They're both equally important in my life, but I was more excited when I was actually able to do my crafts on TV—I felt like I had really accomplished a lot.

VH: *Is there anyone you credit for opening the crafty doors for you?*

TB: A few people—two being my parents. I gave up a pretty high-paying Silicon Valley job to go and not make any money teaching art to kids. They were always really supportive of me following my dreams and doing what I love.

As far as getting my name out there and giving me some of my first breaks in the publishing world, I'd have to credit Jenny Doh, an editor at Stampington & Company, who launched my artwork in the magazine. Also, Teesha Moore,

> Marketing is the difference between not being successful and being successful. That's one thing I learned working in Silicon Valley that really helped me: if you want to be successful, it's all about making your name visible.

a journaling and mixed media artist in Washington, gave me one of my first breaks selling my artwork to a bigger venue and teaching at her retreats.

VH: *Tell me a bit about how you took your passion for being creative and turned it into a livelihood.*

TB: I always knew that I wanted to have my own business; I just didn't know when and how it was going to happen. After I graduated from college, I worked in Silicon Valley for eight years but didn't have a passion for my job, so I quit. The first thing I started doing was teaching art to kids. During that time, I was really able to focus on painting, collage, making journals, and designing clothes. At first, I didn't have a plan; I just knew this is what I wanted to do, but I needed to figure out how to turn it into a business.

Slowly, I started teaching adult classes, and that helped me get my name out there in the paper arts and mixed-media communities. I started locally, but then found out about all these national retreats, so I started applying for those. In the course of a couple of years, I started teaching at some big well-known events, so my artwork was exposed to a larger audience.

Then, I taught at The Art Bar in Southern California. The people from Stampington & Company saw my work there, which helped me get published and start the press side of my business. I also taught and showed my artwork online, which helped garner the attention of book publishers—that lead to writing my first book in 2004. Now, I've taken all of those experiences and turned them into something else.

A lot of my artwork is now licensed for products like Collage Page, a branded art adhesive with Duncan Crafts. Hopefully soon, I'll also be able to license my paper lines and fabric. My career has grown organically without much of a plan. I just always knew that if I was doing what I loved and was passionate about my work, one opportunity would lead to another. It started with me knocking on doors to teach people and just went from there.

VH: *What did you do to design your courses? Did you just have a vague idea like, "I'm going to teach people how to make their first collage"? Or, did you sit down and come up with a curriculum?*

TB: I started by simply teaching projects that I made—the techniques I used for painting and making books. It's kind of grown from there. With all of the different events and places I teach, I'm often commissioned to come up with class ideas. It is a bit like coming up with a curriculum, but more in an artsy kind of way. No following rules, just coming up with creative projects to teach people.

VH: *You mentioned a former career in Silicon Valley. What did you do?*

TB: I started in graphic design, which was my degree, then worked my way through the marketing department. My last job was director of marketing for a software company. I always say that I wouldn't take it back, because it was great training in the business and marketing world.

VH: *How would you say that your marketing experience helped in your current career?*

TB: I think, tremendously. Marketing is the difference between not being successful and being successful. A lot of artists don't take the time to really put their name out there and market themselves. That's one thing I learned working in Silicon Valley that really helped me: if you want to be successful, it's all about making your name visible. It's the same principal in the art world as it is with a Fortune 500 company—you have to be talented and have a good product, but it's important to market it well.

> We all do such unique work, and there's room for everyone. If one of us is successful in what we do it's like, "Yeah, it's another one for our team!"

VH: *Your main medium is collage, which often spans both the craft and art worlds. For you, what's the difference between art and craft?*

TB: I don't see them any differently; they're just two different terms. I know there's a big thing about craft not being a fine art, but for me, it's kind of one and the same. The basis for what I do is trained in art schools. I paint and collage. I think craft is really just the actual making of something. One difference in what I do is that I use my own paintings to create collages, instead of taking magazine images and using them in my work. Everything I use is something I've drawn or painted myself. That could be a difference in an art versus craft, I guess.

VH: *What is the biggest challenge you've faced while trying to make a living through your craft?*

TB: Probably having a steady income.

VH: *I hear that, sister!*

TB: There are times when there's an abundance of jobs and money, and then other times when I have to figure out what to do next, so I'm not eating Top Ramen everyday. It's not really that bad, but you know what I mean.

A big portion of my income comes from teaching. You never know if your classes are going to fill, though, so you also don't know how much money you'll be making. I've been lucky that most of my classes have been full. It's hard to financially plan when you don't know what jobs are a go.

VH: *In my experience, it's almost impossible to plan. Unless you have a salary gig, you never really know how much money you're going to make. When you do finally get the money, it's not like it's hundreds of thousands of dollars, just probably enough to catch up from all the time you weren't making money. It never really seems to work out. That's one of my biggest challenges. There's gotta be some kind of financial planner that deals with freelancers.*

Was there a defining moment when you thought, "Hey, I can make a career out of my passion"?

TB: I think it was when I got an e-mail from F+W Media saying they really liked my work and asking me to consider writing a book. When that happened, it validated everything I'd been working on for so long. When I started writing that book, that's when I knew that I could do this as my career. I also think it gave my parents a sigh of relief that I wasn't just playing and painting my life away.

VH: *Let's talk about community a little. What role, if any, has crafting played in your own sense of community?*

> "
>
> A lot of what I do is very bright and vibrant, as far as colors go, and I use a lot of found items to create my collages. I may paint with the bottom of a jar or things like that.

TB: I've gained a *huge* group of friends nationally and internationally from the workshops that I've taught and from people I've met online. It's all because of crafting or my artwork. I've met thousands of people across the country—but I've also met peers like you, and Jen Perkins, and other mixed media artists. I've grown to know these people through my art. For me, it builds that sense of community where people understand where I'm coming from. I may not see them everyday, but I know I can pick up the phone or shoot them an e-mail, and it's like I've known these people for years. It's that common bond that brings us together: our craft. It's been a really interesting job path, because I don't think I ever felt that sense of community when I was in Silicon Valley; it's a whole different ball game when you're working in the corporate world.

VH: *Do you think that's because we're sort of unique in our industry—if one of us succeeds, then we all succeed? We really do have to band together.*

TB: Totally. I think that's so true. We all do such unique work, and there's room for everyone. If one of us is successful in what we do it's like, "Yeah, it's another one for our team!" It's interesting, because it's always been a sharing community, too. We all exchange business advice; we share contract questions; we help each other get the best of what's out there.

VH: *Your designs tend to stray from the norm of mainstream paper artists. What inspires you and your style?*

TB: Having the freedom to do whatever I want. A lot of what I do is very bright and vibrant, as far as colors go, and I use a lot of found items to create my collages. I may paint with the bottom of a jar or things like that. I get inspired by different things—maybe a picture I took, a color in nature, or a trip that I took. I'm influenced a lot by my life in general—having freedom and giving myself permission to have fun. I think one thing a lot of adults lose when they start doing artwork again is that freedom they had when they were in kindergarten. I always try to get back to that when I'm painting.

VH: *Is that the theory behind* Collage Unleashed?

TB: Yes, it really is. My main goal is to inspire readers to be free in their artwork. It was one of the reasons I didn't want my hands photographed for the book, because it infers one way to do a project. When there are pictures of *only* the project, then readers can translate it their own way.

VH: *Do you feel any kind of sense of responsibility as a feminist woman in a traditionally female community to use your voice as a forum for progression within that community?*

TB: I think so. I do it if I'm asked to, but don't force my opinion on anybody. If I can be an advocate for women entrepreneurs in general, I like to do my best.

VH: *Is there anything else you'd like to say about what crafting means to you or has given you?*

TB: I think it's made me a stronger person and businesswoman today. I truly believe that I can go out there and do anything I put my mind to. A lot of that has to do with having my art out there. When I was growing up, a lot of people laughed because I wanted to major in art. People always assume that someone with that goal is never going to make it. Nowadays, when people ask me what I do for a living I say, "Oh, I paint." That's all I tell them, just to see their reaction. It's always the same. I know they're thinking, "She's just an artist. That's nice." It's a hard job to keep this going; it's 24/7 trying to think of the next career step, but it's validating knowing that I'm doing it. I love what I do and feel very blessed.

For more information about Traci and her projects, go to: www.treicdesigns.com

The Crafter's Studio

In the great tradition of *Inside the Actor's Studio* and James Lipton:

What craft sound or smell do you love?
The smell of brand new crayons, right out of the box.

What craft sound or smell do you hate?
Anything alcohol-based, like inks and permanent markers.

What career, other than craft-world domination, would you like to try?
I would love (one day when I'm retired) to have my own floral shop. I know nothing about flowers, but I love arranging them.

When you burn yourself with a glue gun or cut yourself with a craft knife, what is your favorite exclamation?
I probably just scream.

Words to Craft by:

For 20 years, I wanted to live my life as a full-time artist. When I was 15, I was determined that my future would be filled with bright colors and brushes of every sort. But I listened to people who said artists can't make a living on painting, and after college, I went into

Name: Kelly Basinger

Age: 35 (the more exact answer is 35 years, 7 months, 10 days, 18 hours)

Digs: Irvine, CA

Daily Grind: I was in marketing and advertising for 13 years. Currently, I call myself a full-time artist.

Fave Crafts: Painting is my first love.

More Info: shopboxingday.blogspot.com

marketing and advertising. I would still be in that highly stressful career if I had not gotten sick. Even though I was extremely sick, I didn't know how to cope with long days of isolation. I was used to a life where every moment was filled with activities and people, and there I was at home and sick, no money, no diagnosis. I guess you could call them proverbial lemons. So, of course, I made the sweetest lemonade possible! I've always been a recycler, but with no green to spend, I got even greener! The boxes that my cereal came in made great canvases. The jewelry I had gathered from yard sales could be revamped into beautiful items. Crafting has saved my life and my sanity this year—it offers peace within my being and healing of my physical self.

Name: Christine Hembling

Age: 29

Digs: Ipswich, Suffolk, England

Daily Grind: full-time project manager, but part-time stationery designer and student

Fave Crafts: stationery, simple sewing projects, jewelry, journaling, and crocheting scarves

More Info: papercloth.blogspot.com and craftybride.blogspot.com

Words to Craft by:

For me, the biggest part of crafting has been meeting people. It started online with Craftster, Etsy, Flickr, and blogging, and it's spread to meeting in person. I met a dear crafty blogging friend for the first time this year in London (we live at opposite ends of the country), and it was fantastic. Last summer, I went away to school in York with a group of women I'd met on Etsy to simply craft, make art, drink, and eat chocolate together. It was so lovely to devote a whole weekend to doing what we love. We're doing the same thing this year, and I can't wait to catch up with my friends and meet new people joining us on retreat.

chapter thirteen

Denyse Schmidt

I've been a longtime fan of Denyse's work. Her modern take on traditional craft even inspired me to set down my knitting needles for a little piecework! Her story is as rich in detail as one of her famed quilts. From professional modern dancer, to graphic artist, to world-renowned designer producing gorgeous product lines, Denyse personifies an artist's journey. Although I'd never met her before our phone interview from her Connecticut studio, I hope to take one of her amazing workshops someday. Denyse reminds us of important principles for a crafter to remember: perseverance is key, self-confidence is a must, and simplicity is something to be celebrated.

 VH

VH: *What's your first craft-related memory?*

DS: I was the youngest of four, and everybody in my family had a little bit of an artistic bent, so it seems like I was always making stuff. I remember I had a toy sewing machine, which frustrated me because it wasn't real. I made a lot of doll clothes, but more clearly, I remember making this little zoo out of clay. I must've been about seven or eight. It was during the summertime when my family spent time on the Cape, and my zoo won a ribbon in a contest. I made little tiny animals out of clay, and made the whole zoo in a box. I was really into miniatures. It's funny because recently I've been thinking about exploring that world again, maybe because a quilt is so big.

VH: *That's so interesting, because your work is exactly opposite of miniature.*

DS: Exactly. I think there's an urge to do things that are more manageable somehow, more immediate, and more private. Maybe I'm regressing in some ways, but I still have a dollhouse that my grandfather built for me when I was 10. I used to make all kinds of stuff for it—little eyeglasses out of bread ties, for instance. If you take the paper off, they're really easy to bend, and then I painted clear nail polish across for the glass. I loved doing that stuff.

I have a new studio space across the hall that I'm keeping really empty, and it's going to be my creative think tank. I may bring that dollhouse up and start making little things for it again.

VH: *So your grandfather was crafty too, it sounds like? Although they probably wouldn't have called it that then.*

DS: Yes, and my parents. I think one of the biggest influences on me is that both of my parents had careers. My mother was an educator, a psychologist, ran a school for emotionally disturbed adolescents, and had been an engineer before that, which is where she met my dad. They grew up during the Depression and were very careful about spending money, so they made a lot of household items. My dad made furniture; my mom made all of our clothes, but our things never looked homemade. My parents had a level of skill and craftsmanship that they took for granted. I think they were proud of what they did, but they never called themselves craftspeople or artists. They made things that we needed, and they just happened to be really good at it. For a long time, I just assumed everybody was that way.

VH: *It's funny—you mentioned making glasses out of bread ties, and it made me think about the time I made a headgear for my Cabbage Patch doll out of paper clips, a similar concept.*

DS: Oh, that's great!

VH: *Is there a different moment from your childhood connected to craft that really stands out for you? Something that will always stay with you?*

DS: I remember making a Halloween costume once—I was a tree. I wore a box over my head that I pounded out so it was round. I painted a sheet to look like a tree and hung it from the box, which also had branches reaching out from the sides. I don't think anyone in the neighborhood had ever been a tree. Everybody thought it was weird that I wanted to be one, but I had this vision and made it happen, and it was really satisfying.

VH: *Now, as a professional designer/crafter, is there an equally important moment for you? Maybe it's the moment you realized you could actually make a living this way, or maybe not.*

DS: I have those moments all the time. I don't think it's ever a done deal. I think we're always evolving. It's surprises me how the creative process is just that, and you kind of have to go through all of the steps each time, including the doubt, the fear, and the procrastination. I've gotten better at recognizing the stages, so I don't have big *a-ha* moments.

"

Many people have stories about a grand-mother or an aunt who quilted. They don't have to love the quilts those relatives made to still have a strong tactile, emotional memory of them.

VH: *No, it's like, "This is my neurosis. Period. Acknowledge, and move on."*

DS: This is the creative process. I'm not alone in it. Everybody I know goes through it to some degree. The process is about having the courage or craziness to make stuff in spite of all the difficulties and challenges. The hard part is consistently believing in yourself and persevering.

VH: *Self-doubt is an artist's greatest enemy.*

Is there anyone, in particular, you credit for opening the creative doors for you?

DS: My sister is eight years older, and she was in art school when I was 10. She used to take me to drawing classes with her. I would turn my back on the male models and do my own little geometric drawings. She definitely opened my world to something outside the suburban neighborhood where we grew up. I think that had a huge influence on me.

VH: *Tell me a bit about how you took your passion for being creative and turned it into a career.*

DS: I think my main focus is just persevering. I think I also had good marketing skills and ideas for promoting my work, because I'd been a graphic designer and am very detail-oriented. I still feel as if I'm lacking on the business end—I would like to have more financial security—but I've come to realize not everybody has that, regardless of how financially successful you are. I'm grateful for being small and nimble, and somehow or other, that I'm able to be in a good place.

VH: *When did you start quilting?*

DS: You know, it's funny, I didn't grow up quilting; I grew up sewing. I'd already had a career in New York as a modern dancer and performer, and went back to school for graphic design. I moved to Connecticut and ended up working at a children's book publisher. It paid really well, but was creatively a little stifling. Prior to that, I had become intrigued by quilts. Before I went to Rhode Island School of Design, I had taken some drawing classes at a museum and was really interested in the idea of collage and discovered crazy quilts. I became interested in the quilt as object. Textiles and sewing had always been part of what I did, so I think it was a natural extension of my graphic design work.

VH: *Crazy quilts are also a direct extension of modern dance. Abstract and freeform things are connected, don't you think?*

DS: There you go! I was making a traditional nine-patch quilt for a friend. I was doing the hand-quilting portion and something clicked in terms of the tangible amount of time I had spent quilting, as opposed to the hours spent doing graphic design projects—comparing the space between letters or other elements. So much work, at the time, was printed on paper and thrown out. That had an impact on me.

I began looking at quilting books and realized there were great quilts out there that nobody was referencing anymore—quilts that were made a long time ago, that were more or less traditional, but weren't represented in the commercial or art quilt worlds. People were working from traditional patterns but were mucking it up and using way too many prints and icky colors. They weren't making an artistic statement. There was very little reference to these super simple quilts, where you might see one quirky thing—like the designer ran out of fabric they were using for a flower basket, so they'd use a different fabric in that one pattern. I loved those kinds of quilts and appreciated their spare aesthetic and quirkiness. They seemed really modern.

In my thirties, I was somewhat unhappy with my job and knew I couldn't spend the rest of my life doing it. I also knew there was a contemporary, high-end furnishing and bedding market out there, and nobody was really doing anything with it. It seemed like a kooky idea, but partly out of desperation and ignorance, I pursued it. I was very lucky and happened to be at the right place at the right time.

VH: *Did you write up a business plan and get a loan?*

DS: No, no loan. I kept my job. I had a really understanding employer at the time who let me gradually drop days over a period of about three years. By the time I quit, I was only working two days a week. I couldn't have done it otherwise. I think that if I'd had the pressure of a loan, it would've changed how I did business. To grow the business slowly and keep it high-end was really crucial for me.

VH: *Do you remember your first customer?*

DS: I did a trade show and was expecting to work with interior designers right off the bat. But, at that first show I got Henri Bendel, Saks Fifth Avenue, and Takashimaya as clients. Takashimaya, who I'd never heard of at the time but was, of course, really big, said they wanted to give me some vintage kimono to work with. I was waiting for them to tell me exactly what they wanted, but they said, "Do whatever you want."

VH: *That would make me misty: vintage kimono, and do whatever I want?!*

DS: It was a little terrifying but also good, because I felt like if they had seen something in me, I could do it. I've been lucky to have a lot of great things come my way. I'm a big believer that things don't have to be so hard all the time.

VH: *Quilting has a history based not only on necessity, but also storytelling. In the days of mass production and blogging, what social role do you see quilts filling today?*

DS: It's interesting because I find there's still a strong resonance with collective memory. I feel like we still have a very strong visual memory for textiles in quilts, whether it's from an old shirt we wore or some other personal fabric. Just like certain smells or the grain on a sidewalk can take us back to when we were five, seeing fabrics that way also transports us. It connects us to our history, whether real or imagined.

Also, with quilting itself, many people have stories about a grandmother or an aunt who quilted. They don't have to love the quilts those relatives made to still have a strong tactile, emotional memory of them. I find that really fascinating and think there's something to it, still today, that resonates in people as a grounding influence. Even though there aren't as many people quilting now, isn't it possible that in some sort of collective consciousness that value's still alive? I don't know.

VH: *I also think that because our society is so disposable now, the importance of heirlooms and tangibility has elevated.*

DS: I've been teaching since 2003, but I've definitely seen a rise in the number of people who want to learn. I realize part of it is the current DIY movement, but I also believe that because of our economic and cultural climate, there's a desire to make things again. There's a desire to connect with the process of making something that's also a useful object. What's so beautiful about quilts is that whether you're working with fabric bits or pieces of clothing, it all represents someone. I don't think there's anything else that works that way.

VH: *There's a current debate in the craft community (or perhaps outside of it) about the difference between art and craft. As someone who graduated from art school but makes a living through traditional craft, can you explain the difference, or is there one anymore?*

DS: I don't think there's a difference. Having been trained as a designer, it's a triple whammy. There's the same debate between design and art, but it's all the same thing. It's frustrating, though. My M.O. is to just do what I do. People will define it anyway they want, and the less you struggle against that, the better. Whether we can change the way people define things or not, I don't know. People who work from their own perspective will define things in their own way.

Denyse Schmidt

I think there's something so incredibly cool about the online quilting community—it's the same as a quilting bee: people are sharing their work and what they're discovering, but it's completely global.

VH: *It's interesting. Within the community (and sometimes I think this could be true across the board, because we're always our own worst enemy) there are a lot of colleagues that do not want to be associated with the word craft.*

DS: True. When I started 12 years ago, the Internet barely even existed. To say, "I make quilts" was hard, because nobody had a reference, and they wanted nothing to do with it. I always wanted to carry a picture in my pocket, because that was the only way I knew how to explain what I did.

It's unfortunate that some museums with a craft focus eliminate the use of the word to avoid any marketing problems. I really don't think that's the answer. Again, if you do what you do, and you do it well, the definition will not matter.

VH: *The resurgence of quilting as a popular craft happened way before that of knitting, yet there seems to be way fewer quilting designers who have ventured into modernizing the craft, as you have. Why do you think that is?*

DS: I don't know. It's really hard to make a living as a quilt designer, so maybe that's why there aren't as many out there. I think what inspires me most are older quilts that have a simplicity about them. I think simple is often really difficult for people to do.

VH: *Even in the knitting world, people often think that difficult and obscure are superior, but really, those designs are not wearable by someone with a modern sensibility. Maybe it's the same with quilting. The amount of skill that some quilts take is overwhelming—but would you really put them in your house?*

DS: I'm just drawn to the more simplified versions of things.

VH: *Quilting has, arguably, one of the strongest histories of perpetuating community through family circles and quilting bees. Since the days of village women spending hours together are gone, how do you see the modern-day quilting community being nourished?*

DS: I'm continually fascinated with the whole Internet and blogging thing. I think there's something so incredibly cool about the online quilting community. It's the same as a quilting bee—people share their work and discoveries, but it's completely global because it's not about a community of proximity. It's community of shared interest made possible by the Internet.

I'm also fostering community in our workshops. People come from all over the place to learn. I get people from Australia, California, Chicago, etc. Getting a local person is much rarer than getting people from all over the place. There's something about being in a room with people—that community is a gift.

VH: *During the 2008 presidential election, you created a quilt in support of Barack Obama that raised money for his campaign. I've noticed it's pretty common for artists and crafters to also be politically active. Why do you think that is? Do you think there's a link between crafting and activism?*

> I think what inspires me most are older quilts that have a simplicity about them. I think simple is often really difficult for people to do.

DS: Yes. Because artists and craftspeople are outside of the corporate world, it's a little easier to wear their opinions on their sleeves, I suppose. I did ruffle a few feathers, I have to say.

VH: *I was going to ask you that because, like me, you're in a traditional business, and I sort of side-stepped mentioning the candidate I supported; although, it was probably still obvious. There's got to be a lot of conservative quilters out there.*

DS: Definitely, and I heard from them. I lost some subscribers to my e-newsletter. You know what, though, that's okay. I had some moments of doubt, but on the other hand, I wasn't forcing anything down anyone's throat. I find it really important that I was able to do something I believed in. The whole process was fascinating—how much money we raised in a short time, and getting hate e-mails from people. It was a shocking roller coaster.

I think it's a luxury we have, in a way, although not without risk—but nothing good is. I strongly believed in it. I was inspired by a quilt from the '60s (I'm ashamed to say I don't know the designer) that simply said *freedom* over and over again. I've also seen much older quilts with quotes from the Bible or statements of activism on them. Women were doing that long before we could vote, and I think quilting provided a format for them, a way to make their voices heard. It seemed like the right thing to do, and I'm really proud that I raised some money for the campaign.

For more information about Denyse and her projects, go to:
www.dsquilts.com

The Crafter's Studio

In the great tradition of *Inside the Actor's Studio* and James Lipton:

What craft sound or smell do you love?
I love the smell of fabric, new from the store. I also love the smell of yarn—it's the same smell of new clothes when you go school shopping in the fall.

What craft sound or smell do you hate?
There's not one.

What career, other than craft-world domination, would you like to try?
Some kind of social work or activism. I think it would be satisfying to really give back.

When you cut yourself with a rotary blade or or break a needle on the machine, what is your favorite exclamation?
I probably say, "sh@t!"

Words to Craft by:

Name: Jennifer Ofenstein

Age: 35

Digs: Austin, TX

Daily Grind: mom, quilt designer, and full-time crafter

Fave Crafts: paper piecing, crocheting, stenciling, and costuming

More Info: www.sewhooked.org and ofenjen.livejournal.com

I finished my college degree in 1995 and immediately became a stay-at-home mom. While I wouldn't trade that time with my kids for anything, crafting saved my sanity and gave me something that was truly my own. All these years later, I'm online sharing my original paper-pieced patterns and crafts, connecting with other crafters, and best of all, teaching others how to paper piece and design their own patterns. The *Harry Potter* fandom, especially, has been a saving grace. Since I started sharing my various patterns online (many of which are HP themed), I've met hundreds of Potter fans both online and in real life, and dozens of those have started quilting because of my work. It's been one of the most unexpected but exciting turns my life could have taken. Inspired by the online success of my patterns, I'm working on my first quilting book. Crafting has changed my life for the better, bringing me friends and inspiration, all rolled up in one!

Photo by Tara Rochelle

Words to Craft by:

Name: J. Ana Fuentes Flores

Age: 30

Digs: Los Angeles, CA

Daily Grind: copyeditor

Fave Crafts: sewing, quilting, jewelry making, crocheting, knitting, embroidery, fabric arts, baking, and cake decorating

More Info: www.thegirlwithacurl.com

I'm the 36th grandchild of a quilter who lived to be 102. Growing up in the Philippines, I watched my grandmother piece her pinwheels and Dresden blocks on a manual sewing machine until she was about 98. Many of her 12 children were crafters in one way or another, and most of her 36 grandchildren, especially the women, followed suit. All these numbers convey how, as the youngest grandchild, I often felt dwarfed by the crafting skills of the women in my family. I couldn't start a project without thinking about how precise Tia Deding's piecing was on her latest fan quilt, or about the delicate hand-drawn threadwork of Tia Etta's table napkins. For a long while, I was too intimidated to follow in their footsteps. It was only when I came to the States five years ago that I welcomed my craftster self and discovered what was rich in me: a history of hands picking up needles, quilting, knitting and purling, and bending the will of fabrics. I finally embraced that I was cut from the same cloth as all the crafter-women in my family. Crafting, in all its forms, became my new home.

chapter fourteen

Natalie Zee Drieu

I met Natalie briefly at a Maker Faire in Austin, Texas, several years ago. She had been kind enough to feature my yarn line in the print version of *CRAFT* Magazine, so I wanted to stop by and thank her. Although we didn't get to chat much at the time, we began corresponding through e-mail about various projects. Since then, I've done some writing for the CRAFT website (www.craftzine.com) and, through that, have found that Natalie and I have a lot in common. We've formed a friendship that encompasses both a colleague's respect and a working-mom's compadreship.

VH

VH: *What's your first craft-related memory?*

NZD: I think it was when I was young. My mom did a lot of crafts with me, and I always saw her sewing on her machine, and I wanted to be like her. I remember my mom teaching me how to sew while she made my clothes. When I was 10, I started dressing my Barbie dolls; I would design their clothes by cutting up my old ones.

VH: *Were you hand-sewing or were you just wrapping the fabric and tying it?*

NZD: At first I was hand sewing, but then my mom started to help me on the machine. I would do simple stitches with her watching me, which was really fun! I think that kind of got me addicted. The sewing machine weighed like a bazillion tons back then, but it was such a sturdy machine. I'd always have to bug my mom, saying, "I want to sew now," and she would whip out the machine and be like, "Oh God, this thing is so heavy! Why do you want to do this now?"

VH: *I guess there wasn't any sort of craft room in your home?*

NZD: No, not growing up. But my mom was really crafty because she had learned everything from her sisters. She was the youngest of six children and knows embroidery, sewing, knitting, crocheting—Mom can do everything. Whenever I wanted to learn something, she would just teach me.

VH: *Is there a moment from your childhood connected to craft that really stands out for you?*

NZD: All my memories from childhood really have to do with crafting. When I was 10 years old, I had a great teacher at the girls' club, and I spent that whole summer sewing. She really took her time with us. I still hear her talking to me, and I can remember all the things she told us about working with fabric or working with patterns. We all used vintage Singer machines that were so awesome to sew with. I had no idea back then how great that entire summer would be in my memory.

VH: *Do you know where she is now?*

NZD: I have no idea. I think she must have been in her 20s. I remember my friend Karen and I took the class, and we would love to see her now. I think the class was two days a week, and she would always have her nails professionally done— on the Fourth of July, she would have little flags painted on them, and we thought that was the biggest thing.

VH: *It would be great if you could contact her now and let her know what an impact she had on you.*

NZD: I know! I don't know how I could, though.

VH: *Tell me a bit about how you took your passion for being creative and turned it into a livelihood for yourself.*

NZD: Sure. I sometimes think luck finds you, but you also have to do what you love and go with it. I've always done crafts, and have always been a writer and designer. I've worked for a long time—most of my career, in fact—as a Web designer, which I do for the websites MAKE (www.makezine.com) and CRAFT (www.craftzine.com).

I started my career right after college, at 22, working for a macromedia software company on the Web team, doing Web design for many years. I was kind of known in the industry for writing Web design books, but I was always doing craft stuff to relieve myself of the computer stress. My book editor Steve Weiss knew I was crafty, and we would meet up for dinners and lunches, and I would tell him what I was working on; he ended up going to O'Reilly Media, which publishes MAKE and CRAFT. We always kept in touch, and when I grew frustrated with my job and was tired of being in the agency, I told Steve, "You

> **"**
> When I was 10 years old, I had a great teacher at the girls' club. I can remember all the things she told us about working with fabric or working with patterns.

know, I don't really like what I'm doing, and I need to find a new direction."

It all sort of fell into place from there. Steve set up a lunch for me with Gail, who had just come out with *MAKE* magazine. She and I were soon talking about doing a Web design issue for *MAKE*, and one thing led to another. We ended up in a brainstorming meeting for what would later become the CRAFT site. In short, I began simultaneously blogging on the MAKE site, planning the CRAFT stuff, and started redesigning the MAKE site. I think the key was that I couldn't believe I was going to get paid to write about what I love (crafts) and still work for a place that holds technology high, which was important for me.

It was a perfect fit. All the stuff I was doing on my own time at night (like being in a knitting group with my friends) was now my work, which was pretty fun. I really went for it, but I also knew I needed to use the skills I had.

VH: *So you've basically molded your own career?*

NZD: Yes.

VH: *That's fantastic! We've talked about everything your mom did creatively, but was your dad also crafty?*

NZD: Well, my dad is an amazing cartoonist, but *his* dad encouraged him not to pursue the whole comic book world. My dad actually made up a comic book with his uncle when they were teenagers, and I think he regretted not following that dream. He went into business because it was more sensible, but he always talked to me about his comic books and graphic design books lying around the house. I would go with him on Sundays to the comic book stores in Berkeley.

When I was in college and thinking about becoming a lawyer, my dad sat me down and said, "Do you really want to be a lawyer? You're going to spend your whole life arguing with someone while someone else is trying to negate whatever you're doing. That's not a life. You need to be happy and not do a job just for money. What do you want to do?" He made me realize that being artistic, writing, and drawing, or doing all three of these things, is fulfilling.

VH: *Did you get any of his drawing talent? Do you draw at all?*

NZD: The funny thing is that because I grew up with him and drew pictures for him, he would critique me to the point that I would be so stressed I couldn't really draw anymore. Now, if I sit down and concentrate, I can draw. I don't do freeform very well, but I can draw. My mom will say "Did your dad draw that?" I'll tell her "No, I did," and she says we have the same drawing style. I just don't have time to really sit down and deal with it right now.

VH: *You spend your days writing about crafts for the CRAFT website, but do you still have time to make things yourself?*

NZD: I do sometimes; it's been harder since having a baby, but I always like to have a project for myself. Usually what I'm making is also for the CRAFT site. I think the last unusual project I made (that was for myself and the website) was a dog Halloween costume—I made one for my dog Lulu and her two best friends. They were Star Wars-themed; everyone always thinks my dog looks like a little Ewok, so I made her an Ewok costume and the other two were Darth Vader and Princess Leia.

VH: *I think we designers all turn projects we need done around the house into work.*

NZD: I think so; I always try to. For me, I always have knitting or crocheting projects that I'm working on for myself too.

VH: *You mentioned being in a knitting group before. Do you still craft with people or is it pretty solitary now with work and baby?*

NZD: I don't. We called ourselves The Knittens, and if we all still lived in the same city, I think we would get together. It was like the perfect group—we all worked in the tech or design industries. But then everyone got married, had babies, and moved away, so it's hard, but we still e-mail each other with projects—more so, now that I'm on CRAFT because I send e-mails saying, "This is perfect for you." I miss the face-to-face, because we would sit there together knitting and ask, "How do you get that stitch to go right?" I love that feeling of having access to actual people.

VH: *Yes, knitting is a very unique skill.*

NZD: I have to use a different side of my brain or something. Right now, I'm addicted to crocheting. It was something I never thought I'd get, but now I think crocheting feels easier for some reason.

VH: *It does sometimes. I find that knitting and crocheting fill very different places, because you get such different looks. And sometimes crocheting is way better for certain projects; it's more sculptural; it's also better for things that need a little sturdiness.*

NZD: I've made so many different cool things, but most of what I've made recently has been for the website or for TV shows.

VH: *Is there one craft that speaks more to you creatively than others?*

NZD: Sewing. I can't say that I have a favorite craft—I love everything, and I love learning new things. I'm very, very passionate about that. But I think with sewing, I can be really creative and more freeform. Knitting also holds a very special place for me, because I can really relax while I'm doing it. When things are in disarray, I can just pick up a project to knit and really feel calm.

VH: *Is knitting the only thing that gives you that peace?*

NZD: I think so, because I can keep it anywhere, or knit in front of the TV and feel relaxed.

VH: *As a new mother, are you conscious of creating crafty memories for your own daughter?*

NZD: Yes, I am. I actually think it's because my mom was that way with me. I can't wait to teach her how to knit and sew and for us to do projects together. She's only three months old now, but I have projects saved and bookmarked for when she's older. I think that will be fun.

VH: *How do you handle juggling craft and career with parenthood?*

NZD: I handle it like all of us try to—just do the best I can. I don't think I'd be able to function if my daughter didn't sleep through the night, though, so I feel lucky that she gives me seven hours at least.

VH: *That's great!*

NZD: Yes, it's a miracle! It's definitely helped; otherwise, I'd be all over the place.

VH: *What's the most difficult part of it for you?*

NZD: Of motherhood?

VH: *No, juggling everything.*

NZD: I think it's that I never have a moment to take a deep breath and think for myself. It's always, "Oh, I'm going to do this right now, or I'm gonna have to take care of that." I need to loosen my schedule somehow and just be spontaneous.

Natalie Zee Drieu

> I think the fashion industry itself really notices the DIY movement taking place in the craft industry. It sparked their attention. Luxury brands like Hermes are offering Kelly bags on their site—people can download and print out their own paper versions of the bag.

137

VH: *You also have a passion for fashion, most notably documented on your site www.coquette.blogs.com. The current DIY movement often crosses over to the fashion world. You can find columns on the subject of crafting your own couture everywhere, from blogs to Seventeen magazine. Project Runway has also breathed new life into the once out-of-date sewing industry. Since you span both worlds professionally, what's your view about how fashion influences craft, and vice versa?*

NZD: I think the fashion and craft industries are influencing each other more than ever. Not only do people want to sew their own clothes and make their own fashion, I think the fashion industry itself really notices the DIY movement taking place in the craft industry. It sparked their attention, and they're trying to get more business because of it too.

Luxury brands like Hermes are offering Kelly bags on their site—people can download and print out their own paper versions of the bag. I wonder why anyone would want to do that, but surprisingly, they've got really good buzz about it. So it's interesting how those two worlds are overlapping in some ways. I think with the economy being so bad, we're seeing more people who want to learn how to make or refashion their own clothes so they don't spend as much on new ones all the time.

VH: *We're kind of going back to that make-do mentality.*

NZD: That was actually a theme for the CRAFT website. We called March *mending month.* It was funny—over the holidays, my husband had a sweater with a hole in it, and he was just going to throw it away. It was a great cashmere sweater, and it was his warmest sweater, so he couldn't get rid of it. To save him from being ridiculous, I helped him sew it back up and fix it. He didn't realize I could do that even though I have a whole craft room here. He was just so used to *not* fixing old clothes.

VH: *We've become such a disposable society. Repurposing clothes is not at the forefront of people's minds—but, maybe there's the big shift in that now.*

NZD: People are used to just going to H&M for a new sweater.

VH: *For like 10 bucks!*

NZD: But I'm also seeing a sense of accomplishment from people. They realize it will take more time, but they want to sew their own garments because of the joy of creativity. I especially notice that with teenagers.

VH: *That's a big push for me, because I was that teenager who couldn't afford to have a lot of the clothing my friends had. If crafting had been as popular then as it is now, I could have saved myself some embarrassment. You can basically make couture pieces by just throwing on a great knitted shawl.*

NZD: Right, I know. But in the '80s it was all about buying.

I began simultaneously blogging on the MAKE site, planning the CRAFT stuff, and started redesigning the MAKE site. I couldn't believe I was going to get paid to write about what I love (crafts) and still work for a place that holds technology high.

VH: *True. My mom always made our stuff growing up, because we never had any money. Of course, I just wanted store-bought stuff. I guess it goes in circles. Do you think that more and more people are going back to traditional crafts, and that may be affecting how people look at fashion, production, and responsibility?*

NZD: I would hope so. I really hope so. I don't know if we've arrived at that point, because things are so cheap that people don't need to think about it, but I hope so. I know that some people who aren't part of the craft world go to craft fairs and say, "Oh, the stuff is so expensive." For me, I don't mind paying extra for the handmade, the artistry, and the story behind it.

VH: *You buy less, but you buy better.*

NZD: Exactly!

VH: *The CRAFT website is always really supportive of the craft community, posting multiple links per day to designers' work. In the future, what role do you see the site having in perpetuating that community further?*

NZD: I would hope to see more of a dialogue with our readers. I'd like our community to reach that next level where we post cool projects but also hear what readers want, and give it to them. Tools like blogs, Facebook, and Twitter make that attainable.

VH: *How do you think new media has affected crafting for the everyday crafter?*

NZD: I wish it had been available back then when I was learning all this stuff. Right now, it's wonderful to go online, research how to do one little stitch, and get a video that teaches you something as you work on a project. Or, if you have a question, Ravelry (see page 182) is a great place to post it to a forum. Community is out there; when you're home by yourself and don't really know how to do something, you can quickly learn to do it on the Web.

VH: *Since there are more careers that let you work from home (you and I both work from home), I think the online community has become much more important than it was a decade ago. It's manifested itself through people who are creative. In general, I feel like Facebook and Twitter are my coworkers. For women, that opens our world much wider. A decade ago, women had to choose between career and stay-at-home motherhood, but now there's this weird hybrid because of the Internet.*

NZD: Yes, I feel so lucky!

VH: *Me, too.*

NZD: I went to UC Berkeley in the early '90s and was a mass communications major hoping to work for a newspaper or TV station. I took a new media class and was hooked—I knew it was going to be the next big thing! The Web blew open by 1994, and by the time I graduated, the professor working with my thesis was very apprehensive of letting me focus on the Web. At the end, he said I'd focused on a good thing. He said he learned so much from me and was glad I didn't listen to him about going to work for a newspaper.

The Internet is a medium where stories are told and where you can communicate with people from all over the world. It's so fascinating to me; I still love it, and I love the idea of bringing crafts forward in this new medium. It will go so much further as technology improves. I try to keep up with the tech world, because I really want to bring it into the craft world.

VH: *What is your take on the love/hate relationship between the worlds of general publishing and Web publishing? Who will survive? How will they survive? How will designers and crafters make a living with so much free content online?*

NZD: I don't know. It's like asking, "Is Wall Street going to be okay?" Everything is so volatile right now because of the economy, but I think I'm optimistic. I don't think print will ever completely go away; I don't foresee us all reading digitally. I think there is something about paper that is tactile and helps with learning. At the same time, I strongly believe in the Web. There are benefits to learning online that you can't necessarily get on a page. So, I think we'll find a happy medium between the two things.

As for free content on the Web; that's hard, too. Designers run into the issue of making their work visible without sharing how they're doing it, but people still copy them.

VH: *We've got a long way to go on figuring that out. We need a crafter's union; I keep saying that.*

NZD: So true—just like the Council of Fashion Designers. I don't know; it's really hard. That's what's so interesting about doing things on the Internet. All these concepts are constantly building, so we're living through them and learning from them. I do buy patterns from designers, because I like to support them. I know free patterns are available, but I'd rather spend $7 on something really good that I can make something wonderful out of.

VH: *If there was something as widespread as iTunes, it would be feasible for the patterns to cost less. We have to charge $7, but that doesn't really help because there isn't that go-to place. If there were, and there were millions of people who accessed it, it would be easier to charge only a couple of bucks each.*

NZD: Isn't Ravelry (see page 182) kind of changing that?

VH: *Yes and no, but I mean, you can pretty much find anything you want for free on there, so it's the same conundrum. This is just my opinion, but people go there to search for free things first, and if they can't find what they want, they'll buy. You can't really begrudge people for doing that. It makes sense right now, especially, but there needs to be a way we can keep the career title called designer.*

NZD: I agree.

VH: *Do you have any advice for readers who want to design crafts for Web and print?*

NZD: For submitting work, the key is to be really concise about which project you're trying to sell. Basically, you're trying to sell your project to get it up on a site or in a magazine, so a picture is worth a thousand words. Having pictures really helps the person on the other end understand the project instantly. It's also important to use very concise words when describing what you want to do or write about. I always find those submissions are much easier to respond to than someone writing a long e-mail describing what they want to write about. Just be really clear on the project and how to go about it.

VH: *Is there anything else you'd like to say about what crafting means to you or has given you?*

NZD: I feel so lucky to get to work in an industry where I'm helping people feel good. If you're really into crafting as a career, keep at it. It's not easy, but it's very emotionally rewarding. I've met so many great friends through crafting. I don't think I could ever go back to working in a traditional office.

VH: *I couldn't either. I mean, I would if I had to, but man, I hope I never do.*

For more information about Natalie and her projects, visit: coquette.blogs.com

The Crafter's Studio

In the great tradition of *Inside the Actor's Studio* and James Lipton:

What craft sound or smell do you love?
The clicking of knitting needles.

What craft sound or smell do you hate?
The high-pitched sound of a saw.

What career, other than craft-world domination, would you like to try?
A writer for *Saturday Night Live*.

When you burn yourself with a glue gun or spill beads all over the floor, what is your favorite exclamation?
Oh, f*@k!

141

Words to Craft by:

My brother was born almost three months premature when I was 12 years old. I wasn't old enough to enter the NICU, so for much of the two months he spent in the hospital before he came home, I had to watch him grow from behind a window. One of the things that touched me throughout the time he spent in the incubators was the massive amount of hand-knits floating through the space. Every baby seemed to have his or her own blanket, hat, booties, and more. My brother is now in college, and memories of him being so small seem distant. Thanks to all the people who anonymously knitted and crocheted warmth and love for him and so many others, I've been inspired to do the same. Now much of my knitting time is spent giving newborns just that extra ounce of love and comfort, using simple knits and purls!

Name: Robyn Devine
Age: 31
Digs: Omaha, NE
Daily Grind: slave to the man, student, and writer
Fave Crafts: knitting and crocheting
More Info: craftivist.typepad.com

Words to Craft by:

I've always been creative, and I grew up longing for crafty community! While dealing in antiques in the '90s, I was exposed to vintage glass and vowed to one day work with glass myself. Fast forward through 10 years of knitting, photography, decoupage, jewelry making, and beer brewing. I found myself facing an emotional challenge and realized I needed a new outlet. I knew it was time for glass fusing, so I began making and selling fused glass jewelry.

Name: Nichole Moraila
Age: 34
Digs: Los Angeles, CA
Daily Grind: visual effects coordinator
Fave Crafts: glass fusing
More Info: ohlookwhatimade.blogspot.com

Still longing for community, I decided to start a Craft Mafia in L.A. Every month we host a free craft night at a bar where anyone with an interest in crafting is welcome to have a drink, laugh, talk, and craft. Our first craft night was in January 2008. About 20 people showed up, and the group grows larger every month. People have developed friendships, found inspiration and support, and have started their own businesses. I feel proud to have a hand in bringing this warm craft camaraderie to my city. I've finally found my crafty community!

chapter fifteen

Garth Johnson

Not rain, nor sleet, nor snow could keep this interview down! Garth and I spoke for the first time during his stormy drive with friend Faythe Levine (see page 257) to the Seattle premiere of her film *Handmade Nation*. He's a farm boy turned art academic who constantly pushes boundaries (and challenges us to do the same) between traditional stereotypes and modern statements. Garth's blog Extreme Craft (extremecraft.typepad.com) acts as a virtual arena for "art masquerading as craft, craft masquerading as art, and craft extending its middle finger," reminding us crafters that the world is our stage, and we're here to decorate it.

VH

VH: *What's your first craft-related memory?*

GJ: My first craft-related memory comes from my mother. She was a schoolteacher and somehow accumulated the world's greatest craft collection in old-fashioned '60s pantyhose boxes. I would have to say our house had a hundred flat pantyhose boxes with diligently sorted craft materials: pompoms, pipe cleaners, cut pieces of paper, yarn, spools from old thread. My mother accumulated all these things, and then sorted them carefully; we kids, you know, completely ravished them over the course of childhood and left them a decimated pile.

VH: *They were completely made available, and you had free reign?*

GJ: Yes, absolutely. So I've got to give it up to my mother for enabling that level of creativity and letting us be messy, fun, crafty kids growing up. That is easily a debt that I owe, and will pass on to my own kids when they come along.

VH: *What were your favorite things to make with all those supplies when you were a kid?*

GJ: The spools stand out as a specific memory—coloring things on the spools. I grew up in the country on a farm with a pond, and with the red barn, and the hayloft, with all of these trappings, but with no neighbors. I entertained myself by knitting and making little things for myself. I'm 36 now, so I was in the sweet spot for Star Wars when it came out. I used craft materials to make all sorts of elaborate sets for my Star Wars characters, which I carried around in a purse. I was a pioneer of the man-purse when I was five years old.

VH: *I love that! What was it like growing up around all of that creativity? Do you feel like you were raised differently than your friends?*

GJ: I don't think I ever took it for granted, but I don't think I felt like I was that much different than my friends. I had lots of friends who were provided with all of their toys and entertainment. Some friends were provided with every toy and action figure; I was vaguely jealous of their toys, but completely content to make my own things as well, and make my own entertainment.

One of the things I always talk about when I am talking about my blog is family. Anytime anyone in the craft world talks about what they do, it all comes back to family and history, so I can trace it back to great-grandfathers who were gem carvers, or one who was a blacksmith. When I was growing up, my family participated in every major craft fad that came down the pipes. In the late '60s and early '70s, when I came along, my parents where doing wire art, where you pounded nails into a board and then wrapped wire around them, making elaborate things.

There was macramé—my mother was all about the macramé. Then in the early '80s, there was the stained glass boom, so I was taught to do some of that. My stained glass career ended when I picked up the soldering iron by the wrong end one day.

My mother eventually drifted into quilting and has become an obsessed quilter. My father is more on the *MAKE* magazine side of things, and loves electronics. He can customize cars and works with antique gas engines. I'm still completely in awe of my mother, who is way more of a prolific crafter than I will ever be in my life.

VH: *Do you credit anyone, in particular, for opening the professional crafty doors for you?*

GJ: You know, I have been doing a lot of thinking about how, professionally, I drifted into the world of craft, and I can honestly trace it back to college. I owned a small record label and had my own record store in Lincoln, Nebraska. We were

> I always like to stand up for the brothers when I'm doing my Extreme Craft lecture. I have a very prominent man-craft section where I talk about Rosie Greer and his needlepoint.

always doing T-shirts and posters, playing elaborate shows, and dressing up and doing weird things. I think only recently have I really come to appreciate how much bearing that had on how I think of my art and life. I also went to a traditional art school.

VH: *Where did you go?*

GJ: I went to the University of Nebraska. I started studying illustration in college because that is a nice, sensible career. About halfway through school, they eliminated my illustration program while I was in it. Around that time, I first picked up clay in a ceramics class. Somehow the craft gene kicked in.

I had never really considered it, but something about working with my hands, being able to tell stories and combine illustration with making forms, was huge to me. My first ceramics teacher, Gail Kendall, provided me with a way to create things with my hands, and she encouraged me to think abstractly about those things. You know, the music world also helps me out in terms of how I comport myself within the craft world, and how I frame what I do.

VH: *It's funny—I have interviewed many, many people, and I can't tell you how many times artists have also brought up music and how they promoted it, what they learned from it, how they compared music to their career as a professional crafter or artist. They seem to be very tied together.*

GJ: Recently, I was reading Betsy Greer's book about creativity, and the first chapters are all about what music and punk rock meant to Betsy in her early life, and the light just went on in my head, "Oh, of course." I think I always knew, on some level, that there was a direct connection, but I'm starting to give it more credit.

VH: *I think that kids everywhere, especially boys (since art programs are being cut out of schools) aren't very aware that there are careers in the art and craft industries that are applicable to them, so I'm hoping boys read this book and stories like yours. Please tell me how you took your passion for being creative and turned it into a livelihood.*

145

GJ: It's interesting, and I always like to stand up for the brothers when I'm doing my Extreme Craft lecture. I have a very prominent man-craft section where I talk about Rosie Greer and his needlepoint. Honestly, when I started out, there was a very macho side of ceramics that was overwhelming—in particular, in the early '90s. You would go to a ceramics conference, and it was a bunch of people from the old boys' network trying to outdo each other with their wood firing, and their macho clay calculations, and how big they could make things.

VH: *There is machismo in the pottery world?*

GJ: It's dying out, but the pottery world was totally machismo. It was populated by very alpha males. I tried to bring out as many of my feminine qualities as possible, and tried to drift to the more feminine side of ceramics. It was really surprising in the early '90s. I found a group of little old ladies in Lincoln, and I started taking china painting classes, which really shocked the male-dominated ceramics world. It really tickled my teacher, though. She entirely pushed me to explore hobby-grade glazes, craft glazes, and decals and china painting; all of those things are seen as female mediums.

When I started to take ceramics classes, the valid art was a very macho wood-fired kiln aesthetic. Over the course of the last 15 years that I've been involved in the ceramics scene, those boundaries have really broken down almost entirely. I'm glad, on one hand, to see those boundaries broken down, but on the other hand, I'm sad because it was fun to push against those things, and to try and mix things up and introduce craft elements to the serious ceramics world.

VH: *Do you think there are still plenty of boundaries to push concerning males in the craft community?*

GJ: I think it isn't necessarily about boundaries, but more about meaning. When I do my section of the Extreme Craft lecture, I point to men who explode gender roles. Dave Cole is one example I like to highlight, with his huge knitting machine installation (an enormous flag knitted with the help of industrial equipment). I talk about gender politics, and how he takes a project and makes the ambition of it almost limitless. Then I look back at Rosie Greer and his needlepoint book and point to male quilters—there are certainly plenty of gender roles and societal roles that still exist. I don't ever foresee a day when there won't be fertile territory in exploring those boundaries and those gender roles.

VH: *What is the biggest challenge you've faced in trying to make a living through your craft?*

GJ: Well, I'm a teacher, so I am really committed to education, and I recently secured a tenure-track teaching job. When I got out of grad school, I wasn't sure that teaching was what I wanted to do. I have a graduate degree in ceramics, and I was always interested in exploring digital art and the boundaries between digital art and ceramics, as strange as those may seem. I started teaching after grad school, but I got a job at an architecture firm as a designer, so I spent seven years designing anything that wasn't architecture—doing signage and things like that.

Then one morning, I woke up and realized that teaching was my life's mission and that I needed to get back into it. I devoted myself to hopping on the freeway and taking any far-flung, part-time college teaching job that I could, and my efforts eventually led to the job I have now. There was a huge step between reconciling the part of my life that was an educator and my own studio world. It's all about making things, time management, and getting enough time to explore your own creativity. That's one of the biggest hurdles that I have had to face.

The same issue extends to writing as well. I probably spend more time writing, and thinking about crafts, and talking about other people's work than I do about my own work. So, one of the toughest but most rewarding things, for me, is just balancing the teaching, writing, and making.

VH: *Are you able to find that time to create for yourself, or is everything that you create for a class, for a lecture, or something other than yourself?*

GJ: No, I definitely find time. Participating in the craft community and writing about other people's work has led to increased interest in my own work. When I have a show coming up, or when I have extra time, I force myself to go into the studio and kind of close things off and create things. Writing and teaching really occupy a very similar place for my own creative life. But then, when I finally do get into the studio and shut off the pressures of the outside world, I remember why people find the studio such a fulfilling escape, and why they find it to be such a compulsion and need.

But, I go through periods—I always refer to myself as the Tammy Wynette of the ceramics world. I'll work with ceramics, but it can be such a harsh mistress, and it never does what you want it to do, and it's frustrating. I'll do some projects

> There are plenty of people in the ceramics world who have tendencies toward pyromania, shall I say. It's not necessarily the fact that you're dealing with kilns and fire and heat; it's the attraction, the compulsion of making something that is on the edge of creation and destruction.

and get really angry, and I'll swear it off, but then I wind up crawling back and defending ceramics and standing by my man, as it were.

VH: *Your main medium is pottery. What is it about clay and paint that expresses your voice better than other mediums?*

GJ: Honestly, I have no idea. I describe it by saying that my craft gene kicked in the first time I touched ceramics. I did have a little bit of a history with ceramics before I took classes in college. Once a year in high school, the teacher would wheel out this box of moldy, stinky clay that she had made up from powder. If you have ever been around clay, you know that clay rots. It collects bacteria and molds, so it would sit in this box for the entire year, and then she'd wheel it out.

The teacher really didn't know how to throw pots on the wheel, but we had a pottery wheel that lived on top of a high counter. I would put the moldy clay up on this chest-high wheel, and I'd try to throw pots with no instructions. It wasn't very fun or fulfilling, and coiling and making pots by hand wasn't that attractive to me either. When I was in college, I saved ceramics for my last elective, because I hated it so much in high school. The poor instruction, and just getting on the wheel itself, blew my mind a little bit.

Later, it was the immediacy, speed, and danger about throwing something on a potter's wheel that appealed to me. One of the things I've noticed in the ceramics world (not that I'm a pyromaniac), but there are plenty of people in the ceramics world who have tendencies toward pyromania, shall I say. It's not necessarily the fact that you're dealing with kilns and fire and heat; it's the attraction, the compulsion of making something that is on the edge of creation and destruction.

It was really profound for me, and I don't even make things on the potter's wheel now, but that was the gateway drug for me. It showed me clay was something alive and dangerous, in a way, and it attracted me. The depth of craft and tradition in ceramics also appeals to me. The work I make now deals with taking collector plates from thrift stores and messing with them—I re-glaze them and re-fire other things to them. You wouldn't think that would have anything to do with the processes I've described, but there is a very direct link to the history of ceramic craft that makes my work appealing.

VH: *I don't think that's any different than the current wave of the DIY movement, in general. Whether it's the recycling movement where you turn something into something else, or the knitting or crochet movements where you apply the same techniques your grandmother used to make doilies, but now you cover a motorcycle with it. I think it all comes from the same space; it just evolves.*

GJ: It's one layer. It is a conceptual layer of people's work.

VH: *There's a debate in the community about the difference between art and craft. You play around with the question of what's what a lot on your blog. For you, what's the difference between art and craft, and what message do you hope people*

> The grey area of what craft means drives academics completely nuts, and that's the thing that makes me happiest in the world. Is craft pompoms? Is it the history of Chinese ceramics and techniques?

take away from your Extreme Craft musings?

GJ: I guess the difference between art and craft is whatever I say it is. I tend to use the two interchangeably, but sometimes I use them precisely. I would never want to completely get away from the distinction of the two, because I think it would be a really boring world, which is one of the things Faythe Levine (see page 257) pointed out to me. The grey area of

what craft means drives academics completely nuts, and that's the thing that makes me happiest in the world. Not just the debate between art and craft, but what craft is. Is craft pompoms? Is it the history of Chinese ceramics and techniques?

So the art layer exists when someone wants to engage the art world with what they are making. One of things that drives me crazy in the ceramics world is that people sit back and just make purple glaze travel mugs to sell at their local hobby store; then they sit around bitching that the Whitney Museum hasn't swooped down and given them a one-man retrospective. This is one of my sermons to my students: I think most people in the craft world aren't looking for validation from the art world, but there are plenty of people who are trained as artists (and it's second nature for them) who use craft as one layer of their work. It becomes second nature to engage the art world. So, if you want to participate in the art world, move to New York, schmooze with curators, show in galleries, but don't complain that people call your work crafts if you only lazily show it in craft galleries or in craft situations. You need to embrace new audiences if you are seeking that validation.

VH: *But isn't part of the debate the merit of one over the other. The value seems to go down immensely if you attach the word craft, compared to if you attach the word art to a project. This is why a lot of people in our community have now started calling themselves designers instead of professional crafters—just for respect.*

GJ: Whatever people need to do for their own egos and justification is fine. I've always fought for more design distinction in ceramics, because it is often something that is lacking. Bringing functionality to the design world is a sorely needed thing that has been injected into the ceramic debate. All of the distinctions are so grey right now; I used to be someone who fought and fought for the unvarnished comparison of things, but I honestly think there are plenty of things that are craft and will always be craft. As I said, if distinctions didn't exist, the world would be a boring place.

VH: *What inspired Extreme Craft?*

GJ: I found a bunch of people who were thinking about craft in the same way I was. I always felt a little isolated in the ceramics world, because there weren't many people who were thinking about aspects of crafts and hobby materials in their work. About five years ago, I had a big revelation that all of sudden the fiber world, the knitting world, and all these other craft practices were finding immense power in subverting crafts and thinking about craft materials as a conceptual layer. I started Extreme Craft as a way to do more writing and to keep track of the people that I thought were similar-minded.

VH: *How important is being a part of the craft community to you? How have you been treated within that community? Do you find that you're treated any differently because you're a guy?*

GJ: Community is a funny live product. I was never much of a prolific e-mailer or networker, but when Extreme Craft took off, which was really early in the game, it found an audience. All of a sudden I was included in the craft community, and that has been amazing; it always felt very natural to me.

For more information about Garth and his projects, go to:
www.extremecraft.com

The Crafter's Studio

In the great tradition of *Inside the Actor's Studio* and James Lipton:

What craft sound or smell do you love?
Clove oil used in china painting.

What craft sound or smell do you hate?
Turpentine.

What career, other than craft- and art-world domination, would you like to try?
An emcee or a talk show host.

When you spill turpentine on the floor or break a piece you're working on, what is your favorite exclamation?
Oh, balls!

Name: Josh M. Stewart
Age: 24
Digs: West Chester, PA
Daily Grind: college student
Fave Crafts: ceramic pottery

Words to Craft by:

Ever since my first
pottery class in high
school, I have been
drawn to throw-
ing pottery on a
wheel. It is something
that always felt natural to me.
One moment I particularly remember is when I
had my first real show. It was hosted in a gallery with two other
students, and I was given complete creative control. The turnout was much greater
than expected, and it was a very educational experience that gave me a realistic
perspective as to how much work and planning goes into hosting an art show. I
look forward to many more in the future.

Name: John C. Stewart
Age: 21
Digs: Philadelphia, PA
Daily Grind: college student
Fave Crafts: ceramic pottery

Words to Craft by:

I quickly fell in love with throwing
pottery after taking my first class in
high school. My older brother Josh
and I both excelled in pottery during
our high school years. Unfortunately,
we both decided against a career in
art due to advice and pressure from
our parents. Three years later as a junior
at Temple University (which offers no art classes on main campus), I
realized something was missing from my life. I made the decision to reunite with
clay by enrolling in a wheel-throwing class at the Clay Studio in Philadelphia. It
made such a difference in my life to be working with clay again. I still can't believe I
went that long without throwing, and I hope it never happens again. It has been an
incredible experience to learn with some of the best potters in the country. I have
grown as both an artist and a person due to my experiences at the Clay Studio.

chapter sixteen

Susan Beal, a.k.a. Susan Stars

Photo by Andrew Dickson

I've known Susan for years, thanks to the wonderful Web community this book celebrates. She's a mama, designer, author, editor, activist, and one of four members who make up the crafty cooperative, Portland Supercrafty. Her passion for life and craft are infectious—a reminder, for those of us hustling to live creative lives, of why we do it. Susan and I caught up about motherhood, crafting for profit, and juggling it all, from her home in Portland, Oregon.

VH

VH: *What's your first craft-related memory?*

SB: Probably drawing. When I was little, I'd make drawings of everything that came into my head, like a dress I'd love to have or a doll that I wanted. I couldn't use my parents' camera because it was fancy, so I'd prop my stuffed animals up and draw them. I still look at a box of crayons and immediately get ideas.

VH: *You're the second person in this book to mention a box of crayons, which I find so interesting!*

SB: The box of 64 Crayolas is the best!

VH: *You know the branding for that product really worked, because we all still remember the name and crayon count.*

Is there a moment from your childhood connected to craft that really stands out for you?

SB: When I was in elementary school, my favorite craft was making paper dolls—kind of like drawing, but a little more grown up. I would draw sheets of paper dolls, and I remember showing them to my friends at school; they got so excited and asked if I'd draw a sheet for them. I remember one of my friends who was a boy wanted one—it was so cool because boys were usually into trucks and machines, but we got excited about drawing this sheet of superhero paper dolls. My most special memory is probably just drawing those dolls and sharing them with my friends.

Another memory I have is of my grandmother, who was an amazing seamstress. She made doll clothes and would encourage me to do the same with fabric scraps, only sewing by hand. I would hang out with her for the afternoon while she was sewing something for me or my mom, and then we'd use the scraps to make little matching doll dresses—either my amateur versions, or she'd make real ones on the machine.

VH: *Now as a professional designer/crafter, is there an equally important moment for you? Do these two very different moments hold the same weight of feeling for you?*

SB: One really exciting moment was to see people wearing my skirts or jewelry that just came out. I have a vivid memory from when I used to make custom skirts and sell them on my website. This woman in Kansas City ordered a plain skirt from me. She e-mailed me saying that she really loved it; then she e-mailed me again a few months later, wondering if I could make her a maternity version. I went to the fabric store, got a maternity panel, and made up a simple style to send her. She said it was perfect and that she'd been wearing it just about everyday, because it was exactly like something she'd wear even if she wasn't pregnant.

About four or five years later, I was at a coffee shop in Portland, Oregon, and this woman came up and asked me if I was Susan. She recognized me from my picture online and had just moved to Portland from Kansas City. She asked if I remembered making a maternity skirt for her. She had a baby in a sling and a toddler and said she wore that skirt all through both of her pregnancies. I thought, "Wow, what a cool circle." Then, about six months after that, I was pregnant and went to a consignment store in my neighborhood looking for stuff, and all of a sudden, I found my own skirt on the rack! She had nicely told me that her family was complete, and she was happily back in regular clothing. I guess she'd traded it in for credit, so I bought it back and wore it through two-thirds of my pregnancy!

VH: *That's the full circle of craft, if I've ever heard it! As a new mother, are you conscious of creating crafty memories for your own daughter?*

SB: I've always thought how fun it would be to make stuff with my daughter when she's older. My nephew is seven and *loves* making stuff and drawing. He's really into designing stuff in his head, and then we'll try to bring it to life. He's so creative that it's made me really excited for when my daughter's older.

> I remember one of my friends who was a boy wanted [a paper doll]—it was so cool because boys were usually into trucks and machines, but we got excited about drawing this sheet of superhero paper dolls.

153

Photo by Susan Beal

I've been really busy since my pregnancy, though, and haven't had a chance to sew her the adorable things I've always thought about, but I did make her a Harry Potter Halloween costume. She's got a shock of dark hair, which was the deciding factor for choosing that costume. It was really fun. I've also had a really great time taking pictures of her, photography being sort of peripheral, but it's the kind of thing that I look forward to doing more and more.

My friends hosted a baby shower for us, and we got together and painted all-in-ones and bibs. It was really nice getting together and making these cute things for the baby. I've hosted two showers since then, and it's been so great to have an opportunity to make things for them. It makes me dream about making stuff with my daughter when she's older.

VH: *How do you handle juggling craft with parenthood?*

SB: It's going pretty well. There are definitely some limits on my time that weren't there before. I'm sure you can relate—there are some days that you don't go outside, or you barely stop to eat because you're busy writing or making something. It kind of consumes your whole life. With a baby, you really do have to become more balanced, even though it's not necessarily restful. It definitely gets me out of my hard-core, deadline-oriented pattern. I find it so much fun to take time to play with her when she's just waking up from a nap, and I've gotten something done while she was asleep—then I have her all over again. It's a real treat coming back to her after that break.

It's hard, though, saying no to projects. It's been a real gift to be able to contribute to other people's projects, or to do things that are more time and labor intensive, but I've had to say no to some things I wouldn't have had to a year ago. There are some real advantages to focusing on creative outlets outside your own work, like raising a baby and doing things that are more focused on the household.

VH: *That's interesting. Do you find parenting to be a creative outlet?*

SB: I do, but there are hard and challenging times that seem to steal my creative energy. At the same time, just having my baby in my life is inspiring in a lot of ways. She brings me a lot of fresh energy—it's been personally creative, but obviously not a work boost. I think, if you're creative for a living, there's something nice about being able to do something that's not for a blog post or a magazine tutorial—but doing something that's just fun for the household, for the baby, or for a gift.

VH: *Please share how you took your creative passion and turned it into a livelihood.*

SB: I started out making and selling jewelry and skirts. After college I went to a six-month, intensive jewelry class specializing in silversmithing and casting. I always loved making jewelry. In middle school and high school, I'd take things apart and put them back together; I'd re-string beads on dental floss and make it up as I went along. I was so drawn to it, so once I got the chance to go to school for it, it was really exciting to finally have my skills catch up to my enthusiasm. After that, I started selling small lines of my jewelry and skirts.

The first time I ever took my skirts into a shop was when two friends of mine took over a small jewelry and clothing boutique and asked me if I wanted to bring anything in. I brought in four skirts, and soon after I got home, I got a message from one of the owners telling me that a girl came in, tried on one of the skirts, fell in love with it, and bought it on the spot. The owner kept repeating, "She looked so cute in it!" It was such a cool moment, because you never know what's going to happen when you take those first little tentative steps—when you open a small website store or bring things to a retail outlet—whether or not people are going to be drawn to your stuff. It was really exciting. It helped so much to have support from friends who owned stores or from people trading links with me, once I got my website up and running.

I wrote an article for *ReadyMade* magazine in the spring of 2002 about how to start a small business and what had worked for me. They ran the article with my Web address, and it turned into this exciting thing where I was writing part-time and making steady sales from my site. It was a transition for me to think that I could actually make a small, part-time living from craft, instead of it just being a labor of love.

Slowly, I got the chance to sell at more stores, do fashion shows, and put catalogues together for my jewelry. Crafting really put me in contact with so many great people. I've since transitioned from selling wholesale and retail to doing a lot more writing, but it's been so great being a part of this mutually supportive craft community. I love the fact that you can bump into someone on the street wearing your stuff. I love doing trades at craft fairs, helping organize events, and having people respond with so much great energy. Also, as a customer, being able to support other people's handmade lines has been a real pleasure. There's something so exciting about buying things made by hand, knowing that someone put their good energy and time into it, and knowing that you probably won't see anyone else wearing it.

VH: *Do you have any advice for readers who hope to craft for profit?*

SB: Really, just be patient with yourself at first. If you open an Etsy shop, your own website, or start bringing catalogues to stores, be ambitious, but don't set unrealistic goals that will be disappointing if you can't meet them. Not to discourage anyone from thinking big, but if your first bit of craft sales are slow, don't take it personally. Once you have your feet wet, just make sure you stay connected with the community, because it's such a great source of support and help. Organize a craft show with a group of people, or cross-promote each other, and swap tips. Baby steps are important, and you don't want to burn out in two months after investing a lot of money.

VH: *Out of everything you do, is there one craft that speaks to you the most creatively?*

SB: My favorite is still making jewelry. I love it because, like I said, I've always been drawn to it, and because it's kind of the magpie craft in that it's a shiny, colorful, and very luxurious *optional* craft. Some delicious knitted thing will keep you warm. A great pair of handmade pants or silkscreen shirt will cover you. Jewelry, though, is so optional. I love that it's the kind of thing people ornament themselves with just because they want to. My second stable craft is Gocco printing, and I love sewing and paper collage.

VH: *You're a part of a core community that has not only been a source of crafty nourishment for you, but also an inspiration to the creative community at large. Will you talk about Portland Supercrafty—how it started, its philosophy, and where it is today?*

SB: I had lived and crafted in Portland for several years, when I met a woman named Cathy Pitters at a small sale that we were both doing. I really liked her stuff and since it was a quiet afternoon without much traffic, we started chatting about different ideas. We thought, "Why don't we try to organize a sale?" We stayed in touch about it, and it turned into this sale called Riches at Roomsky's, which went on for several years at a small coffee house.

Around the same time, I met Torie Nguyen on the Get Crafty boards. We hung out a few times and started crafting together. Then I met another woman named Rachel O'Rourke backstage at a show, and we bonded over the hairspray ridiculousness of the event. I had the idea to get us all together, so we could help each other. It crystalized into the four of us meeting regularly, talking about co-advertising strategies in *BUST* or *Venus* magazines, and sharing tables at sales under the name of Portland Supercrafty.

Then, a publisher at Sasquatch Books e-mailed us out of the blue because they liked our website. They asked if we'd potentially be interested in writing a general craft book. We were so excited about it! We put together a proposal that they loved, and the next thing we knew, we had this six-month whirlwind of putting together an 80-project book that spanned everything from sewing vinyl,

Photo by Susan Beal

to recycled crafts, to shrink art. It was our chance to go in a zillion different directions and write essays about things like craftivism, crafts of the past, and crafty disasters—things that were really important to us. There's so much enthusiasm packed into that little book, and it turned out to be this communal achievement. We've done some great events with it and taught some fun studio classes.

Over the past couple of years, three of us have had babies, so it's been a little harder to meet up, but we still collaborate on stuff whenever we can. The group has been an unbelievably positive part of my life, so I'm always excited when we connect.

VH: *During the 2008 presidential election, you threw yourself and your craft into promoting Obama. I've noticed that the art and craft community tends to be pretty politically active—why do you think that is?*

SB: I think part of it is that people who are passionate about crafts, also tend to be passionate about what's important to them. For a lot of people, that passion isn't politics, but for those who are into politics, I've noticed a surge of creativity. A friend of mine runs the Obama Craft Project, which I love—it spotlights work that happens to be made by people who are like-minded about this one movement.

I think, too, that people are truly excited to help in both big and small ways. If you're already making jewelry, you can donate 10 percent of your sales, or donate money from a special collection. It's an empowering opportunity.

VH: *Don't you think this particular campaign was fairly crafty in and of itself? I don't mean that in a literal way, but it had a very indie feel of running itself—that grass roots, get your hands dirty, whatever it takes kind of thing. Anyone who's tried making it in a band or making a living crafting knows that's how you survive.*

Sort of on the same topic as activism, do you feel any kind of sense of responsibility as a feminist in a traditionally female community to use your voice as a forum for progression within that community and beyond?

SB: Definitely. My main avenue for that is my personal craft blog, West Coast Crafty (westcoastcrafty.wordpress.com), which I love, because I don't have any advertisers and it's not edited. It's just what I feel like writing about or what I'm passionate about.

I've done small fundraisers to benefit Planned Parenthood and the Los Angeles and Portland Food Banks. I am very much a feminist and part of that means sustaining the value of what we're doing so that it isn't just an aimless hobby. It's the kind of work that really produces results—whether it's a handmade piece that's beautiful or valuable; whether it supports your household; or whether it's a meaningful gift.

As a woman, I feel very connected to traditional *women's work*, but now we have an arena where artwork is looked at more critically and considered a serious business. It's a pretty major industry too, and I think it's finally starting to shift over to where people are taken seriously. For instance, Kathy Cano-Murillo (see page 68) has this pretty incredible opportunity to do her own craft supplies line and exhibit in a major museum show. Kathy's just an example, but I think it's really cool that people who were, maybe 10 years ago, producing zines, or knitting, or writing free pieces for websites, are now on their fifth book. Vickie, the way you've transformed what you do into this really cool public, sustainable business (that your career has blossomed around your passion) is amazing. The fact that the possibility even exists now is something I never considered would happen.

VH: *Although things are a little rough in the economy right now, I think we're really lucky to be part of this crafting era.*

SB: I believe that even though times are tough, people still want to support small businesses when they can and not always buy cheaper, mass-produced things.

For more information about Susan and her projects, go to: westcoastcrafty.wordpress.com

> As a woman, I feel very connected to traditional women's work, but now we have an arena where artwork is looked at more critically and considered a serious business. It's a pretty major industry too, and I think it's finally starting to shift over to where people are taken seriously.

The Crafter's Studio

In the great tradition of **Inside the Actor's Studio** and James Lipton:

What craft sound or smell do you love?
Since we mentioned it earlier, I'll say I love the way a box of crayons smells. I also love the sound of a sewing machine.

What craft sound or smell do you hate?
Toxic glue—it's nasty.

What career, other than craft-world domination, would you like to try?
One thing I miss is working as a copyeditor. I really like that work. I love that feeling of working with a page of someone else's writing.

When you burn yourself with a glue gun or poke yourself with a needle, what is your favorite exclamation?
Probably a curse word. Sometimes I get so pissed that I don't have anything to say.

Words to Craft by:

My mom always worked on her loom, sewed clothes, or made something while I was growing up, but when I caught the craft bug, nothing came easy. Patterns didn't make sense, and finishing seams made me queasy. But I was hooked, so I winged it. I used found objects to make mosaics, made a quilt from thrown-out fabric swatches, and started sewing my way. Sewing was much easier when I wasn't worried about the right way to do things. My skills grew organically until I was really good.

Due to a long-standing obsession with bags and my new sewing skills, I made my own diaper bag after the birth of my first son. A friend begged for one, and word spread like wildfire that I was making custom bags. It wasn't long before I found myself with my own sewing business. I'm still a one-woman shop and take one order at a time. Most of my days are devoted to my two little boys, but I sew almost every day and love to invent new designs. A half-yard of fabric, a sewing machine, a corner of the living room, and the courage to make mistakes is all it takes to make something spectacular.

Name: Kate McFaul

Age: 28

Digs: Benicia, CA

Daily Grind: stay-at-home mom and part-time crafter

Fave Crafts: sewing, quilting, and knitting

More Info: www.katemcfauldesigns.com and katemcfauldesigns.blogspot.com

Words to Craft by:

Sewing and crafting really make me happy and help me relax. For some time, I went away from my favorite hobby. I thought sewing took too much time, and when you have two kids, you don't have enough free time for yourself! Then I met Amela Spahic Savic, a.k.a. Narya. She also has a demanding job, but she squeezes in some sewing after putting her baby to sleep and before going to bed! I thought I would give it a try! Now I sew almost every week—sometimes more, sometimes less. Plus, Amela became one of my best friends! Our friendship started because we had the same hobby, but from our sewing talks, we have learned a lot about each other, our lives, hopes, and dreams. We hope our friendship will continue for years and that one day we will be two fit and happy grandmothers teaching our granddaughters to sew. Of course, that will happen after many, many productive years of running our own craft business!

Name: Selma Žiga, a.k.a. **Ramona,**

Age: 34

Digs: Sarajevo, Bosnia, and Herzegovina

Daily Grind: telecommunications engineer

Fave Crafts: sewing, paper crafts, fabric jewelry

More Info: byramona.blogspot.com (written in Bosnian, but you can see the photos)

chapter seventeen

Wendy Russell

Wendy's an actress, designer, producer, and writer. She's also made it her mission to spread the crafty gospel whenever possible, so I was thrilled when she called me up to be a guest on her HGTV Canada show, *She's Crafty!* I'd never been to Vancouver before and was really happy that the folks in her neck of the woods seemed as passionate about being creative as people in my 'hood. At the time, the transition of security protocol between our two countries was just taking place, so it was unclear whether or not I'd need a passport. Since mine had expired, we rolled the dice—and lost. When I reached Seattle, I was told that I couldn't fly into the country, but I could drive. So Wendy's production company (Love Your Work Productions) scored a car for me, and I took off for a kinder, gentler land. Waiting for me upon arrival was a hotel room with a beautiful view of the Pacific Ocean and a flask engraved with my name and "Most Impressive Arrival." I knew that Wendy and I would be fast friends.

Photo by Pink Monkey Studios

VH

VH: *What's your first craft-related memory?*

WR: When I was in kindergarten, we made name tags. We used big, orange construction paper cut into a flower shape, a pipe cleaner stem, and a glue stick to apply the all-important *mug* photo in the center of the flower. Super cute— and I still have it to this day! According to the female parental unit, however, she had me finger painting with chocolate pudding at the ripe ol' age of 10 months. Ah! That explains my penchant for all things chocolate.

VH: *It's funny that you mention the pudding-paint thing. My friend Noelle just told me that her 4-month-old was doing that at his daycare. It seems like the consistency would be really great for sensory development, not to mention that*

> I love that my grandma and mom taught me as a kid the importance of recycling and using what we had on hand.

finger painting is a fantastic introduction to creativity. I guess the proof really is in the pudding, since here you are, years later, making a living being crafty!

Is there a moment from your childhood connected to craft that really stands out for you?

WR: Maybe not just one moment. My grandma Kate always used to make us the most amazing things—one year, a dollhouse, and another year, her version of the Cabbage Patch doll. But as a kid, I didn't appreciate her crafts. I wanted the *real* Barbie dollhouse and the *real* Cabbage Patch doll. It wasn't until I was in my late teens that I realized the depth and importance of what those gifts meant to me. My grandma inspired me to make things for people by hand; for her it was as easy as breathing. My mom also made a lot of our clothes. My sister and I often matched, much to my chagrin. It's never cool to have your little sister dressed the same as you. My mom crocheted us matching yellow- and rust-colored hoodie jackets. I knew then, at such a young age, that these sweaters were borderline cool, but they were *so* not my colors. And any ounce of redeeming coolness was null and void because my sister sported the identical garment.

Mom also made our Halloween costumes every year—my favorite was an angel. I wore one of her dresses (in hindsight, I wonder if it was actually a tablecloth), and she crafted a halo from tinfoil and pipe cleaners. Classic. I love that my grandma and mom taught me as a kid the importance of recycling and using what we had on hand. It's part of who I am as an adult, and that makes me really proud in a world that is so quick to dispose. I really care about how things come in and go out the door at my house. I'm so nuts about recycling that I will pick paper or cardboard out of the garbage when my husband just *happens* to forget to toss it in the recycle bin. Now, as a home décor designer and teacher of crafty goodness, a handmade gift is the definition of pure love for me. Thanks Mom and GK!

VH: *Now as a professional designer/crafter, is there an equally important moment for you, or one that stands out as a defining time in your career?*

WR: People would often come over and comment on the décor items in my home, saying, "Wow, that's so cool. Where did you get that?" You can see this coming a mile away—I made whatever they were commenting on. That was certainly the beginning of believing I could make cool things that appealed to lots of people. Then people started offering to pay for the things I made. Or if they were crafty, they would ask me to teach them how to do it. I really liked the teaching aspect. It felt comfortable for me and was über-satisfying. But then came the dreaded non-crafty period in my life, where I was so busy trying to be an actress. I had (temporarily) tossed crafting to the curb. Note to self: Don't stop doing what you love. Don't stop doing what fulfills you creatively. Even if it's for six months or a year. No matter how much is on your to-do list. No matter how many dishes are in the sink or how much laundry has piled up. Creativity is more important.

VH: *When did you start to think, "You know, I may actually be able to make a living doing what I love?"*

WR: When I read *The Artist's Way* by Julia Cameron, without a doubt. There's a whole section in there about never using the word *try*. You don't try; you either do or you don't. When I would run into people I hadn't seen in years, and they'd ask the inevitable, "What are you up to these days?" I'd reply, "Oh, I'm trying to be an actor, you know." The minute I stopped saying *try* and told people that I was an actor, I got 10 commercials in a row with a film or television role thrown in there. As Yoda says, "Do or do not. There is no try." Words to live by.

VH: *Who do you credit for opening the crafty doors for you?*

WR: My mom and grandma Kate. Both are very crafty, creative, talented, beautiful women.

VH: *How did you overcome that stigma and turn your passion for being creative into a livelihood? Did you have a professional mentor that steered you in a certain direction?*

WR: Well, going back to *The Artist's Way*—I read that book about 10 years ago, and it gave me permission to unabashedly live a creative life. At the time, I was struggling with an eating disorder, and one day I had an Oprah *ah-ha* moment. I realized that I was so busy waiting for Hollywood to call that I had stopped crafting for a few years. I wasn't being creative at all—you can't call jumping up and down in a room full of producers, auditioning for a toilet paper commercial, creative. I felt empty, and the disordered eating was filling that hunger. The next time I came home from an audition, instead of eating cookie dough, I made gifts for friends and family. That same week I heard Oprah say, "Ask the universe how you can serve." For me, not only did that mean I had to continue to create with my hands, it meant teaching and sharing creativity with the world. My hope was that someone feeling the same would be inspired to invite creativity into their lives and have the opportunity to heal—crafting had made that much of a difference in my life, so I was sure there were others out there who needed creativity, too!

That privilege manifested itself in the form of hosting and producing *She's Crafty*. I knew it was something I needed to do to heal. When I pitched the show to HGTV, I had 10 minutes with the director of original programming (five minutes to pitch and five minutes afterwards to chat about it). I had worked with Jan Miller (world-famous pitching coach and a particularly excellent human being), who encouraged me to share my very personal story with whomever I was pitching. Her reasoning behind this disconcerting (to me) piece of advice was that I had five minutes for them to connect with me and believe in me as a host. They needed to know that I was deeply connected to the subject, because that ultimately translates into passion and authenticity on television.

VH: *Your passion for general creativity is truly impressive, but is there one craft that speaks to you more than another?*

WR: I can't say that there is. I once heard someone describe themself as having craft ADD, and that statement totally resonates with me. I tend to get bored really quickly, so I hop from one project to another. If I can't generally do it in an hour or less, all bets are off. Although this cool chick named Vickie Howell taught me how to knit a few years back. It's my favorite thing to rock out on when I'm traveling!

VH: *I'm so happy to hear that you've continued knitting. That makes mama proud! What's your favorite thing about crafting?*

WR: It's my meditation. I find it healing and peaceful. It clears the clutter from my mind and makes space for new creative ideas to come in. On a potentially irrelevant note, I reconnected with dancing, too. It's my other form of meditation. Those are really the only two things I can say that I'm actually fully present for. Eckhart Tolle would be proud. It's funny—I had no clue how much I missed crafting and dancing and how much my body was craving them until I got back at it. There definitely had been a little voice in my head trying to push me, but I guess I wasn't listening.

VH: *Over the years I've had the opportunity to meet a variety of crafters who are also musicians, writers, actors, graphic artists, etc. I've found that if a person expresses creativity in one way, they more than likely are interested in multiple forms of it. I believe that all things creative are linked together. Do you find that to be true for yourself? Are there non-handicraft, creative aspects to your life?*

Photo by Pink Monkey Studios

WR: Yes. That's pretty much me, in a nutshell. Thanks to Julia Cameron's inspiring writings, I'm an actor, television host, writer, producer, home stager, stylist, organizer…and closet rock star. Oh, and one day I envision playing Donna in *Mamma Mia* on Broadway. Gotta figure out that whole "Canadian in America" thing. I swore when I was a kid that I would move to Hollywood, not realizing it was in a different country. I just thought I could move anywhere, without question. Not so much. I'll let you know how that works out.

VH: *Really? I didn't know you were so into Broadway. Keep me posted, and I'll be first in line for a ticket!*

Do all of these things you do, interchangeably, fill the same creative space within you, or is each one just a piece of the whole?

WR: Interchangeably, they all fill the same creative space—absolutely. I get as much of a sense of satisfaction from decorating someone's house as I do singing karaoke or sewing a pillow. They all satisfy my hunger for creativity. I love the variety and never get bored—remember my comment about my craft ADD! Don't let people tell you that you can only have one hobby—you can do everything you love.

VH: *Canada is known for being very supportive of the television and film industries, often funding portions of shows and films. Is there the same financial support for the craft arts?*

WR: In a word, no. There is a little bit of financial support for the craft arts, but it certainly is not funded as well as film and television. We quickly became Hollywood North in the '80s: Our dollar sucked compared to yours, and

> "
>
> I once heard someone describe themself as having craft ADD, and that statement totally resonates with me.

Vancouver really resembles Seattle, so our government gave producers incredible financial incentives to shoot here. It was easy for Hollywood to want to film here. So, no, we're not nearly as well-funded in the craft world, and it is a bit of a delicate subject for our artisans, so let's move on.

VH: *Has the huge resurgence of craft that's taken place in the States over the past 10 years occurred to the same degree in Canada?*

WR: Yes! We're so influenced by the States. We're kinda like America's little sister. Everything you do is cooler. Everything you have is cooler. And we want to be just like you (minus the guns and the health care, but anyhoo). With books, magazines, and at least 50 percent of our television programming coming at us from the States (don't quote me on that percentage—I'm ballparking), we know exactly what's shakin' down south. Keep in mind, though, our population is a tenth of yours, so it's all relative.

VH: *Speaking of how different places are influenced by different things, what role has crafting played in your own sense of community?*

WR: Thanks to the Austin Craft Mafia, crafters around the world experience a great sense of community. These fabulous gals inspire and welcome others on the planet to form their own Craft Mafias, with the goal of supporting each other in our creative endeavors. I was one of the inspired, and set out to form the Vancouver Craft Mafia in 2005, which became another important part of my healing process. What I love about the community is that we *get* each other. There's an innate understanding when it comes to venting about our creative blocks or business tribulations—an understanding without judgment or scrutiny.

VH: *Wow, it's really lovely to hear that the Austin Craft Mafia was an inspiration to you. You've never told me that before. Sniff, sniff. Just out of curiosity, how did you even come across our group?*

WR: Wow, I can't remember, it's been so long. *Bust* magazine? The Internet? It was one of the two, for sure. I remember traveling to the States for vacations and would make sure that I stayed at a place that had the DIY network, because I was so inspired and excited by what was happening in television for crafting. And then I'd go home so bummed that we didn't get these cool shows in Canada. At the time, we only had Martha repping the craft world up here, if you can believe it! I'm still shocked that we don't have as many shows. The only one that played here was *Craft Corner Deathmatch*. Classic, really. I do enjoy Jason Jones as a host.

VH: *You're in the rare position of not only being a professional crafter, but also a celebrity because of it. Do you see your role as an example of how the industry and our society are evolving, or are people just more aware because of media avenues like the Internet?*

WR: The current (horrendous) state of the economy is an absolute testament to what the crafting community has been aware of for years—decades, really. Buy locally. Buy handmade. Recycle. Reuse. Revamp. Stop buying so much crap! I believe the recent resurgence of crafting came from a generation that was sick of shopping for the same old cheap T-shirts from Indonesia and earrings from China—a rebellion of sorts. People were craving originality via creativity. As a community, it's fundamentally important for us to continually bring about awareness when it comes to being globally conscious and responsible. Ironically, this recession presents that awareness to our society at a rapid-fire pace. Hopefully, now, everyone will think twice before they make another mindless purchase at a big box store.

VH: *Answered like a true Canadian—you avoided the vanity part of the question. I agree with you about the motivation behind the current craft movement, but I think what I'm more curious about is whether or not you think that achieving fame for crafting is something that's possible now because the societal view of crafting as a career is shifting? Or, do you think it's just a product of designers being able to reach more people because of Facebook, Twitter, YouTube, and other social networking outlets?*

WR: Vickie Howell, you crack me up. I hardly consider myself a celebrity. I think that's why I avoided that part of the question. My brain went, "Irrelevant to you, Russell. Move on to answering the industry/society portion of this exercise." Well, society isn't necessarily shifting, but the good news is that people who love crafting are infinitely inspired, and perhaps now have the courage they didn't have before, because of how social networking outlets embrace craft. People are seeing craft shows on television, shopping on Etsy, reading *Bust* and *ReadyMade* magazines, watching craft instructionals on YouTube, and saying, "Hey, I can do that!" I think it's so cool. The more creative we all are, the better world we live in.

VH: *Do you feel a sense of responsibility as a feminist woman in a traditionally female community to use your voice as a forum for progression?*

WR: I think women should use their voices as forums for progression regardless of their community. As a mentor, I personally feel a deep responsibility to inspire and support all women to do what they love, be creative, be fearless, and then just do it (thank you, Nike, for that). The more we're happy and creatively fulfilled, the better the world will be. That's progression!

VH: *Well said, my friend!*

Is there anything else you'd like to say about what crafting means to you or has given you?

WR: It's given me health, peace, and balance.

For more information about Wendy and her projects, go to:
www.wendyrussell.com

The Crafter's Studio

In the great tradition of *Inside the Actor's Studio* and James Lipton:

What craft sound or smell do you love?
Rubber cement. A classic.

What craft sound or smell do you hate?
Burning plastic.

What career, other than craft-world domination, would you like to try?
Rock star. Period.

When you burn yourself with a glue gun or spill beads all over the floor, what is your favorite exclamation?
Can I have more than one? Because it's so dependent on the company I'm keeping, if ya know what I mean. Sweet mother f*&^! Crapity von crap! Sweet Jesus (pronounced in Spanish—hay-sus)! Mother of pearl!

Name: Cat Susch

Age: 43

Digs: New York, NY

Daily Grind: technology executive

Fave Crafts: knitting, spinning, and crocheting

More Info: www.letsknit2gether.com

Words to Craft by:

In the fall of 2001, I had been knitting for many years, but was lucky if I finished one or two projects a year. On September 11, I saw the World Trade Center burn and collapse right outside my office. My sister worked there, and I spent most of the day distraught, wondering if she was still alive. I found out later that she had escaped and made it out of the city. When I got home, shaken up and stunned, I picked up my needles and cast on for a sweater. I knitted my anger, sadness, relief, and all my other feelings into the Stockinette stitches. This sweater became my way of moving forward with life a stitch at a time. As I worked on the sweater's cables, the world around us tried to pick up the pieces and figure out what to do. All of this became as twisted as the cable pattern itself. After I completed the sweater, I started something else, and I've had a project going ever since. I'm still trying to knit my frustration, stress, and joy into the stitches. Now as a video podcaster teaching knitting, I hope I can pass on my experiences.

Words to Craft by:

The women in my family were never crafters. My great-grandmother had her own syndicated newspaper column; my grandmother worked for the newspaper and later became a teacher; and my mother holds a master's degree and is a teacher. The women in my family hardly even cook! I taught myself all the crafts I know, or have sought out other women to teach me.

When I was pregnant with my daughter, a fellow teacher taught me to knit, and I ran with it. After I moved back to the Navajo

Name: Molly Ferriter

Age: 36

Digs: Sanders, AZ—northeastern Arizona on the Navajo Nation Indian Reservation

Daily Grind: teacher, but working on a master's degree and raising my toddler

Fave Crafts: knitting, embroidery, and crocheting

More Info: desertstitcher.blogspot.com

Nation Reservation to teach elementary school, I held weekly knit nights. My neighbor and I taught several women to knit, many of whom were traditional Navajo rug weavers. I also remember knitting in my classroom when our adopted classroom grandma taught kids to weave on cardboard looms. She only spoke Navajo, and I only spoke English, but we sat together and made textiles. For me, crafts connect women from different cultures, times, and locales. Crafts have been women's work since the dawn of man, when women made pottery or textiles for survival. Now it's for leisure, but that thin thread is carried through generations, and as my daughter grows up, she will see me make things and craft.

chapter eighteen

Jackie Guerra

Jackie and I met when I was doing a cross-promotion for *Knitty Gritty* on her show, *DIY Jewelry Making*. Our two big personalities equaled a whole lotta host on one show, but we sure had fun shooting that episode! It's always such a treat to hang out with someone who digs being creative as much as I do, and that day with Jackie was no exception. Actress, writer, designer—she's a triple-threat with more charisma in her pinky finger than most have in their entire bodies. I had the pleasure of gabbing with her again from her Southern California home about gaining community, losing weight, and living *la vida crafty.*

VH

VH: *Do you come from a family of crafters?*

JG: Kind of. It's strange, because I never would have said that 10 years ago. When I started hosting *Jewelry Making*, it was like the stories came floating to me, and I realized that, yeah, my mom was the Mexican Martha Stewart.

VH: *You never noticed?*

JG: I definitely noticed, but it's so weird. This is the story I always tell people: it never occurred to me that everybody didn't make stuff. I had this moment when I first got out of college, where my good friend from high school and I (she was making a lot of money, and I wasn't) went shopping, and she was casually trying on a necklace. Literally, the stupid necklace was $840. The materials probably cost $60, and you could make it in maybe two hours. She was like, "Oh, I have to have this necklace!" and pulled out her credit card to buy it. I looked at her and went, "Are you loco? Seriously, for about $60 and two hours you could make that." And she goes, "No, *you* can make that." Vickie, it was the first time in my life that I realized everybody doesn't walk into a store and think they can make what they see. So the short answer is yes, I do come from a family of crafters; the long answer is that I never realized it until I was about 22.

VH: *What's your first craft-related memory?*

JG: It's making jewelry, funny enough. When I was really little, every summer I would go to Mexico to spend time with my family. My grandmother and my aunts and I would go to all the *mercados* and look at all the handcrafted jewelry and clothing. I remember being seduced by the beads, and all the amber and amethyst that the indigenous women in Mexico work with. Then, I would come home and try to make jewelry in the way that kids do; I would string beads and color macaroni and things like that. When I became a Girl Scout, I had to get my arts and crafts badge, and I was like, "Oh, I'm for sure going to make jewelry. That's what I'm going to do!"

We lived in Brazil, and my mother and I met this woman named Aldieza. She was basically covered head to toe in all this incredible jewelry, because the tribe she came from in Brazil still traded and bartered in beads and handmade crafts. She taught me the very basics, like how to close a loop and how to attach things, and I was in love. It gave me that same feeling that, I guess, some people feel when they rock, or play an instrument, or sing, or whatever—it was this flood of creativity. Of course, I got my Girl Scout badge with flying colors, but I also went on this spree of making jewelry.

I went to Catholic school where you had to wear uniforms and everybody looked the same, so by making cool jewelry, my friends and I could look different but kinda match. I remember feeling so cool. It sounds so dumb to say, but every time somebody said, "I like your necklace," and I'd tell them I made it, the feeling was so empowering. When I look back on it now, I know it's so important for kids to have something like that. I definitely suffered from high self-esteem as a kid. There was nothing I didn't think I could do, or make, or figure out, or deconstruct or reconstruct, and it's all because of making jewelry and the learning process.

VH: *It's so great that you had that perspective about it, and that feeling of empowerment was instilled in you so young. I remember similar situations, but we had things made for us basically because we couldn't afford to buy a lot of stuff. For me, it was often a source of embarrassment when I was little. It wasn't until I was older that I embraced it, and I'm hoping this book will help pre-teens and teens*

Jackie Guerra

171

find something, whether it's jewelry or knitting or sewing, that they can add to the basics they get at Target, or Old Navy, or wherever. You know, some kind of couture piece—because it does make you special, and not everybody can do it.

JG: I just don't want to come off as holier than thou, but I think it's one of the saddest things—I was telling my husband, Bill, this story. I do a lot of work with the Girl Scouts. Specifically, there's a branch of the Girl Scouts called *Soy Unica, Soy Latina*. They're trying to recruit more Latinas because it's culturally not the norm. I always speak to the girls and then do jewelry-making workshops with them. I give them kits and walk them through it, and it's fun! I mean, there should be nothing stressful about jewelry ever—not receiving it, not making it, not giving it, not thinking about it—it should be exciting, and fun, and an expression of yourself.

There was this one little girl in Colorado who looked at me and goes, "I don't want to do this." And I was like, "Why would you not want to do this?" She said, "'Cuz mine is going to be stupid and everyone is going to laugh. Everything I make is stupid." It was such an epiphany for me and an eye-opening moment, because when I was a kid, it never occurred to me that anything I made wasn't anything other than *wow*, because there is no right way or wrong way, it's just your way. Who cares if 20 people don't like it, if it matches my outfit in this moment, I'm rocking it, and I rock.

VH: *But that must have been something that your parents gave you.*

JG: For sure. Definitely. It's so funny—I was thinking about this interview when I was stuck in traffic, and I thought about my poor mother. When I tell you, Vickie, there is nothing I made that that woman didn't wear, it's 100 percent true. I remember one time, in particular—for some reason, I had this fascination with bobby pins when I was about 10 years old. I decided it would be super cool to paint bobby pins with different colored nail polish and then hook them together and glue them to make these crazy chains. How about, my mom actually wore them to church. She would rock the necklaces.

I think about her now and go, "Wow, God bless her," because never once did I give her something that ended up in a drawer somewhere. So for sure, my confidence has a lot to do with the fact that my parents *ooohed* and *aaahed* and encouraged me to be creative. But beyond crafting (and I think it's a residual effect of crafting) my parents encouraged us to be expressive.

VH: *I've seen a common theme, not necessarily by the professionals that I've been interviewing, but more by the hobbyists: they were told really young, mostly by teachers, that they sucked at being creative, and that whatever it was they made wasn't very good, or that they would never be an artist, or that kind of thing. It makes me so angry, because a lot of these people didn't pick up anything creative again for 20 to 30 years. That is just heartbreaking, and so irresponsible.*

> When I started hosting *Jewelry Making*, it was like the stories came floating to me, and I realized that, yeah, my mom was the Mexican Martha Stewart.

JG: Very irresponsible. Believe me, my husband is a teacher, and we talk about this issue all the time. It's amazing how much words affect people. I've always been (this will shock you) very chatty. It's not as if I just like talking for the sake of talking, I genuinely enjoy hearing people's stories, and I've always been really curious. The comments on every single report card from when I was a kid were always, "Jackie's favorite word in the English language is *why* or *how*." And that really is true.

As a kid, I was always interested in other people and would strike up conversations with strangers. I never learned the concept of "don't talk to strangers." So, I was always very expressive verbally, and I was in Toastmasters, on the debate team, and took speech classes, and all this stuff. You know that my biggest dream in life is to sing? If you said pause, rewind—you can start over, and you can have one talent that you'll be great at—I don't care if I never made five cents, just to be able to do it, I'd be a mariachi singer. One hundred percent.

VH: *That is one of my dreams, too.*

JG: Really?!

VH: *Not mariachi. I'd probably be a lounge singer or maybe follow in the footsteps of Joan Jett. One or the other.*

JG: So you totally get it.

VH: *Please! I've carried around a guitar that I don't know how to play for 15 years, just because I like it there.*

JG: I, of course, own a microphone for no apparent reason.

VH: *Of course. You never know when you're going to need it.*

JG: You never know. When I was in tenth grade, I auditioned for the school choir, and you had to sing the scales. Well, I didn't know. So I get in the room with the piano guy, and he starts hitting the piano and says, "Do this." So I do it. And then the teacher looked at me as said, "Okay now, let's do it for real." Do you know that as seriously confident as I am, as cool as I am with myself, to this day, I am so self-conscious about singing. It's crazy. So when I hear that story about people who don't do things for 20 years, that's how I am with singing. Words totally matter.

I also want to say, in terms of people being rejected, especially young girls, tweens, and teens; I think the things they often get criticized for are the things that make them unique. I think it's really important that when somebody says something critical about something you make or like, that you understand why. Why would they take time out of their life to say something nasty? It's similar to what we were talking about in terms of people being irresponsible with their comments. Do those nasty little creeps deserve airtime in your life? I don't think so.

VH: *As a child, you don't understand that though.*

JG: Right, I say this only because when I speak to Girl Scouts and high school kids, it's one of the main themes. If somebody else's life is so empty that the only thing they have to do is talk about you and what you're doing, then you've given them a purpose in life and can move on.

VH: *It probably speaks loudly to their own insecurities.*

JG: Absolutely.

VH: *Do you craft with anybody now? Do you still craft with your mom?*

JG: My mother passed away unfortunately, and when she died, it was the rebirth of me and my love of jewelry making, because I had done it with her, and it was such a connection for us. She died very suddenly and unexpectedly, and she was definitely my touchstone and my cheerleader. I went through a phase where I was completely depressed. I couldn't come up with a reason to get out of bed—it all shut down. My husband (fiancé, at the time) and my dad literally saved my life with jewelry making. They went downtown and bought a bunch of jewelry-making supplies for me, and came home one day. They were trying to get me to do something other than just lie around and be sad. It took me a few months, but the first time I sat down and started making jewelry after my mother died was the most cathartic experience.

It was bad enough to deal with the fact that she died, but it was also like this joyous part of me was gone, because she was the one who did a lot of this stuff with me. When Bill and my dad brought the jewelry-making supplies home, for the first time, I looked at jewelry making as more than a source of confidence,

> I use crafting, specifically jewelry making, to celebrate and commemorate special events. I think it's very important for me to give a part of myself to people that I care about.

empowerment, income, and a way to define myself and share things with other people. For the first time I became aware of its therapeutic effect, because literally, Vickie, as I sat at the table—I know this sounds dramatic, I'll just start crying—but every bead that I strung, or every time I wire-wrapped something, or connected one stone to another, it took me out of my sadness. It just made me laugh as I thought about the crazy stuff my mother and I had made over the years, and some of the crazy-ass jewelry that

I made for her, which was, let's just say generously, *interesting*. I just laughed and cried, and I understood her even more. I'm going to start crying….

VH: *It gave you a piece of her back.*

JG: Yes, for sure, and I think more importantly—and what I would want for other people—is that she gave me the ability to create. She gave me this gift of learning to make jewelry and feeling very confident in my abilities, which made me want to learn more and do more. It's also a connection that's going to live beyond either of us, and nobody can take that away.

VH: *You were a known TV and film actress before you began hosting the show. What made you decide to venture into the world of craft television?*

JG: You know what? It's one of those moments of: do what you love and the universe has a way of telling you what you should be doing. I was asked a few times to go on a show called *Celebrity Hobbies;* it was on HGTV. Every time I was scheduled to appear, something would happen. I was making a movie or the production schedule got changed. And they always wanted me to do something

crazy, like go to a batting cage or something weird like that.

I kept telling my agent, "Like, really? I just want to make jewelry. If they can work that out, I'll do the show." Finally, they decided to come to my house, and I would make jewelry. I remember thinking (and I'm sure this will unleash no shortage of criticism), but I remember thinking, "This is going to be the most boring segment *ever* on *Celebrity Hobbies*—to film somebody making a piece of jewelry! I mean, why don't you come over and watch me paint my walls!"

Ironically enough, the day I was supposed to do the segment, a friend of mine came in from out of town, and my other friend decided to play hooky from work and come over for the taping. So I had a house full of people, besides the crew that was there, and I tell you it was one of the most fun things I'd ever done. At that point, I had two movies in the theaters, I was on two television shows, I was doing stand-up comedy all over the country. I had a lot going on and no shortage of people going, "Oh, that's great," but there was something so unbelievably comfortable, and normal, and right about this. It was just a blast.

It never occurred to me to do a show. About a month later, I was in San Diego helping my cousin give her home a facelift. I was literally outside sanding a door, and I got a phone call from my agent saying the executive producer of *Celebrity Hobbies* wanted to talk. Barry Gribbon calls me, and we have a lovely conversation; about 20 minutes into it, he goes, "So, um, I showed your segment to the DIY network and told them we should do a whole show about this stuff. It's coming up to be a big deal—the world of crafting."

VH: *Hopefully he wasn't in charge of pitching, because that sucked!*

JG: Can I tell you, and you will appreciate this having worked for that network, that *was* the pitch! Literally, they showed them my segment and said, "She had a lot of fun, and the crew was really interested, what do you think?" And they were like, "Will she do it?" He called and asked, and I agreed! Vickie, it was the greatest gig I've ever had. We did three shows a day for two weeks—knocked out all those shows. I met the *most* amazing people and learned so much.

VH: *Would you do the show again?*

JG: Oh my God, in a heartbeat! Despite the nuttiness. Yeah, oh my God, yeah.

VH: *And the saaad pay.*

JG: Believe me, I made less on those shows than I was paying my agent in commission! Seriously, my hair and makeup glam posse made more than I did on that show, but I didn't care. It was so much fun.

VH: *On a new topic, your Hispanic heritage seems to play a big role in some of the non-craft-related projects you take on. Do culture and craft also mix for you?*

JG: Absolutely. You know what I think it is, Vickie; I think it's similar to a discussion I just recently had. I spoke at this lesbian, gay, bisexual, and transgender event the other night, and this girl came up to me afterwards who couldn't have been more than 18 or 19 years old. She's a young lesbian woman who is not able to talk to her family about it—she's a Chicana—it's a whole cultural thing. And she was asking me sort of the same thing: Do I feel my politics seep into everything that I do? And the answer is yes. I feel like your culture, your politics, who you are—it flavors everything you do.

I am incapable of making Porterhouse steak; mine's always going to be *carne asada*. I can learn, but I think whether you're talking about politics or crafting—your culture, what you value, and what you know are all embedded in who you are, and therefore, reflected in what you do. People who say, "This is Latino. This is not Latino."—that's bullshit. We are all textured and layered; we are all a tapestry of our life experiences and nobody is one thing. The fact that I'm Mexican-American obviously affects who I am, because it has dictated a lot of my experiences. Am I going to deny that my people tend to be a little overly accessorized? Hell no!

VH: *What role, if any, has crafting played in your own sense of community?*

JG: Huge. I use crafting, specifically jewelry making, to celebrate and commemorate special events: birthdays, weddings, graduations, an expression of love, friendship, and family bonds, all those things. I think it's very important for me to give a part of myself to people that I care about. To make them a piece of jewelry is the best way, the best expression of who I am. It shows how I feel about them and defines the moments in our lives. It's also something that can be passed on and takes on meaning and value way beyond its cost. To give yourself or somebody else a piece of jewelry that you've made, to me, is the ultimate expression of love. I know some people say it's food; I say making jewelry is just as instantly gratifying as chocolate, but without the calories.

> When I became an actress, every time I started a new role—your wardrobe and the look of the character are so important—I always forced myself to make something for my character as a way of understanding who this person was.

VH: *That's how I feel about giving handmade stuff in general, too.*

JG: One of the reasons I was so upset when I thought that I had missed the opportunity to be part of this book is because I think two things are really important in terms of building community. I get asked the question a lot, "If you could buy it, why would you make it?" That's so offensive. In terms of building community, there is such a history in crafting, especially for women.

My husband and I recently went to the National Museum of Anthropology in Mexico City—which, if you ever have a chance to go, not being ethnocentric—it's just unbelievable. The history of women and crafting is so beautiful and amazing. When we think of women in history, we think about how we didn't have the right to vote until the '20s, and about the suffragist movement, and how we were second class citizens and couldn't own property, but you know what? Two hundred, three hundred, even one thousand years ago, we were making jewelry. We were queens, and empresses, and heads of villages, and our identity was directly connected to the baskets that we wove, the clothing that we made, and the jewelry that we created.

VH: *The difference being that there was value in it then. That's what has changed over the decades; things considered women's work lost value.*

JG: For sure, crafting took a hit, because it was thought of as something your grandmother did. But I think our generation and younger women are not making tissue cozies. We're making really badass stuff that, not only do we want to rock, but other people do too. It's interesting and fun. I think that when it comes to building community, people need to step up and own their talent. It's such an important lesson for us, as woman, to learn for ourselves and to pass on to the girls and boys behind us.

People can say, "Eh, jewelry. You can live with it, you can live without it." And you know what? That's 100 percent true. I don't think jewelry is going to end the war, but I do know the world is a better place when women feel good about themselves. It's scientific data that when you feel like you look good, or you like the way you look in something, you actually do better. If you put on a piece of jewelry that you've made, you're gonna feel empowered, excited, and proud. When you put on a piece of jewelry made by somebody who loves you, you're gonna feel special, beautiful, and proud, and you're going to have a little pep in your step.

So maybe jewelry can't change the world, but the women who wear it can. The women who make it are definitely changing the world one bead at a time. I think it's really important to not allow crafting and being a designer, being an artist, to be dictated by the antiquated images we all reject. Young girls and women should see their own handiwork as not just a source of pride, but particularly, a source of income. Like I said, jewelry making definitely gave me confidence as a child, but as a teenager it was a source of income. If not for jewelry making, I would never have traveled around Europe.

When I was in college, I wanted to travel with my friends who were all going

> Maybe jewelry can't change the world, but the women who wear it can.

to Europe, but I didn't have the money or a job. But I did know how to make jewelry, so I went to a store, bought beads and made jewelry, and sold my stuff at flea markets. I made enough money to pay for my trip, and that was really empowering. When I became an actress, every time I started a new role—your wardrobe and the look of the character are so important—I always forced myself to make something for my character as a way of understanding who this person was. All of this is reinforced in acting, because part of telling a story as an actor involves the way you physically look, and that's true in life. We tell people a lot about who we are by the way we dress, and jewelry is a perfect way for women and men to express their individuality.

VH: *Let's change gears a bit. You've been very vocal about your battle with weight over the years, specifically documenting it in your book,* Under Construction. *I interviewed another craft TV host for this book who shared how crafting helped her with her own food demons, by giving her something else to feed her soul. I was wondering if your passion for jewelry making played a role in the success you've found in body empowerment?*

JG: Absolutely. Oh my God, not only did it play a role, and continues to play a role in helping me keep weight off, it played a huge role when I quit smoking. Because the number-one thing you have to do when you quit smoking is replace the hand-to-mouth thing, which is why a lot of people tend to gain weight. I just forced myself to make jewelry.

I don't say it was easy; I don't say there weren't two or three weeks where I was nothing but a walking/talking grouch, but it was making jewelry that gave me a place to go that wasn't smoking and wasn't eating. It's so Zen and so therapeutic and—I can't say this enough—there should never be anything stressful about creating. So, to be able to spread out my shiny stones, and shiny crystals, and put patterns together was a great way to replace the hand-to-mouth, whether it was food or cigarettes.

This is something that I talk to people about all the time. I do a lot of motivational and inspirational speaking, certainly for people who have gone through massive weight loss or are considering it. I always talk about the importance of doing something physical to replace the eating. It's shocking how much free time I have, since I quit smoking and quit eating so much. It's a great way to fill that void, and again, crafting is really empowering. The more you do it, the better you become.

For more information about Jackie and her projects, go to:
www.jackieguerra.com

The Crafter's Studio

In the great tradition of *Inside the Actor's Studio* and James Lipton:

What craft sound or smell do you love?
I love the sound of crystals and beads and stones touching and clanking together, and of course, the last *snap* of wire being cut as I finish a piece of jewelry.

What craft sound or smell do you hate?
I hate the sound of trays filled with 3mm Swarovski crystals hitting the floor! It's Dante's Inferno, for sure.

What career, other than craft-world domination, would you like to try?
I'd like to be a daytime talk show host or mayor of Los Angeles. But I could also be talked into food taster, fundraiser, clothing and accessories buyer, home decorator, chef, ambassador to Mexico, and/or belly dancer!

When you drop beads all over the floor or break a jewelry finding, what is your favorite exclamation?
Un-f*@*ing-be-lieve-a-ble.

Words to Craft by:

For several months, a small group of my friends and I collaborated on a charm necklace project. None of us had ever met in person, but we knew each other from various online groups. This project made us feel extremely close: it's remarkable how much kinship you feel when you've never met in person but share a common goal. We decided as a group to auction off our necklace to raise money for breast cancer research. Each participant made a charm in an ocean color palette. The charms were sent to me, and I assembled them into a complete necklace. The real fun started as we passed the necklace around the group! We each wore it to a special event—everything from art openings and reunions, to a concrete convention—and had ourselves photographed with it. We used a Yahoo group to keep in touch throughout the project and to share our stories as the necklace was passed around. The stories from our dates with the necklace and the reactions of those who saw it were quite gratifying. People stopped us on the street, crossed crowded rooms, and even chased us down to get a better look. Everyone sensed that there must be an amazing story behind it.

Name: Cyndi Lavin

Age: 48

Digs: New England

Daily Grind: artist and blogger (about arts and crafts, of course!)

Craft of Choice: mixed media jewelry

More Info: www.jewelryandbeading.com

Words to Craft by:

While I am now an avid loom knitter, if I look into the way-back machine, I remember starting with needlepoint, candle-wicking, and cross-stitch. The girls in my elementary school learned these skills while the boys did mechanical things. I would rather have been with the boys, but without that start, I might have missed a lifelong love of craft. One of the first projects I made was a little needlepoint caterpillar that came in a kit with a frame. I gave it to my aunt for her birthday, and she hung it up in her dining room where everyone who entered would see it.

Recently she sent it back to me with a catalog containing an ad for my loom knitting book. I knew why, and it brought tears to my eyes. She wanted me to have it because she expects that soon she won't be around to keep it safe. She wanted me to know how proud she was of me then, and still is. It warms my heart to know my aunt thought so much of my first little crafty attempt that she treasured it all that time. It now hangs in my own house, and every time I see it, I think of her.

Name: Denise Layman

Age: 38

Digs: Ohio

Daily Grind: mom and knitter

Fave Crafts: loom knitting!

More Info: www.knitchat.com

chapter nineteen

Jessica Marshall Forbes

In 2006, Jessica and her husband, Casey, launched a website meant to be a one-stop organizational tool for knitters and crocheters around the world. Prompted by Jessica's frustrations with the lack of resources available on the Web, and created from Casey's computer wizardry skills, Ravelry (www.ravelry.com) filled the stitcher's bill as a pattern archive and personal database. Little did they know that a year later, their little project would become a *huge* social networking site, essentially the Facebook of the knitting world! I spoke with Jessica from their Boston home about what it took to make Ravelry the powerhouse it is today, and how it will continue to evolve in the future.

VH

VH: *What's your first craft-related memory?*

JMF: I always kind of liked being creative. When I was little, I mostly just fooled around; my grandmother taught me how to knit when I was young, like a lot of grandmothers do. But you know, it was the '80s, and I have this awful photo of myself with crazy bangs learning to knit with my grandmother. I was wearing some sort of awful thing with suspenders. I made a blob of some sort, and I threw it away and was on to something else. I actually did cross-stitch for quite a while when I was younger. I did a few panels, but when you're a kid, you don't stay on things for too long. But yes, my first craft memory would be learning to knit with my grandmother.

VH: *Was anyone else in your family crafty?*

JMF: That grandmother actually was a big quilter, so I'm surprised she's the one who taught me to knit. I never really saw her knit, other than that one time. She made quilts for everyone in the family. We all have pictures holding our quilts up, and she had a little photo album that she would carry around to show off her grandchildren with their quilts.

VH: *Did you ever ask her why she taught you to knit and not to quilt?*

JMF: I'll have to ask my mother, but maybe I saw knitting somewhere and my grandmother said she knew how to do it. Ironically, my other grandmother was a big knitter and would send us mittens every winter with the strings attached. I would always get the bright pink ones, acrylic of course.

VH: *Have you made yourself a grown-up version?*

JMF: I actually have, and I put the strings on them and everything. It was great when I was traveling by subway, because you're always pulling your mittens on and off during Boston winters. Everyone picked on me because I had kids' string going through them—but I didn't lose my mittens!

VH: *Who, if anyone, do you credit for opening the crafty doors for you?*

JMF: I think it was my husband, which is really funny, because I wouldn't call him a crafter. He's the one who first came up with the idea for Ravelry, because he had the technical skills behind the scenes of what we wanted to do. It was his idea to bring everyone together in one place, and to have database information, and all that stuff. So I think he inspired me with that idea of a bigger picture. I had always been dissatisfied with trying to find information on the Web, and not being able to find something that I had seen two days ago. My husband has a different sort of brain; he is very creative, but I wouldn't call him crafty. He has that analytical/computer science brain. He said, "We can do this together," and I think if it wasn't for him having that idea, we wouldn't have made the transition. We always wanted to work together on something, but we never knew what it would be.

VH: *Let me skip to talking about Ravelry, since you brought it up. One of the focuses of this book is community. You've become a ringleader of the fiber community by founding your social networking site. Tell me more about how it got started and what your vision is for the future of it.*

JMF: We started talking about Ravelry back in 2005, and it basically came out of being on the Web, having friends all over the world, blogging about craft, and talking to people. We knew there was a super active and incredibly inspiring community out there, but it was very difficult, at that point, to find information; it wasn't really organized at all. Someone knitted a sweater and put nice pictures of it on their blog that other people would see. They'd want to knit it, so they'd buy the same yarn and try to make the sweater. But there wasn't really a way to search for that information.

> We literally could not have done Ravelry without everyone coming together and helping us build it. We had the structure, but it didn't make any difference until it was filled.

Another issue is that I might finish up a project and want to make a sweater that I saw online months ago, but maybe I didn't bookmark it, and now I can't find it. After hearing me swear at the computer a few times, Casey said. "That's something we can do. We can build a site so people can share their photos and bring everything together in a searchable way."

We posted the idea on my Frecklegirl blog in 2005 and talked about what kinds of things you could search for, and we added a little drawing. We asked people what they thought, and the response was really great. I didn't have a huge blog following, either. I wasn't like January One or Yarn Harlot, or anything like that, but my few thousand blog readers thought it was a good idea.

I was working full-time as a study abroad advisor then, and Casey had a very busy job also, doing computer things. We shelved the idea; it was a hard, busy time for us, and we thought we'd do it some other day. Two years later, Casey had a different job that was not really using his skills, and he was pretty bored. I had since quit my job and was going to school part-time, trying to figure out what I wanted to do for grad school. We were in a different space, and we had a couple of friends who kept bugging us every six months about our blog idea: "Hey, are you guys ever going to do that really good idea—come on, do it!"

Then we got an e-mail from Kelly Sue DeConnick, who had been blogging on the Web for a long time; we call her our muse. She said, "Listen, this is what you are doing. Here's an idea for the main boards on Ravelry: do yarn, for the love of Ravelry, and needlework on the net." She got us thinking about it again. In the beginning of January, when we were excited for the new year and had a lot of energy, Casey sat down and started plugging away. We started working together and building what it would be.

VH: *Did you have any funding for it, or was this just you guys in your living room?*

JMF: Basically, it was the latter. When you start a website, luckily, you don't need a huge amount of money. People mostly pay for the technical side of things, and Casey had all that. At the very beginning, our main investment was time—and it was a lot of time. Casey was working full-time and would be up until three or four o'clock in the morning; he'd get up again at seven-thirty to go to work. So until he quit his job in June, it was pretty crazy.

Being in school still, I had more time to work on things, so I'd do it while he was at work, and then he would come home and play around with it until the wee hours. At some point, I looked at him and said, "Honey, I love you, and I'm your wife first. We have to decide if we're going to do this or not. If we are, you have to quit your job, because I can't see you walking around like a zombie." He would fall asleep on the bus.

VH: *What allowed him to be able to quit his job, though?*

JMF: We had enough savings to last until September, and we thought, what is the worst thing that can happen—we'll give it a shot, and Casey can get another

> My husband has a different sort of brain. He has that analytical/ computer science brain. He said, "We can do this together," and I think if it wasn't for him having that idea, we wouldn't have made the transition.

job in September if he has to. It was a different kind of economy.

VH: *That is still a big leap of faith.*

JMF: Yes, but Casey had had six jobs since 2000, when he graduated from college. He gets one fixed up, and is bored with it in six months. His hobby is getting jobs.

VH: *Is he bored with Ravely yet?*

JMF: No, he's not. He's pretty busy, and the most important thing for him is to be challenged, and he certainly is challenged with Ravelry.

VH: *Absolutely! Just from poking around on it, it seems like there are always new balls coming at you; there are always new requests and things that need to be done—and they need to be done faster, bigger, now.*

JMF: Casey fosters that kind of environment; if the site doesn't change every few days, he gets all twitchy and says, "It's stagnant, it's stagnant." I'm like, "Casey it's been a week, it's okay."

VH: *What's been the biggest challenge in this huge undertaking of running a social networking site?*

JMF: In the beginning, it wasn't going to be a social networking site; we hadn't thought of it that way. We try to think of it as three different things now: it's an organizational tool; it's also a database where people research projects and yarns; and the social networking stuff was thrown in at the end. After we thought we had everything in place, people looked to us and said, "I have questions I need to ask someone, and I want to meet other people, and you guys have to add a forum."

We dragged our heels for a while on the forum stuff because we hadn't used an online forum much. It was like opening a can of worms, because it would take a lot more time to moderate, and we hadn't figured out how we would oversee something like that while still maintaining the environment we wanted. We wanted it to be welcoming and feel cozy, but as it got bigger, we realized we weren't going to be able to maintain a cozy atmosphere on a site with 100,000 people. The groups and forums came out of that, and it's good because people can

still talk to each other in a cozy little space. I think, in terms of challenges, there's just always something different going on—and that's a good thing, as well.

VH: *What's the most exciting thing that's happened to you since Ravelry's inception?*

JMF: It's the reception from people. The community has been so unbelievably supportive of what we are doing. We literally could not have done Ravelry without everyone coming together and helping us build it. In the beginning, we had this database with nothing in it. We had the structure, but it didn't make any difference until it was filled.

VH: *One thing I wanted to bring up is friendship; I'm sure you've seen tons of that on Ravelry, and that it has happened to you—it's happened to me often over the years. I've become friends with people I probably would have never spoken to in other circumstances. We may have nothing else in common on the surface, except for knitting, crocheting, or a particular craft; but thanks to the Web, we can reach out. It opens up this dialogue where you figure out that we're all human beings. It ties us together and gives perspective on how much we need community right now—not to get all hippie-philosophical on you. I think Ravelry has done a huge service to that philosophy.*

JMF: We hoped that would happen, but you can't really build that, technically. It happens organically, but it's nice to provide people space to talk and let them have the freedom to make groups as they wish. There are groups for pretty much anything you can imagine online. It's really amazing to see kids counseling each other through divorce, or to see people who have relatives with breast cancer talk to each other about treatment methods and how they are dealing with the illness.

Whenever I start to feel a little overwhelmed by day-to-day tasks, I end up looking at these cool groups or cool conversations that are happening. That's what keeps our work going, and we hear that stuff when we go to events. People say they connected with someone they lost touch with back in grade school, and now they see each other every week. Or they've moved to a new location where they don't know anyone, and now they have a wonderful knitting group they go to every week, where they've made real friends. It's pretty awesome. Right now, we just don't have those kinds of communities locally, based on churches or community centers.

VH: *There aren't quilting bees or knitting circles to the same extent that there used to be. And I think that since we've had a resurgence in knitting and crocheting, people are longing for that, especially professional women who are used to being in a competitive environment with other women. It's so nice to have a place where all that stuff is set aside, whether it's virtual or physical.*

One of the main questions I've heard over the years is, "How can people best promote themselves," whether they want to have a small part-time business, or sell a couple of patterns here and there, or if they want to become the next Debbie Bliss. Would you mind sharing a bit about how people can use Ravelry to promote themselves?

JMF: Sure. There are actually a lot of ways. The simplest way is by advertising on our site (not to be self-promotional, but it's extremely inexpensive). You can get ads on Ravelry for five dollars a month. The people on Ravelry really click; they are very active, so even getting your name recognized is great. If people see you on Ravelry, you can definitely get the word out about what you are doing. That's the simplest way.

The other thing you can do is find people that are interested in what you're doing—we have groups for so many things. If you are making stitch markers or bags, there are groups for people who like tools, and groups for people who are crazy about bags. If you go into a group and say you have an idea for a business and would like to get people to start using your stuff, they'll give you feedback. One thing we have noticed with Ravelers is that they are very involved, and they will give you their opinion whether or not you want it. In the meantime, there are a lot of people on the site, and if you want to get something started, there's a captive audience.

VH: *What about the shop?*

JMF: Oh, yes. If you are designing patterns, we do provide a pattern delivery system. Instead of doing something on your own site, where you pay an outside service to deliver the document to people, you can do it through Ravelry. Subscribers will actually get the pattern within their pattern library. I don't know about you, but I have a computer full of PDFs, and when I'm trying to find something, I can't find it. You can always do it through Ravelry, and your customers will be able to save it in their notebooks; it will be available to them whenever.

> In the beginning, it wasn't going to be a social networking site; we hadn't thought of it that way. The social networking stuff was thrown in at the end.

VH: *Do you do any crafts other than knitting, or is that really your focus?*

JMF: Well, I have learned to crochet. I'm not super great at it, but I know how to do it. I actually just signed up for a potholder swap, so that'll get me going.

VH: *Do you spin also?*

JMF: Yes. I really like doing that. It's a different process—very calming, and if I want to get in the meditative zone, it's a great craft. Other than that, I have started sewing some, but I'm not really great at that either. I got a new machine and a new weekend sewing book, and there are a few projects I want to make. It's different; it's more immediate than knitting, which can take months.

VH: *What are your favorite types of projects to work on? Are you a lace gal, or do you prefer quick, fast, and easy?*

JMF: I like everything, really. It's very much about the combination between how something feels and the colors. Right now I'm working on a yoke sweater made out of silky wool that is this springy, bright turquoise color. You know, up here in Boston, we barely touch spring; there is no green here. I think the projects I do depend on the time of year, but what really inspires me is colors and textures.

For more information about Jessica and Ravelry, go to:
www.ravelry.com

The Crafter's Studio

In the great tradition of *Inside the Actor's Studio* and James Lipton:

What craft sound or smell do you love?
I like the sound of my metal knitting needles clanking against each other.

What craft sound or smell do you hate?
I don't like wet alpaca; it smells so bad.

What career, other than networking-world domination, would you like to try?
Knitwear designer.

When you drop a stitch or make one sleeve longer than the other, what is your favorite exclamation?
F@ck!

Words to Craft by:

My best friend Betsy taught me to knit at a swim meet in Fort Lauderdale. It was a perfect storm of summer sun, loosely spun wool, and hours of downtime on the pool deck. Something clicked (and not just my bamboo needles). Knitting just made sense to me. Over the years, it's provided hours of pleasure, a chance to meet new people around the world, and tangible creations to hold in my hands, something that my day-to-day job of pixels and programming doesn't afford me.

However, it was through the digital ether of the Internet that I reconnected with an old acquaintance who had also picked up knitting. For male knitters, a minority in the crafting universe, keyboards and broadband connections are the sole means for hanging out together. Luckily, WonderMike lives nearby, and together we participate in our local scene as well as the growing online community of photos, blogs, and the occasional real world event. As members of the not-so-fairer sex, we're trying to do more than knit socks. We're two voices in the wilderness, offering a guy's perspective with Y KNIT, a knitting podcast. We do our best to encourage more men to knit and add a dash of male spice to the vibrant stew of the United States of knitting.

Name: Stephen "hizKNITS" Houghton

Age: 35

Digs: San Francisco, CA

Daily Grind: online marketing guru for delicious organic goodies

Fave Crafts: knitting

More Info: www.hizknits.com and www.yknit.com

Words to Craft by:

I didn't learn to drive until I was 30. I was too afraid to learn, but once I did, I realized I had always been terrified to try new things, so I dove headfirst into new experiences. I tried my hand at being single. I learned to swing dance and roller skate. I then spent four years skating as Kitty Kitty Bang Bang on the Hotrod Honeys as a member of the Texas Rollergirls. Based in Austin, it was the first flat-track roller derby league in the U.S., founded in 2003.

After retiring, I was left with a lot of free time on my hands. I took a knitting class and took to it like fish to water. I've been knitting for less than two years but always approach new projects with fearlessness. I'm addicted to knitting—socks, sweaters, gloves, lace, anything! And I have an enviable yarn stash. I formed a multi-craft group called Arts & Drafts that meets weekly at a local coffee bar on Thursday nights. We pride ourselves on welcoming new crafters and have taught many an unsuspecting coffee shop patron to knit. These days I go by Knitty Knitty Bang Bang—it burns fewer calories and causes fewer bruises—but it is just as thrilling and fulfilling!

Name: Rachel Kieserman, **a.k.a.** Knitty Knitty Bang Bang

Age: 37

Digs: Austin, TX

Fave Crafts: knitting

More Info: kkbb.livejournal.com

chapter twenty

Diana Rupp

Diana and I have known each other since the sweltering hot summer of 2005, when the Austin Craft Mafia had a booth next to hers at the Renegade Craft Fair in Brooklyn. I was immediately drawn to her gorgeously hand-dyed yarn and edgy haircut! Diana has such a cool vibe about her, one that makes you want to sit at her feet and learn from her. Appropriately, she's a natural teacher living the dream by running her own craft school, the Make Workshop, in New York City. I phoned her there to chat about her love of knitting, her past in the fashion industry, and her future as a clog-making hopeful.

VH

VH: *What's your first craft-related memory?*

DR: I remember embroidering with my great-grandmother when I was probably about four or five years old.

VH: *Was anybody else in your family crafty?*

DR: My mom was the super, over-the-top, pre-Martha crafter. She made everything from a full-length veil and dress for my Barbie, to diorama sugar eggs at Christmas. She did a lot of cake decorating and made me the most amazing birthday cakes. She made us matching outfits, and she canned things—it just went on and on.

VH: *Do you consider your mom as the one who opened the crafty doors for you?*

DR: I think so. She taught me that you can make anything and do it really well. Anything that you put your hand to, as long as you do it with love and energy, can be made beautiful and meaningful.

VH: *Did you always want to be an artist?*

DR: No, I really thought I was going to be an academic. It's interesting to me that I always loved making things; I always loved reading and writing; and I loved teaching. I taught English for a while before realizing that I could do both: I could teach people to make things. It was sort of this synergy that came together.

VH: *Was it intimidating having a mom who was so talented and driven with her passion, or did it encourage you?*

DR: It totally encouraged me! She would take me to the fabric store and let me pick out a pattern and some fabric, coaching me through. She must've shown me how to thread her sewing machine 800 times, over, and over, and over! She was always patient and supportive. I wouldn't say she was driven as much as a little obsessive. I think that people's strengths are often also their weaknesses. That OCD-type of person can really get into the repetitive and meditative aspects of making things.

VH: *Do you still craft with her?*

DR: Yes, definitely. She had forgotten how to crochet, so we went out and got yarn and a hook and got right back into it. She's also a fine arts photographer and loves to collaborate with me on things. It's pretty cool.

VH: *Do you collaborate on projects often?*

DR: As often as we can. She lives in California, and I live in New York, so it's hard.

VH: *I want to talk a little bit about how careers in the craft world are viewed by society today. Although we've come leaps and bounds over the past decade, society still doesn't place much value on handicrafts, especially as related to a career.*

DR: You know, I have a lot of things I've been thinking about regarding this topic lately—like with the whole rise of Etsy. I feel like so many people out there are basically starting their own sweatshops. I think it's a real trap to think you can support yourself making something, when the market won't give you the value of your item.

I started out doing hand-knitted things. I love, love, love to knit, and I loved selling the stuff that I made. In terms of actually being profitable, though, it's not realistic. That sounds so negative, but I think there are really smart ways that you can position yourself so that you are able to have a career in this world.

VH: *If you're going to hand-knit and not hire machine knitters, you have to make ridiculously high-end pieces that you can sell at wholesale for $200 or more, that would then be sold at retail for $400. Not many people can pull that off.*

> I was teaching all of my friends and co-workers to knit. I got in big trouble at my company— my boss said I couldn't teach one more person to knit.

DR: It's difficult. I always encourage people to go to the small business administration in their area and come up with a small business plan.

VH: *Is that what you did before you started Make Workshop?*

DR: Yes, I did. Honestly, though, my business is not profitable. I shouldn't say that because I'm actually really successful.

VH: *Let's come back to that. First, though, tell me about how you took your passion for being creative and turned it into a livelihood.*

DR: First, I was a fashion editor. I was producing things for photo shoots when I realized I could make customized items instead of shopping for them. Then, I started doing a line of hand-knits and planned on launching a product line around them. I took classes through the small business administration and really started thinking of different businesses I could start. I was also teaching all of my friends and co-workers to knit. I got in big trouble at my company—my boss said I couldn't teach one more person to knit.

VH: *Because it was affecting productivity?*

DR: I was a senior writer, so I had some flexibility, but I was holding knitting sessions at my desk and told people to tell me if my boss was behind me. One time he was, and he wasn't thrilled. But I realized I had a passion for teaching people, and that it was a better use of my time and talent to teach people to make things for themselves and for people they love. I really like teaching people who don't have creative careers or who need something to help with stress. You know, they just want to do something fun and creative.

VH: *So, you were working and teaching on the side. When was the transitional moment when you quit your proverbial day job and started your own business?*

DR: It was so exciting, and I always encourage people to do this. My best friend got laid off from his job, and he wanted to move to New York. I told him to take me with him!

VH: *Really? That's ballsy!*

DR: Yes. I went to New York—I had no where to live, didn't have a job, didn't really even have money. I just gave myself permission to not get a job. That was in July 2001.

VH: *How do you do that without giving yourself permission to not also starve?*

DR: Well, my friend fed me. I had *some* money, and he helped me out. Within two months I was teaching knitting and sewing, and by February, I'd opened Make Workshop. I think starting from scratch is really helpful. I was lucky I was able to do it at that point in my life. I didn't have a husband, or kids, or any responsibilities. I just went for it.

> My career is a total labor of love, but I'm not lying when I say I go home at night and think, "Oh my God, I can't believe I get to do this for work. I had the best day!" I'm so thankful.

VH: *I would love to talk about how the craft community is perpetuated at Make Workshop, since it seems to be such a hub.*

DR: I think it's a very social place for a lot of people who come to meet other like-minded people, and to talk and be inspired by the things other people make. Again, I don't think they're necessarily the super-crafty types of people that one might associate with the new crafting movement—they probably wouldn't even identify themselves as crafters or as crafty—which I actually think is really good.

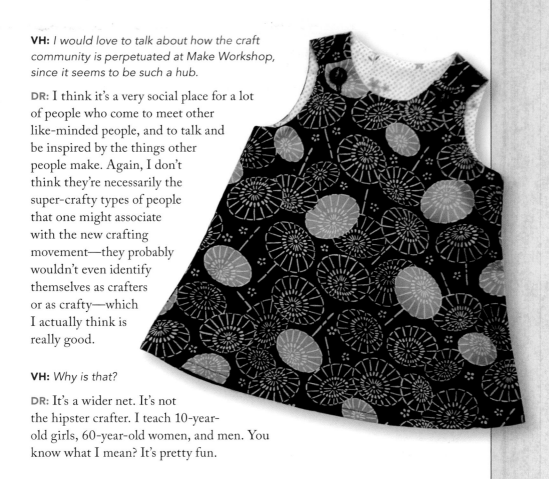

VH: *Why is that?*

DR: It's a wider net. It's not the hipster crafter. I teach 10-year-old girls, 60-year-old women, and men. You know what I mean? It's pretty fun.

VH: *I think that's sort of the key thing about community. I was just talking to Kathy Cano-Murillo (see page 68) about how, years ago, we were so adamant about saying indie crafter, punk rock crafts, and announcing that we're breaking the mold of grandmother crafters, etc. Similar to how feminism worked, we definitely haven't won the battle; instead, we're kind of at a place where we realize that one of the biggest gifts craft gives is that it fills the gap between different generations, different social statures, and different life spaces. On Knitty Gritty, I loved seeing the punk rock girl sitting on the couch with her grandmother as they knitted together.*

DR: That's why I always shy away from the hipster label. My publisher has pushed that on me at times, and I'm like, "I'm not cool!"

VH: *Let's go back and talk a bit about profit versus success. I was having a conversation about a year ago with friends of mine who've written a business book for women. They were discussing success and profitability, and I talked about how, in my business, it jumps from year to year. Some years I do well, and some years I do terribly. They said, "Well, then you need to re-examine your model for success." I told them that I consider myself successful because I get to stay home, pick up my kids from school, do what I love, and don't have to work a day job. That's another thing that might be different in our industry than in others—what we base our success level on.*

DR: I think that's totally true. My career is a total labor of love, but I'm not lying when I say I go home at night and think, "Oh my God, I can't believe I get to do this for work. I had the best day!" I'm so thankful. That's the dichotomy. I'd never want to encourage someone to do something like I'm doing without thinking about it long and hard first.

VH: *How are you able to continue making a living in a business that isn't technically profitable? Do you continue to do the teaching, yourself?*

DR: Yes. I do most of the teaching myself. Also, my book is doing incredibly well. My rent doubled this year, so it's difficult being an independent businessperson in New York without going retail.

VH: *Is that something you'd ever consider—having a little boutique?*

DR: Maybe. I've flirted with it a few different times, but I'm sort of anti-consumerist. I'd love to develop product I believed in and felt that people could really enjoy, but we'll see.

VH: *Has the economy affected class enrollment?*

DR: I've noticed that with a lot of the less expensive group classes, enrollment's down a bit, but the private and specialty classes like shoemaking are doing really well.

VH: *You have a shoemaking class? I love that so much! I think my life would be perfect if I knew how to make shoes.*

DR: Well, they're easy to make! We had a reporter from *Elle* magazine take a class, and she knocked off a pair of Manolos. It can totally be done!

VH: *That's enough to get me on a plane!*

You mentioned earlier that you started out as a fashion editor, which comparatively, could be a wee bit more glamorous than working in the craft world. What caused you to change your path, other than the love of teaching you spoke of before? There's more prestige involved in being part of the fashion industry.

DR: When I did fashion, I was in San Francisco working with local designers. I used real people as models, so it was more down-to-earth than the high-end fashion world. I produced a runway show once; I remember these designers were fighting, and I said, "Um, hello, we're playing Barbies. Calm down." I find fashion to be fun, but I don't take it very seriously.

VH: *So it wasn't a difficult transition for you at all, then?*

DR: No.

VH: *What's your favorite thing about crafting?*

DR: Just being really present for however long I'm focused on creating something. I also love the process of starting out—you make something and maybe you're not so happy, but you work through it. You might even make *mistakes*, but that's what makes the design totally original. I also, in terms of my teaching life, love seeing what people can do. I host parties where I give everyone the same supplies, but when each person comes up with something unique and incredible, it's inspiring.

VH: *You've written a sewing book, but you also dye yarn and knit, among many other things. Is there one craft that speaks to you more creatively than the others?*

DR: I have this fantasy of making clogs, and I haven't been able to achieve that yet. My boyfriend's actually an industrial designer, and he's helping me figure out how I can produce one-of-a-kind clogs. That's my Holy Grail right now. I'd like nothing more than to pack my bags, go to the Netherlands, and apprentice with a clog maker. That would be amazing!

VH: *I've found that if people express themselves creatively in one way, they more than likely are interested in multiple forms of creativity. I believe that all things creative are linked together—do you find that to be true? Are there non-handicraft, creative aspects to your life?*

DR: I enjoy making anything; it could be making a meal. It doesn't matter what I'm making, craft or otherwise; I just love the act of producing something.

VH: *Do people from all over the country come to Make Workshop?*

DR: Actually, from all over the world. I've had a lot of Australians lately—they're awesome. A lot of teachers come from there and from Canada. Then, I get a lot of travelers and tourists coming through New York who decide to take a class.

VH: *I'm always curious to know if craft is viewed differently by people around the world or around the country. For instance, is it seen differently by people in the Midwest than it is by people on the coasts? Is it defined differently in Australia than it is in the United Kingdom?*

DR: I think so. I was dating a guy who lived in Iowa. In his tiny town of 10,000 people, there were multiple fabric stores and a sewing machine dealership. From my perspective doing a book tour, in certain areas, craft is still something that's handed down to you from your family. I think that's much more true in the Midwest than it is here. In many countries kids learn how to knit as part of the school curriculum. In Europe, that practice is a little more present. I also think there are certain periods in people's lives when they craft more, like for weddings or when someone's having a baby.

VH: *Also in grief. This was a huge topic after 9/11. Not to sound insensitive, but it was a good time for the knitting industry, because people really worked out their sadness by working with their hands.*

> Everyone's an artist and craft is art. Being a craftsperson is honorable, and we should all be proud of it!

DR: That's how it got started in New York. That fall, I think people were just desperate for a feeling of comfort.

VH: *And to produce something positive out in the world, even if it was as small as a pair of booties. It was a way to be active.*

As a feminist woman in a traditionally female community, do you feel any responsibility to use your voice as a forum for progression?

DR: I am a feminist. I really like the idea that everyone has talent, and that we can support one another, because there is a certain amount of competitiveness in the craft world. I try to keep my head down in terms of getting into that dynamic. I think it's really important to value what used to be considered the domestic arts. I taught a series of classes at the Museum of Art and Design, and they had changed their name from the Museum of Craft—they spent millions of dollars to do so. I don't think there's anything wrong with crafting. Everyone's an artist and craft is art. Being a craftsperson is honorable, and we should all be proud of it!

VH: *Is there anything else you'd like to say about what crafting means to you or has given you?*

DR: Crafts have given me the opportunity to meet tons of amazing people. I never get tired of it!

For more information about Diana and her projects, go to: www.makeworkshop.com

The Crafter's Studio

In the great tradition of *Inside the Actor's Studio* and James Lipton:

What craft sound or smell do you love?
The whirl of the sewing machine.

What craft sound or smell do you hate?
Petronius. It's a shoe-making glue. It's nasty.

What career, other than what you do now, would you like to try?
I'd love to be a public school art teacher.

When you burn yourself with a glue gun or drop stitches in your knitting, what is your favorite exclamation?
I might drop the F-bomb if students aren't present.

Words to Craft by:

In third grade, I was an avid finger knitter—I made many headbands and bracelets. Then one day, I decided to try something more challenging. Using mint green and black yarn, I finger knitted two chains to create a yarmulke for my dad. With the mint green yarn, I made one long chain, coiled it around, and sewed it together to create a circle (the main part of the yarmulke). Then using the black yarn, I finger knitted another chain and sewed it around as decorative edging. Despite the colors (and the not-so-perfect sewing), my dad actually wore this to temple for the high holidays! I believe he only wore it out once but kept it in his tallis bag from that point forward.

For reasons unknown to me now, I eventually stopped finger knitting and didn't learn how to knit on needles until after college. That's also when I learned how to crochet, and I haven't stopped since! I lost my dad in 2006 and the yarmulke is now in my possession. In addition to being one of my earliest creations, it serves as a source of support and inspiration for all my current crafting.

Name: Beth Shorr

Age: 29

Digs: New York, NY

Daily Grind: talent coordinator at *The Daily Show with Jon Stewart*

Fave Crafts: knitting and crocheting

More Info: bshorr.etsy.com

Words to Craft by:

The first needle art that I started was knitting. I have been sick for about three years now, so I was homebound for my last year of high school. I turned the television on to *Knitty Gritty* one day. The show got me addicted, and I later got into crocheting. The medical condition that I suffer from is POTS or Postural Orthostatic Tachycardia Syndrome. A lot of girls and some guys I know with this and other dysautonomia conditions knit and crochet because it's the only thing that keeps us sane. It's a very relaxing art, and we can make things for other people we know from far away.

Name: Alicia Reardon

Age: 19, going on 20

Digs: Danville, KY

Daily Grind: college student

Fave Crafts: knitting, crocheting, painting, sketching, and photography

We have an amazing organization known as DYNA. It's a non-profit organization that allows youth to hang out with other kids with the same problem. It's not limited to the United States. DYNA reaches youth across the world, from Chile and Argentina, to New Zealand! Without this organization, I wouldn't be able to connect with people who share the same crafting interests as me and still understand what I'm going through.

chapter twenty-one

Travis Nichols

I first met Travis when he designed fellow Austin Craft Mafia member Susan Koehane's Sasquatch wedding reception invites. Yes, you read me right. My friends are quirky like that. Since then, I've had the pleasure of getting to know him (and his work) through shared craft fair booths, and we've crossed paths at many Austin events. It's been wonderful watching his career grow and stem off into a diverse resumé of accomplishments that any creative soul would be proud of: published cartoonist, professional crafter, musician, and novelist. After about a year had passed since I'd seen Travis, I caught up with him via phone from his home in San Francisco, California.

VH

VH: *What's your first craft-related memory?*

TN: In second grade, I used to make pop-up books in school with a couple of other kids, just for fun. I learned how to make springs out of paper by folding pieces over on themselves. Then, I would pop out stuff like monsters, swords, or things like that.

VH: *Is there a moment from your childhood connected to craft that really stands out for you?*

TN: Indirectly, my mom and dad always encouraged us to be creative and make things.

VH: *Were they artists themselves?*

TN: Yes. My mom's now a full-time photographer, after teaching for 30 years. My dad was primarily a musician. My uncle was an artist. So art is always something I've been around, and people have encouraged me to do it.

VH: *Do you have a memory as a professional artist that will always stick with you?*

TN: When I had my first solo art show, I realized that aside from just making crafts and art, I really like putting shows together and packaging the things I do into presentation form.

VH: *Was that the first time you also presented craft pieces, versus just showing your paintings?*

TN: Before that, I'd been making comic books and other craft things, more so than painting. I got back into painting, though, and also incorporated handmade greeting cards and little door hangers. Since then, I always incorporate my craft stuff along with my art. If you can't buy a painting, then there'll be cheaper items you can pick up—something for everybody.

VH: *Did you go to art school or are you self-taught?*

TN: I did not go to art school—I kind of wish I did, though. I went to Texas Tech University, and my major was studies in fine arts and technology: graphic design, photography, music technology, and science fiction as literature. I also went to New York for an internship, where I worked for a magazine and was going to art galleries everyday. When I came back to Lubbock, Texas, I opened an art gallery with a friend. I don't know if I could have done that if I'd gone to an art school, especially in a bigger city.

VH: *Why not, because the gallery scene would've been over-saturated?*

TN: That, and it would've been too expensive. I don't ever want to regret where I went to school, because I got involved with the music scene in Lubbock, and that experience got me where I am today. I'm okay with that.

VH: *You're not doing too shabby these days, I must say!*

TN: I think I'm doing okay.

VH: *For artists and crafters, thinking we're "okay" is good. Huge, even.*

TN: For me, I never let myself get excited about anything for too long, because I don't want that to be the peak.

VH: *And you wait for the other shoe to drop.*

TN: I'm always like, "Okay, that's good, but now what's next?" My mom always says, "Aren't you so excited?" I say, "Yes, it's okay, but now what?"

VH: *I do the exact same thing. I'm afraid it'll all go away if I stop to celebrate.*

TN: The first time I got a comic published in *Nickelodeon Magazine* was really exciting, but it just made me wonder where I go from there. It was a big deal, but I didn't want it to be the biggest thing I ever did.

VH: *Do you credit anyone in particular for opening the professional crafty doors for you?*

TN: When I worked for Jennifer Perkins (see page 57), I learned a lot about the business side. I owe a lot of my knowledge to her. I wouldn't have met her, though, if I hadn't started making crafts, moved to Austin, and got stuff in Parts & Labour, a local store that solely sells handmade items. Working for her taught me a whole lot about how to run a business and what you can do with it.

VH: *What about personally? Who really got you started in a creative way? Was it your parents, or was there someone else who influenced you growing up?*

TN: Well, there are my heroes, if that's what you mean. Jim Henson, Paul Reubens, and Shel Silverstein are a few of my biggest heroes.

VH: *Those are good! What about in your family, though? I've interviewed other crafters who've credited a grandmother, aunt, etc., for sitting down and crafting with them. Was that the case with you, or did you come into it on your own?*

TN: I think a little bit came from my mom. As recently as a few years ago during the holidays, we made soap, candles, or paper—which is probably my favorite thing to do. It's so much fun! I collect scraps and then, at some point, turn them into new paper.

VH: *Tell me how you took the leap with crafting—from something you just loved to do, to something that you could actually make a living out of.*

TN: As an aside, before saying anything personal, I think we've definitely moved away from the how things were done for thousands of years. Things used to be made by hand because that's how they had to be made. Now with factories and industry, it's out of our minds to think of making clothing, books, or paper ourselves. It's easier now, but I think we've lost an important quality, and there's a lot of waste in production.

VH: *It's contributed to our society becoming completely disposable.*

TN: Exactly. There's a big disconnect between ourselves, and the things we use, and the food we eat. People don't know where food comes from. People don't know where their clothing comes from. That's something I've always thought about. When I look at greeting cards in the grocery store I think, "Okay, where did this come from? I know someone designed it, but the trees came from somewhere, and the paper was sent somewhere to be printed. There's no personality to it anymore." I'm always inspired to buy things that have been actually touched by the person who thought of them.

VH: *Do you think that because consumers are far removed from the process, they're also removed from responsibility?*

TN: Yes. I think when you can buy something that's one of a million copies for one dollar, versus something more expensive that's been handmade by one or two people, it's a lot easier to turn a blind eye.

VH: *Agreed. Let's go back for a second to what we were talking about before. Was there something that happened to you—some kind of break—that made you feel like, "Hey, I may be able to make a living out of this!" Or was it just something you'd always known you would do?*

TN: I always knew I wanted to do it, but one of the bigger moments for me involved Nickelodeon. I do a lot of comic conventions where I sell my comics and crafts, and I don't even remember where I was—somewhere on tour playing a show that wasn't going very well. I got a call from my mom, who said there was a message on her answering machine from Nickleodeon; they were going to buy a comic I had submitted. It was right at a moment when a show wasn't going well, and I felt like things weren't really happening for me. Then, I get this call from a magazine I grew up with and loved, and it made me think, "Wow, I may be able to pull this off."

VH: *You've mentioned that you're a cartoonist and crafter. For you, what's the difference between art and craft?*

TN: It's weird, because there are a lot of overlaps. Many artists will have little figurines or little objects at their shows that are still art—and I don't know if it's called that because you can give something a higher value if you label it *art*. Maybe it's craft once you can duplicate it? But there's also craft that's absolutely one-of-a-kind, so it's hard to say. Maybe you can't wear art—unless it's jewelry—in which case....

VH: *That's tough. Technically, what Hope Perkins of Hot Pink Pistol does, with painting portraits on clothes, would be considered art. Those portraits happen to be of people like Biggie Smalls, but that's neither here nor there.*

TN: If you talk to art history people, they'd say the big divide came when art was made for art's sake. Before that, you'd make something because of function—there were artisans. Then, there became people who were just artists, who weren't making useful things.

> If you talk to art history people, they'd say the big divide came when art was made for art's sake. Before that, you'd make something because of function—there were artisans.

VH: *The current argument would be: Now that we've already established that necessity doesn't matter as much, the worlds of art and craft have become a convergence of something larger.*

TN: How do you define the difference then? If there's a craft that isn't useful, does that make it art?

VH: *If that's the case, there are a whole lotta Popsicle stick projects out there that would fall into the art category.*

TN: This is a hard, terrible question.

VH: *The reason I ask is because there are several people (some of whom we know well) who have a real problem with being called a crafter. They want to be known only as an artist or a designer, which is what many crafters call themselves now. I make a point of calling myself a craft designer, because it's irritating that some people feel they need to take the word craft out of the equation to make their work valuable. I've even known people who've hosted what are technically craft shows, but they refused to refer to the projects as crafts, opting instead for something like multi-media collaborations. There's still a huge gap in the value that's placed on one over the other, so what I'm trying to get down to is, what's the difference now?*

TN: I think people who have a problem with the term don't want to be confused with what our grandmothers would think of crafting. Now, though, people like Jenny Hart (see page 31) balance that divide awesomely by taking a traditional grandmother-esque craft like embroidery and turning it into something that's completely modern.

VH: *I feel like the anti-grandma thing is an out-of-date way of thinking. Really, crafting, which we often learned from our grandmothers, has brought back heritage. It's still your roots, remembering where you come from.*

TN: Exactly. I like that.

VH: *So, we're back to Point A: how do we divide the two?*

TN: How about we don't?

VH: *You mean, "Why can't we all just get along?" Moving on, what's your favorite thing about crafting?*

TN: Fundamentally, I like making things that are fun. The greatest reaction I could get, whether it's a craft, a painting, or a comic that I've made, is when people get a laugh out of it. I realize that if the whole world went to crap like *Mad Max*, we wouldn't need anything I make, but having fun is important. That's something that motivates me.

> For me, writing a song, drawing a comic, making a painting, or making a craft—it all feels the same. There are the same elements to all of it.

VH: *I've found that if people express themselves creatively in one way, they more than likely are interested in multiple forms of creativity. Do you find that to be true for yourself? Are there non-handicraft, creative aspects to your life?*

TN: I really think that's true. For me, writing a song, drawing a comic, making a painting, or making a craft—it all feels the same. There are the same elements to all of it. There are ideas, there's manufacturing, then there's sharing. Sometimes I'll have an idea first, and then feel out what would be the best way to express it: through painting, song, craft, or whatever feels right. Sometimes they overlap. I may draw a comic that's based on a song I wrote.

VH: *I didn't know you're a musician, too.*

TN: I guess, for longer than anything else, I wanted to create music. The other stuff was always a part of it. I'd sell crafts and comics on tour, because it was a good way to make money when I wasn't making enough at shows. Even if someone wasn't into my music, they might think, "Hey, that's a nice greeting card. I'll pick that up."

VH: *So instead of flipping veggie burgers to make ends meet while you were pursing a music career, you made cards and comics.*

TN: Yes. I've always tried to come at it from different angles. If one thing starts lacking, something else can pick up the slack.

VH: *How have you been treated within the craft community because of your gender, and also because being a cartoonist sometimes falls into a different category? I suppose you're in a different position than some other men in the industry because you lived in Austin, where it's not all that peculiar for a guy to make a living crafting. Out in the big world, though, it would be.*

TN: As far as the crafting community goes, I felt immediately welcomed by it. Being able to share booths with the Craft Mafia was fun. Although maybe you just invited me because you wanted someone with upper body strength, in which case you're definitely barking up the wrong tree. Seriously though, I felt like I had an advantage, as if white males need another advantage in society. I remember several years ago, I posted a tutorial on Craftster (www.craftster.org) for a Care Bear costume I made, and I still get e-mails about it at least once a month. That was *years* ago. I think it benefited me to be one of maybe 10 guys posting on the boards.

> I actually have to make good stuff now, instead of just being able to get by because I'm a guy.

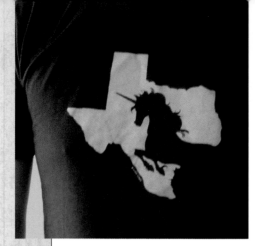

VH: *It was a bit of a novelty then, but that seems to be changing now, due in large part to community. There are boards, groups, Internet hubs, and things that nurture genderless crafting. Do you find that you're coming across more male counterparts now?*

TN: It's more normal now. I actually have to make good stuff now, instead of just being able to get by because I'm a guy.

VH: *What has been your biggest source of creative community in the craft world?*

TN: Being in Austin was amazing—meeting so many people who were actively making crafts as hobbies or as full- or part-time jobs. There was a real sense of community, even if you weren't part of a specific group.

VH: *Have you found that community where you live now, in San Francisco?*

TN: I haven't, but for me, community is all over the place, and I connect with it on the computer—which is good, because if you live in a town with like 35 people, it's hard to find that community locally. As lame as it is to talk about how neat the Internet is, it really is helpful.

VH: *See, I don't think it's lame at all. As much as it's killed some of us in terms of making money, it's also been a huge asset. Personally, I would never be where I am today if it wasn't for the Internet. You can't really bite the hand that fed you.*

You wrote a book called Punk Rock Etiquette. *The philosophy around the punk and indie craft movements seems fairly similar. Is that true in your experience?*

TN: Yes. Both are about doing something for the sake of loving it—not to be a rock star or the most famous person in the world, but rather to do something you love without asking permission. I wrote the book to encourage people to take the tools available, and really go for it. If all they can do is break even, that's still awesome.

VH: *So, it's the philosophy of "insert your creative choice here." It can be about promoting your band or your jewelry business, because the same motivation is behind it.*

TN: Yes!

VH: *You said you've had advantages within the community, but perhaps outside of it, do you find yourself ever having to fight stigmas against being a male crafter? Or does it seem more acceptable to people because you're also an artist?*

> ❞
>
> **Fundamentally, I like making things that are fun. The greatest reaction I could get, whether it's a craft, a painting, or a comic that I've made, is when people get a laugh out of it.**

TN: I hope you're not *hoping* for that in asking the question.

VH: *No, I really hope you don't have to deal with it. I'm the mother of two boys, and I want them to proudly identify themselves with whatever makes them happy.*

TN: It's kind of surprising, considering I make things with unicorns and rainbows, but I've never felt any kind of prejudice. I feel like I should've been beat up a lot more. Maybe people just don't want to mess with me.

VH: *It's that upper body strength you referenced. I think it's encouraging, though, that your experience has been positive. Maybe we're progressing as a society. Is there anything else you'd like to say about what crafting means to you or has given you?*

TN: One of my main goals is to hopefully inspire other people to think about where materials come from, how they're made, and to create things responsibly. It's important to do something you can feel good about, because you've made wise choices—even when it comes down to packaging. There are easy solutions, and there are better solutions. I use recycled paper, and I print with vegetable ink. When I need to use bags, I use biodegradable plastic. I feel like I can sleep better if I know I'm spreading a message of less waste.

For more information about Travis and his projects, go to:
www.ilikeapplejuice.com

The Crafter's Studio

In the great tradition of *Inside the Actor's Studio* and James Lipton:

What craft sound or smell do you love?
Ooh. I was not prepared for that. Can we talk about ethics again? I have this white paint that smells really good. Only the white smells good, like vanilla.

What craft sound or smell do you hate?
I don't like the smell of polymer clay after I've used it. It stays on my hands, and it won't go away. I also don't like envelopes that I have to lick, especially when I have to close 50 of them. You'd think I could just get a sponge or something, but that never seems to occur to me.

What career, other than craft- and art-world domination, would you like to try?
Sometimes I just want to be an organic or succulent farmer.

When you burn yourself with a glue gun or spill paint all over the floor, what is your favorite exclamation?
Balls!

Words to Craft by:

Name: Dave Lowe

Age: 42

Digs: Los Angeles, CA

Daily Grind: illustrator, designer, and television art director

Fave Crafts: general, but often recycling things into something new

More Info: davelowe.blogspot.com and www.davelowedesign.com

It begins by making stuff from pipe cleaners and construction paper. You advance, using paper towel or toilet paper tubes in a diorama. Peeling dried white glue from your fingers becomes a bad habit. Soon you're wrapping a balloon in dipped newspaper papier-mâché or melting crayons in cupcake tins. Artistic avenues open with colored pencils, acrylic paints, inks, and canvas. Unique and different materials present themselves: stone, wood, foam, hand-pressed paper, polymer clay, exotic fabric, and yarn. New tools come into play: hot glue guns, rubber stamps, crafting irons, crochet hooks, and rotary drills. Your brain swells with creative overload—and it's only Monday morning, working in the art department of a craft and decorating TV show.

Words to Craft by:

Name: Shayne Rioux

Age: almost 33

Digs: Columbia, MD

Daily Grind: mom and blogger

Fave Crafts: fuse bead portraiture

More Info: www.transcraftinental.com and www.geekcrafts.com

When I started blogging for Geek Crafts, I came across numerous fuse bead crafts made with Perler and Hama beads. You know, all the old 8-bit video games work perfectly with fuse beads. So I started thinking about other geeky things I could make with beads. I was making a list, nothing exciting, and then Mr. T popped into my head. I searched for a good photo, imported it into PC Stitch (cross-stitch design software), ordered a ton of beads, and got started. Mr. T is a whopping 18 x 22 inches, and he is spectacular. I plan on framing him in a fancy-pants, ornate gold frame. Since then, I've made patterns for more celebrities I admire: Elvis Presley, Frida Kahlo, Patsy Cline, Michael Landon—okay, I'm not sure how much I admire Michael Landon, but the pattern is awesome. And now, Pandora Kitten's Portrait Emporium has come to life. I've been crafting since I was a little girl, trying all different mediums. I feel like I've finally found my craft-istic calling. Thank you, Mr. T.

chapter twenty-two

Alex Anderson

Alex and I had never

actually met before our phone conversation, but because we'd had the pleasure of working with the same supervising producer, Kelly Mooney, on our respective shows, we felt like long-time acquaintances.

If you're part of the quilting world, then Alex Anderson is likely a household name. She's written several books, hosted 12 seasons of HGTV's *Simply Quilts*, and co-hosts *The Quilt Show*, a successful, studio-quality Web show with fellow quilter Ricky Tims. Alex has worked her way up in the industry from stay-at-home quilter (and mom) to the head of her own company. Her enthusiasm for her craft is as infectious as her accomplishments are successful. She truly loves quilting, and perhaps more importantly, absolutely adores the community it cultivates.

VH

VH: *What's your first craft-related memory?*

AA: That's a really difficult question. I was just presented with an award, so I dug back into pictures, photographs, and things like that—and there are actually pictures of me trying to knit at my grandma's knee (probably at age four or five), but then during the same vacation, I'm at my other grandma's knee learning to stitch. We also found Barbie clothes that I'd made. I probably wouldn't have remembered any of that if I hadn't found those things. The first thing I *really* remember is a needlepoint piece I made in fourth or fifth grade, or my first sewing experience on a machine around that same time.

VH: *Is there a moment from your childhood connected to craft that really stands out for you?*

AA: Hmmm, it's interesting because my mom didn't sew. She was very artful in the way she lived, but she didn't sew. I had people all around me who did, though. I vaguely remember sitting under our neighbor Mrs. Kelly's quilt frame. I had to be in first or second grade, if not younger. Then for eighth-grade graduation Mrs. Kelly gave me a thimble. I think these sorts of textile experiences were more commonplace when I was growing up than what the younger generation was exposed to. It was more of an integrated lifestyle then.

VH: *Yeah, that may be. Although now, I think it's sort of cycled back again, and the current generation will see a lot of creativity from their parents.*

Now, as a professional designer/crafter, is there an equally important moment for you?

AA: Yes, oh yes. I was an art major in college graduating with a general degree, but drawn to textile and design. One month prior to graduation, I realized I needed a unit to graduate. I went to my teacher and asked if I finished a quilt that my grandma had started in the '30s, could I get that unit? She agreed. You might say that was an important moment, but what was more profound was my experience at a quilt show at the Oakland Mormon Temple. I walked into a room and saw quilts hanging as art, and it was a life-changing moment. It nearly sucked the breath out of me.

VH: *Was that the first time you'd thought of quilting as an art form?*

AA: Yes, and I knew that I could move in that direction! I didn't have to be a weaver. I didn't have to be a potter. I didn't have to be a painter. I could be a quilter.

VH: *What, for you, is the difference between the word* artist *and the word* crafter, *or the words* art *and* craft?

AA: In the quilting industry, there's been a tremendous push-and-pull.

VH: *I think in the craft world, in general, there has been.*

AA: In quilting, it would be the *traditionalists* versus the *art quilters*. I really wanted to be on the art side because, after all, my degree was in art. I found, though, that my secret pleasure is sitting at the machine and doing traditional pieces that could be equated as craft-oriented pieces. I think that even though a crafter may not associate with being an artist, it's all generated from the same place. As long as you're creating with your hands, and it comes from your heart, that's all that matters.

VH: *Do you think that in the past crafters just haven't felt license to put themselves in the same ranks as artists?*

> I walked into a room and saw quilts hanging as art, and it was a life-changing moment. It nearly sucked the breath out of me.

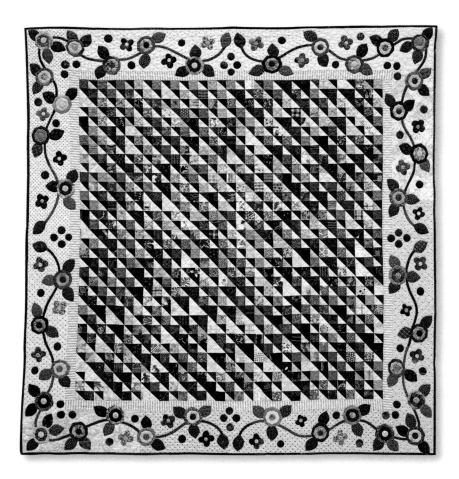

AA: For crafters, I don't know. For quilters, I see the tug-and-pull more between the traditionalists and the art quilters. When you say *crafter* to me, quilting doesn't even come to mind.

VH: *But if you go to the bookstore, quilting books will be in the craft section, and probably not in the art section.*

AA: Yes, they will, won't they?

VH: *This is a debate I've been having with people. My argument is that the lines have blurred as the value of craft has risen. It used to be considered only women's work that was done out of necessity, but now it's evolving into a form of expression.*

AA: This is a deeper conversation. I have a friend who's a quilter. She would very much like to be engaged in the art community. The high-art community, whoever that is, has made it very difficult for her. It's exactly what you're saying!

VH: *There's discrimination against the word* craft.

AA: Against the word *quilt*, too. The Oakland Museum had a quilt exhibit, maybe 25 years ago, called Women's Lives, by Julie Silber. It was a profound exhibit. I don't know how difficult the struggle was for her to get it there, but it was their most highly attended exhibit ever. The argument I've heard come up in the past is that museums will succumb to quilting because they're just going after the buck. I really don't dwell on those things, though.

I do have another story. My son's best friend growing up is now the webmaster for my personal site. He went to the University of California, Santa Barbara. He said I should come down to the university and talk to the students about quilting, because the guest speakers they bring in get a nice little chunk of change. I said I'd love to come down and talk to the students about how to make money in the field of art—How do you package yourself? How do you present yourself? How do you move forward? He said, "They don't want to hear that. If that's what you're going to do, they won't hire you."

So they have all these students getting art degrees, and they're positioning them to not make money. I don't get it. This probably wraps into some of the stuff you're thinking, right?

VH: *It does. I also think that we are sometimes our own enemies in the community. I have a lot of colleagues who refuse to call themselves crafters because they're artists, even though they work in embroidery, collage, etc., because there's a stigma attached to it.*

AA: You're A-one, exactly right. Honestly, my personal goal was to make a living doing something I love passionately—even in the old days when I was a stay-at-home mom and could just bring in a little extra money. It started out as a way to pay for family vacations, then a way to help put our kids through college. I didn't have the privilege to be able to think of it the other way, but I wouldn't have wanted too, either. Had I stayed in that box of being an art quilter, of which I was *struggling* to do in the beginning, I wouldn't have been able to spread the fairy dust of wonderment and joy that quilting brings to people's lives.

VH: *Is quilting your only crafty medium?*

AA: Currently, yes. I have experimented with woodworking, though. I've also done bobbin lace. I've done it all! But when I found quilting, I found my home. It was like walking through a door and knowing I'm supposed to be there.

VH: *Who, if anyone, do you credit for opening the crafty doors for you?*

AA: Probably my parents. My mom has a very good eye, and my father would let me go in his wood shop and try things. Nobody ever said, "You can't do that." When I needed something, I got it, even though we weren't a wealthy family. I got a sewing machine for eighth-grade graduation when my parents didn't really have the money.

VH: *Although we've made great strides over the past decade, society still doesn't place much value on handicrafts, especially as related to a career.*

AA: Oh, okay, let me tell you this! You're sitting on an airplane, and the person next to you says, "What do you do for a living?" I answer, "I am a quilter," and the response is only, "Oh."

VH: *But if you said, "I'm a TV host of a quilting show, you'd get a totally different reaction."*

AA: Yes! So that's what I do.

VH: *I do that too, because I want people to think there's value in it! It's so sad, though.*

AA: I know! I'll say, "I'm an author; I'm a fabric designer; I'm this and that. Oh yeah, and I hosted this show on HGTV for 12 years." How sad that I have to say that!

Then, if you go to a party and tell people you're a quilter, they'll say things like, "I need a quilt made, and I can pay you $50." They haven't a clue! I will say this—because quilting, and knitting, and probably crafting is mostly a woman's sport, it's grossly undervalued and underpaid.

VH: *As long as it's considered only a woman's sport, it will be that way. Tell me a bit about how you took your passion for quilting and turned it into a livelihood.*

AA: I have to tell you that at the beginning it wasn't a livelihood. I did have the privilege of a husband that made a decent-enough living that I could stay home and raise the kids—but I also remember that he got paid once a month. We'd pay all the bills, then I'd have $50 to feed the family for the rest of the month. I was naive enough, and it was early enough in the game, that I thought, "Well, I'm going to go teach at the local quilt shop." It was a matter of putting one foot in front of the other. My first quilt was published, then another one, and so on. The path laid out before me was very serendipitous. Now, I think some people come into the industry thinking, "I want that"—but I paid 15 years of dues before I did a book, or a show, or anything else. I was really kind of disappointed, though, with the money. I thought, "Oh, I got a book deal, I'll make tons of money." Well, that's not how it works.

VH: *Yeah, tell me about it. I'm currently writing three books and barely scraping by.*

AA: Someone in the industry who I greatly respect said to me, "You will never make money from one thing. It's a little bit of this and a little bit of that, and it all works together as a whole." I think there's real truth to that. Being on HGTV was obviously the tipping point. It was nothing I thought out, nor something I wanted to do, but my husband, John, encouraged me. It wasn't something that was even in my game plan.

> Someone in the industry who I greatly respect said to me, "You will never make money from one thing. It's a little bit of this and a little bit of that, and it all works together as a whole."

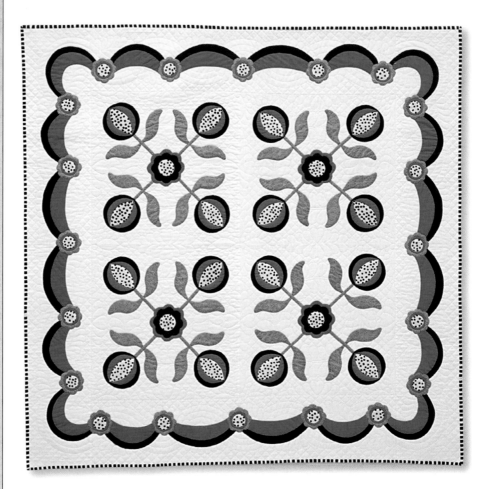

VH: *Why wouldn't you want to do it?*

AA: Because all I wanted was to be a professional quilter who traveled and made money that way. John asked, "What do you have to lose?" I said, "Making a jerk of myself in front of people all over the United States." Little did I know, it would be the world. Honestly, that first season, I got hate mail because I didn't know what I was doing. I didn't know how to be a TV host! I didn't even want to do it. After 12 seasons though, I'm doing my own thing. Thank goodness my husband pushed me through that door!

VH: *How did the opportunity come to you?*

AA: I was approached by the production company. HGTV was desperately trying to fill airtime, and after the company produced the second season of *The Carol Duvall Show*, they pitched a quilt show. HGTV agreed to buy 13 episodes—they were *desperate* for airtime filler. The producer went to her sister (who was more immersed in the quilt world) and asked who'd written a book within the last year, that also hasn't been pegged with a specific style, who's also entertaining, but still knows the language of quilting.

VH: *So you wrote your books first?*

AA: One book—and the next thing I knew, I was on a plane to meet the executive producers. The whole first season, I thought I had the flu, but the whole experience just had my nerves going. It was terrible.

VH: *Quilting has a history based not only on necessity, but also on storytelling. In the days of mass production and blogging, what role do you see quilts filling socially?*

AA: Explain what you mean.

VH: *It used to be that people quilted because families needed blankets. Or, if you go back to the turn of the twentieth century or earlier, quilters lacking formal education told stories through quilts as an alternative to writing those stories down. Times are different now. People don't need to make their own blankets, because it's probably more expensive to make them than it is to buy one from a big box store. We also don't need to tell our story through quilts for the historical record, because we can write whatever we want, anywhere we want—and probably have mass viewers on the Web. So, the position of quilting has changed, and I'm wondering if you still see a social value to it.*

AA: I don't think the position has changed at all. Quilts are made for many, many different reasons. Quilts are made to make political statements, to celebrate the arrival of a new child, or to work out grief for loved ones who are ill. For instance, after 9/11, I found myself paralyzed. I could not sew for five months. I would sit at my machine and just stare at it. Then there was a whole group of people at International Quilt Market who were working out their grief from the event through fabric. So, I think it's deeper than telling a story.

VH: *What's your favorite thing about quilting?*

AA: If you'd asked me that 30 years ago, it would've been the discovery of quilts as textile art. Maybe 20 years ago, it was walking into a quilt store and getting a rush from all the fabric. Season to season, what I love most about quilting evolves and changes. Right now, it's the people. I love being able to sit and sew. I love being able to do what I do. However, when people come up to me and tell me how they got through a horrific experience in their lives because of quilting—that means everything to me.

I look at the people quilting has brought into my life who I wouldn't have had the opportunity to meet otherwise. Maybe I would've thought, "They're not like me." But the fact of the matter is that they are like me. You peel the skin away from a quilter, and no matter what they look like on the outside, they're just the same on the inside. They are the best, best, best group.

> Season to season, what I love most about quilting evolves and changes. Right now, it's the people.

VH: *The main focus of this book is community. Quilting has, arguably, one of the strongest histories of perpetuating community through family circles and quilting bees. Since the days of village women spending hours together are gone, how do you see the modern-day quilting community being nourished?*

AA: Oh, the Internet! First of all, you've got these incredible shows all over the world. We've got the ability to fly and get there—and quilters do get there. So we're not stuck in our little villages. It's a very global craft. I remember walking into a show of Japanese quilts about 15 years ago, and it knocked me on my pins! I entered the show thinking I would win because my quilt was so awesome, politically correct, and everything it needed to be. Then I came face-to-face with the Japanese quilts and realized I had to step up my game.

VH: *Japanese crafts in general kick our asses all over the place.*

AA: I know! I thought, "Ok, so mine looks like kindergarten work!" You've got this whole global exchange now that's tightening up the button on what we enjoy today versus 20 to 30 years ago. I would say that global communication is the way the community's being nourished most.

VH: *In the knitting world, we still have knitting groups. Is that still happening with quilters, even though it's a less portable medium?*

AA: Absolutely! We have guilds. A guild might support anywhere from 50 to 700 people. Around 25 years ago, guilds contained mini-groups that met once a month to share tips and chat. Those still exist, but we also have global groups via the Internet.

VH: *Through hosting HGTV's Simply Quilts and authoring several books on quilting, you're in the rare position of not only being a professional crafter, but also a celebrity because of it. Do you see this as an example of how the industry and our society are evolving, or are people just paying more attention to what's always been there because of mass-media avenues like the Internet?*

AA: I think it's because of TV. What television has done for all of the industries is wonderful, and it saddens me that the networks are walking away from it. I think that having a TV show does give validity to the industry. I mean, the only time I get recognized in my small town is when I'm at a quilt market. I remember the first time I got recognized outside of that—it was after I got my wisdom teeth pulled and had blood and gauze hanging out of my mouth.

VH: *That's always how it happens! I had someone come up to me in an airport bathroom while I was literally on death's door, coughing. They came up to shake my hand, and I thought, "Do you really want to shake my hand right now? I just coughed into it!"*

What do you see the future being for crafting in the media? A resurgence of TV programs or more Web shows like your current project?

AA: I think there will be more Web shows. I think TV's in trouble. They have ignored the demographic that built them. I do understand that advertisers dictate who they want to brand. They want to brand 20-year-olds who will then create loyal viewers for the next 50 years. I get that. But us baby boomers are the ones who have time to watch TV and the money to spend on our passions.

VH: *True, but I honestly don't think the two are mutually exclusive. I was consulting for a big craft company who said that they needed to splash pictures of me, or someone younger than me, all over their ads. I told them I disagreed and encouraged them to create an ad with me, or someone like me, next to Carol Duvall (see page 50), or someone like her. There's value in that. It's about spanning the gap, not alienating people.*

You're one of the few people in the demographic we were just talking about who has really taken advantage of the Web through your own site, podcast, and Web show. Will you talk a little bit about how you've gotten a group of people who may not be tech-savvy to embrace the mediums you're now a part of?

AA: I built up trust with these people. I go out there and do shows and lay out the cause. I say, "Folks if you want it, this is where you've gotta go." And you know what? We own it. Once we get quilters through the door and on our site, they are hooked. They love it!

For more information about Alex and her projects, go to:
www.alexandersonquilts.com

The Crafter's Studio

In the great tradition of *Inside the Actor's Studio* and James Lipton:

What craft sound or smell do you love?
I *love* the smell of fabric!

What craft sound or smell do you hate?
The sound of my machine breaking.

What career, other than quilt-world domination, would you like to try?
A belly dancer? I don't know, something where I might be fit.

When you break your machine or or slice yourself with a rotary cutter, what is your favorite exclamation?
It's called the language of quilters—it's X-rated. You can't publish it.

Words to Craft by:

An elderly neighbor taught me how to knit when I was six. That kind woman gave me her elegant old-world craft, along with needles and a skein of beautiful yarn the color of raspberry sherbet. My grandmother, a crafter and resourceful person who could fix, clean, or create anything, taught me to crochet not much later.

I didn't work on a serious project until I was 27 and expecting my child. I learned how to follow a pattern, choose the right yarn and tools, and to block. I knitted one traditional going-home outfit and crocheted a more contemporary jacket and blanket set. When my little boy was a few months old, I held him out for my grandmom to see, smell, and touch. She was bedridden with cancer and was about to leave us. When she looked at the baby, she gently stroked his hair and said, "Don't ever fuss at him. He's so sweet. Such a sweet little boy." That's how I think of knitting and crocheting— with sweetness and kindness. When my husband and I are cross, I hear my grandmother's words and pick up my knitting to calm my heart.

Name: Jennifer Mansfield Peal

Age: 47

Digs: Dallas, TX

Daily Grind: songwriter, musician, and entertainer

Fave Crafts: knitting and crocheting

Words to Craft by:

I love what I do for a living, but it saddens me how much technology has taken over the favorite parts of my job. Handwritten notes have turned into e-mails. Thumbnail sketches and paper mock-ups have been replaced by PDF files. You can't hold a finished website in your hand or slip it into a portfolio sleeve. Crafting has given that back to me.

Name: Julie Kundhi

Age: 38

Digs: Lincoln, NE

Daily Grind: freelance graphic designer and writer

Fave Crafts: knitting and sewing

More Info: www.kundhi.com

I love the feel of soft wool moving through needles in my hands, and the smell of freshly pressed cotton on my ironing board. I get warm inside whenever my daughter asks to wear the hat and mittens I knitted for her. I love it when I get compliments on a purse that I sewed myself. It feels good to give handmade gifts, to give a part of myself, my creativity, and my time. Technology isn't all bad, though. I take photos of my work and share them online with other crafters. Through the Internet, I have met so many wonderful people, both locally and virtually. It has its place in my life. Just not in my craft room.

chapter twenty-three

Sandi Genovese

Sandi and I became

fast friends in less than ordinary circumstances. We met in Vermont on a shoot for a television holiday special we were co-hosting, along with four other craft personalities. While on the set, in a beautiful winter home in the center of snow-covered trees, we experienced the worst blizzard in Vermont's recent history. Snowed in overnight with cast and crew, we all hung out by the fire, sipped wine, and chatted. It was the best possible scenario in an otherwise unfortunate situation. Sandi is best known as the host of DIY's *Scrapbooking* show. She's also an author, a prolific paper arts designer with a multitude of licensed products, and has been a spokesperson for companies ranging from Mrs. Grossman's to Kodak. Living in different parts of the country, we don't see each other much these days, but we got to catch up from her studio in Laguna Beach, California.

VH

Photo by Cheryl

VH: *What's your first craft-related memory?*

SG: When I was in fifth grade, my neighbor gave me my very first paid job drawing a cowboy and cowgirl for a mosaic wall hanging she was creating. She used planks of wood, really garish gold piping, and colored gravel to create these pictures, but needed artwork to use as the outline. A restaurant had commissioned her to make this particular piece, but she realized she didn't know how to get a large image onto planks of wood. She hired me to draw directly on them, and when it was all done, she took me to the restaurant where they were hanging the pieces. I felt so proud!

VH: *What a cool memory—how nice that you were validated at such an early age! I know how important that is, because my own artistic son doesn't get the same rewards that his athletic brother receives through games and awards. I try to display his artwork or write articles using projects we've collaborated on, so he can see the value in being creative. I think we do feel that value when we see our work someplace where other people can also appreciate it.*

SG: To me, it was so cool. The restaurant had wood chips on the floor, so there was a strong smell of cedar when you walked through the door. To this day, when I smell cedar, I'm right back at that restaurant with that feeling of pride and happiness.

VH: *Is there a moment from your childhood connected to craft that really stands out for you?*

SG: Growing up, we didn't have a junior high school in our district. We went to elementary school through eighth grade and then straight to high school. In seventh grade, in an effort to bring art to us (because the teachers were only teaching main subjects), my teacher Mr. Sweeney gave us charcoal to sketch with outside. I had these shoes that were wicker with a flower embellishment. I guess I loved the texture, so I took them off and drew my shoes. I loved how the drawing turned out. When Mr. Sweeney was going through everyone's art later, without filtering his reaction, he said, "I let you guys out to draw nature! You're the best artist in the class, and you do this?!" He meant to be angry with me, but when he said that, it was the first time I ever thought of myself as an artist.

> It was my dad who really worked with his hands. To this day, I have furniture in my house that he built. I'd see something that I liked somewhere, and he'd take a look at it and then make it.

VH: *It's been a common theme in these interviews that people bring up the impact a teacher's words had on them at a really young age. You're one of the first who's had a positive memory in this vein. I noticed specifically with the non-professional crafters who've told their stories for Craft Corps that there were so many who said a teacher once told them they'd never be an artist, or that they were terrible at creating art, so they didn't touch anything creative again for 20 or 30 years! Breaks my heart.*

Who, if anyone, do you credit for opening the crafty doors for you? Is anyone in your family creative?

SG: Yes, my mom would sketch and draw a bit when we were on vacation. She always wanted to be a dress designer but had a job during the war and then had us, so it never worked out. I was this tall, skinny stick, and finding stuff to wear that was long enough in the arms and legs was really hard. My mom made clothes for me but didn't need patterns. I would tell her what I wanted, we'd go get the fabric, and I'd always love the stuff she came up with.

It was my dad, though, who really worked with his hands. To this day, I have furniture in my house that he built. I'd see something that I liked somewhere, and he'd take a look at it and then make it. Watching him create had an effect on me. My parents were supportive of my creativity in a very general sense. They never said that it wasn't okay to try something, or that something didn't look good if it wasn't the norm. They were really good about just letting me find myself.

VH: *When did you start scrapbooking?*

SG: I think the first scrapbook I made was after I graduated from the University of California, Santa Barbara. My brother had just graduated from high school, and my sister had graduated from flight attendant school. My parents decided they'd splurge and take us all on our last family vacation together to Hawaii. I took the pictures from that trip and put them into a scrapbook. I hand cut "Hawaii or Bust!" out of construction paper and used floral patterns for embellishment. It's so crude and ugly, and yet, it was probably my first *real* scrapbook.

VH: *Is there another craft that speaks to you creatively as much as scrapbooking does?*

SG: Actually, as much as I love scrapbooking, it's so personal. I use photographs for everything and even wrap gifts with them—I was a card maker long before I was a scrapbooker. I'm licensing products now, and many of those products are cards.

VH: *Are those through Mrs. Grossman?*

SG: Through her, it's mostly embossed stickers, ribbon embellishments, and a few card kits. I also have boxes of all-occasion cards on QVC that are through C.R. Gibson. They sold out right away, so they've ordered a lot more. That was cool. Since they've continued to do well, they asked me to create a second batch of all new designs.

VH: *You send out these amazing Christmas cards every year. Do you make all of them personally? Do you feel pressured to?*

SG: I do. I make them every year. Once I come up with the design, I go back to a company I used to work for that makes dies. I'll have a custom die made for the things I can cut out. The cutting out goes quickly. It's the assembly that's killer. I enlist my dad's help, since he lives close by. For me, a card is called a card because it can lay flat and be sent in an envelope. That's really the only requirement. Nearly all of them open up, though, in some kind of dimensional way. I like them to be interactive, so the person who gets them can play with them a bit. I just like my cards to be fun.

> Well, it seems as though the person who initially made crafting more upscale was Martha Stewart. Whether or not her style was like mine, it said to everybody that crafting is personal and creative.

Photo by Cheryl

VH: *Tell me a bit about how you took your passion for being creative and turned it into a livelihood.*

SG: You know, it wasn't intentional. It wasn't like, "Gee, I'm going to start a business." Right out of college, I went into teaching fifth and sixth grade. Art was always something I really loved, so I left the classroom after eight years to run the curriculum labs. It was a place where all the teachers came and provided ideas to create educational learning aids for K–12 classes. For instance, I would design a game that would help older kids practice multiplication in a way that was age-appropriate.

I discovered that the kids loved art, but for teachers who were less creative, it was really hard to come up with something to teach every week. I realized this was something that needed to happen in the lab. I needed to create an Art-a-Week project that all the teachers could come in and use. I'd heard there was a die cutter that would make cutting easier for teachers—they wouldn't need to do everything by hand. I found a local company, and the owner (who's one of the most artistically talented and wonderful ladies I know) came out to the curriculum lab to show me the machine. She saw how I had decorated the lab and asked if I did freelance work.

When you work for the school district, you have summers off, so I did some freelance—a lot of company logos, silk-screening, and stuff. Anyway, the owner of this company hired me to illustrate a newsletter they sent out to their customers and to create their display projects for trade shows. I started playing around with their die-cut machines and let them know that they didn't *only* work on paper! I bought Dr. Scholl's foot pads and made rubber stamps out of them. She was blown away! We struck up a friendship, and it wasn't long after that when she hired me to work full-time. It was one of those cases where one thing led to the next. That's how I got a job at Ellison.

VH: *How did you get the DIY* Scrapbooking *show gig?*

SG: While I was at Ellison, I had written a couple of books on how teachers could use the equipment to create learning aids for the classroom. The president of Ellison came to me and said, "We'd like you to write a book that's geared more towards crafting." I told her that I thought scrapbooking was going to be really popular—this was back in 1996. When you think about it, everybody has photos. I wrote a book called *Memories in Minutes*. I was demonstrating in the Ellison booth at the Craft & Hobby Association trade show, and Terry Ouellette (a.k.a. Terri O, the current spokesperson of CHA) was there covering the story for a station in Arizona.

She was going to interview me showing projects from the book in the booth, but when we realized that I lived in California and she lived in Arizona, I ended up just going out and doing a couple of segments live. At the same time, Carol Duvall (see page 50) saw the book, plugged the address into her GPS, and showed up in the Ellison parking lot. She called up and said, "I don't know if you know who I am, but is there any chance I could come in and see your projects?" She came in, really liked them, and booked me to do two different segments. It went really well—I enjoyed her and the crew—it was so much fun! They had me back many more times.

In the process, whenever Ellison booked me at trade shows, they also arranged for me to do segments on local news shows around the country.

> Carol Duvall saw the book, plugged the address into her GPS, and showed up in the Ellison parking lot. She called up and said, "I don't know if you know who I am, but is there any chance I could come in and see your projects?"

I enjoyed it. To me, it was kind of like teaching. I ended up doing a segment on *Good Morning America*, and the people from *The View* saw it. In turn, they had me on their program to do a scrapbook for their 100th show. They referenced the scrapbook all throughout the episode, and at the end, they said the viewer who made this says anyone can scrapbook—they interviewed me about how to do it. The folks at the DIY network had already planned on producing a scrapbooking show but were still looking for a host. They just happened to see me on *The View*, so they called and asked me to send a tape. That was it.

VH: *Wow, it was a long road to get there, but that's fantastic!*

SG: Yes, and somewhat accidental. I guess it's a testament to letting things just happen, if they seem to be going in a certain direction.

VH: *As a veteran in the craft industry, have you seen the view of crafting change over the years in both society and the media?*

SG: Well, it seems as though the person who initially made crafting more upscale (not so much pipe cleaners and google eyes) was Martha Stewart. Whether or not her style was like mine, it said to everybody that crafting is personal and creative. For me, she was the person who showed that making it yourself didn't have to look as if it were done by a fifth grader; it could be beautiful. The beauty of it was that it was custom and personal. It seemed like, up until she came around, crafts were almost something people did to save money rather than something they used as a creative outlet.

VH: *Do you think that perception has stayed true, or has it waxed and waned?*

SG: It seems like most things go in cycles. It's hard for me to be objective, though, since I'm so immersed in the craft industry. When I was shooting the show, though, people on planes would always ask me about what I do. When I told them I was going to Knoxville to tape a show about scrapbooking, I could tell they immediately assumed it was a small, local cable show. There is a little bit of a stigma.

VH: *I get the same thing, almost like a pat on the head. Switching gears a bit, what's your favorite thing about your craft?*

SG: I love that feeling when you get an idea, when you're brainstorming, and then start playing with paper (in my case) to see if it works. It gives me an adrenaline rush.

VH: *In the knitting and sewing worlds, we have Stitch 'n Bitch groups. Since scrapbooking and card making aren't as mobile, how does community manifest itself in the scrapbooking world?*

> I love that feeling when you get an idea, when you're brainstorming, and then start playing with paper (in my case) to see if it works. It gives me an adrenaline rush.

SG: There are people who get together in groups to paper craft. Initially, when there were lots of new stores, many of them had late-night craft sessions giving customers access to tools and each other. Many storeowners told me over the years that, frequently, the people who took the classes could've taught themselves. They came just as much for the community as they did for the project being made. I think it's similar to what you're describing with knitting.

VH: *Before you became a well-known leader in the industry, how did you seek out your own craft community?*

SG: Mostly, if I had a big project to do, I'd get my friends to come over for dinner and assemble things with me.

VH: *Is there anything else you'd like to say about what crafting means to you or has given you personally?*

SG: For me, I can lose myself in it. It's that same feeling I got out of college when I was playing my guitar and singing in clubs—time just flies. The last time you remember looking at the clock, it was four or five hours ago. It's such an internal enjoyment. Thinking of something and then wanting to make whatever you see in your head (or, in the case of music, that you hear)—it's just so fulfilling!

For more information about Sandi and her projects, go to:
www.sandigenovese.com

The Crafter's Studio

In the great tradition of *Inside the Actor's Studio* and James Lipton:

What craft sound or smell do you love?
The sound of ripping paper.

What craft sound or smell do you hate?
The sound of water or soda being spilled and ruining a project I'm working on.

What career, other than craft-world domination, would you like to try?
Something with music—I don't know what. Maybe songwriting.

When you spill that soda or cut yourself with a craft knife, what is your favorite exclamation?
Oh, you can't print it. I curse like a drunken sailor. I just say, f*$k, f*$k, f*$k!

Words to Craft by:

I have always been artistic, and if I'm not creating something, I feel like I'm missing a piece of my soul! After marrying my husband Jason, a naval submarine officer, moving all over the place, and having a baby, my passion to create grew stronger. I started creating whimsical submarine art when I discovered there really was a market for it, but no one was producing it. I've created artwork for submarine wives and children all over the country! I feel like it's a special reminder of husbands and daddies who may be at sea. I am very proud of our military personnel, and I think my artwork shows it. I try to create joyful pieces that celebrate the military family and lifestyle. I love what I do!

Name: Rebecca Williams

Age: 27

Digs: Groton, CT—the submarine capital of the world!

Daily Grind: artist, SAHM, Navy wife, and former special education teacher

Fave Crafts: painting and making mixed media pieces of submarine art

More Info: shaywilliams.blogspot.com and lovelyyellowribbons.etsy.com

Words to Craft by:

I remember talking to my husband when I first wanted to make greeting cards. He had an odd look on his face and said, "I think this is a great idea, but here's the deal: You can never purchase another card from Hallmark or any other greeting card company. You must make every single card you will ever need." This was difficult because it usually took me at least an hour to pick out the perfect card at my local retail store. I wanted to read every card—I would laugh out loud, so loud, people thought I was losing my mind. It's been six years; I'm still making cards and have not purchased one card for any occasion, and I always have that perfect card in my stash! I love making cards. My eight-year-old daughter is now the VP of packaging. I have to admit, my goal is to have both kids grow up to work in the art world. It's fun and fosters a creative mind!

Name: Tisa Jackson

Age: 34

Digs: Round Rock, TX

Daily Grind: I work full-time as an executive assistant and serve on the executive PTA board at my son's school.

Fave Crafts: handmade cards and stationery

More Info: tisasspot.blogspot.com

chapter twenty-four

Margot Potter

Margot is a driven crafter

who's made a name for herself as the Impatient Beader. She's written successful jewelry books, designed for worldwide companies and publications, and can be seen regularly as a guest on the home shopping channel, QVC. She's constantly hustling (a skill that's imperative as a professional crafty-type), reinventing herself, and surprising people with her latest ideas. She's known for being a straight shooter with a passion for her craft. Although Margot and I have since met in person, this was our first conversation after running in the same professional circles for several years. I spoke to her from her home studio in Pennsylvania about everything from how she got started in the business to her possible future as a cabaret singer.

VH

VH: *Do you come from a family of crafters?*

MP: I come from a family of fine artists, going all the way back on both my mother's and father's sides. My mother has always been crafty and artsy, so I grew up surrounded by that. I never really thought of myself as an artist, though. They were really the artists, and I just made stuff out of stuff.

VH: *What's the difference, do you think?*

MP: This is the big, philosophical question. I'm not sure there's as much of a difference as people think there is. I think one difference people perceive is that crafters are kind of being derivative. We're more about a task or a skill set, where artists are being more creative. I think that line has been blurred over time.

VH: *I also think that separating the two really devalues craft. I've seen a lot of really crappy fine artists, and a lot of kick-ass crafters.*

MP: I agree. I mean, things that people are calling *craft* I'm thinking should be in a museum!

VH: *Exactly, but I think that if you put the word* art *next to* the word craft, *people often think of one being associated with talent and the other with skill.*

MP: Yes, which I think is misguided.

VH: *Which is our job to change, dammit!*

MP: It is. Before I started this career, I had a gallery where we sold fair trade handicrafts from all over the world. The biggest battle I had in educating my customers was explaining the value of these crafts that they'd see. They thought a lot of our stuff was weird, but I'd explain that it's art and an expression of culture. I got to the point where I was so tired of trying to defend what I thought were beautiful handmade things that I finally just said, "Enough."

VH: *There's also value in sustaining communities, which I think is something that's missed by society. It's not missed as much when referring to third world countries that have programs and co-ops—there's acknowledged value with that. However, people now make their living here in the United States by making handicrafts. The value is equal, just different.*

MP: It is different. One thing for us was that we saw a lot of fair trade initiatives— they were missionaries going in and trying to help, but they were encouraging people to make what I saw as watered-down, airport art. Nobody was bringing in the really cool stuff—you know, stuff that was really edgy, different, and spoke to some of the mysteries of the culture. That became our mission, and I loved it! Everywhere you go in the world, there's beautiful art being made that's powerful and that opens dialogues. There's so much more to it than people perceive when you say the word *crafts*.

VH: *Let's talk about your beginnings. Is there a moment from your childhood connected to craft that really stands out for you?*

MP: Well, this is a funny story that I tell. When I was a little baby in my crib—I guess I always had the impetus to create—I reached in my diaper and painted on the wall.

VH: *These are things you should maybe keep to yourself.*

MP: Right. I just have always, always wanted to make things. Whether it was with a box of crayons, with mud pies, or making clay sculptures. I didn't know what I was doing, but I wanted to do it. It's always been there.

VH: *Now, as a professional designer/crafter, is there a moment equally important for you as the aforementioned diaper moment?*

MP: For me, the moment was when I realized I could make this a career, and I finally said to myself, "Hey, you know what? You're an artist."

I got commissioned to do a design for Beadalon. The company wanted me to make something out of wire, and it became an obsession. I wanted to make this multi-dimensional, sculptural piece that looked like a real vine with 3-D flowers and a crystal dragonfly. When I turned it in, they totally freaked out. They thought it was incredible and asked me to make more. I was like, "Uh, ok."

In the meantime, we closed our business, and I lost my job at QVC. For a year, I'd been talking to my husband about how to turn making jewelry into a career. I didn't know how to do it, and he thought it would never work, that I couldn't compete with cheap labor from overseas. The wire piece was the epiphany for me. When it was so well received, I thought, "Hey, I can do this. I can write instructions. I can write books. I can teach people how to be creative."

VH: *Does your husband work for Beadalon?*

MP: He does now, yes. Beadalon had been coming into our store and buying things for their catalogue, but still, it didn't connect for me. I didn't see it as a career; I just thought they were buying my finished goods.

VH: *Do you think that has anything to do with what we were talking about before— the value placed on craft?*

MP: Yes. I really believed in my heart of hearts that I wasn't an artist. I was just making jewelry. I didn't see it as being valuable enough to make a living at it.

VH: *What did you do for QVC before the career change?*

MP: I sold Tiffany-inspired lighting. I auditioned to be a host—my background is as an actor—and I got really close but was a little too funky for them. They suggested that I sell Tiffany lighting, though. I did that job for three years, and even designed some night-lights for them. Again, still not thinking of myself as a designer.

> Something I've learned from the Amish (and that crafters should take to heart) is that they do not undervalue themselves *at all*. I think a lot of crafters forget to calculate their time and creativity when they're pricing things.

VH: *So you're making stuff for a national audience and it doesn't occur to you that you're an artist. But when you make a necklace for one company, it finally clicks that you are? Interesting.*

MP: I know, right?

VH: *You were classically trained as an actress, as you just mentioned. Where did you go to school?*

MP: I did my undergraduate work at Kennesaw State University. I'm a vocalist, and they had a theater department where I was working toward a music major.

VH: *You touched a bit on this before, but how do you use what you learned in school in your career as a craft spokesperson?*

MP: For one, I'm really comfortable in front of people, whether it's doing demonstrations, being a guest on a TV show, or hosting things. My comfort in front of a camera in a live, unscripted setting (because of my years in the theater and my habit of thinking on my feet) makes me a unique entity. You're like that, too, because you have a background as a host. Not everybody in the industry has that, so it sort of sets you apart.

VH: *Although, more and more, people seem to be gaining experience now—maybe just because they're dabbling in it with YouTube. When I started (and I'm sure you can say the same thing), really, nobody our age was crafting on-camera.*

MP: Maybe that was because it was Carol Duvall's domain (see page 50), or maybe it's because a lot of artists are introverts. Then a new generation of extroverts appeared. We're much more willing to wear our art on our sleeves now.

VH: *Which is a vulnerable place. For me, I just sort of assume there will always be people who are more and less talented than I am, but my job is primarily to get people creative.*

MP: I just think of it this way: I'm completely unique. Even though I have the same skill sets as some other people, what I have to offer is *so* different that there's room enough for all of us to find success. I'm all for supporting one another in doing that. I really hate situations where people are bitchy and competitive— that's just such a lack of maturity.

VH: *I think it's tougher now. At the time of this conversation, the economy is at an all-time low, and like many other industries, the craft industry has been kicked in the teeth. Craft programming and magazines have been the first to go, so it's even more of a challenge to fight to make a career out of what we do.*

MP: True. I'm sitting here in my home studio brainstorming ways to stay afloat.

VH: *I do that too, every day. There's also a big debate in the publishing world*

> I've been thrift store shopping for 26 years. People who thrift are always bringing things home and repurposing them. It's just what we do— we're crafty kind of thinkers.

that really affects us: How do we make money when there's so much free content available on the Internet?

MP: I struggle with that on my blog. I've been offering free projects, lately. I'm hoping people like it and think, "Well, maybe I should buy that book." The other side of the coin has me wondering if Web traffic is worthwhile, or if it's just people who like free stuff.

VH: *I really don't know the answer. I made the decision to offer small, simple projects for free and save the bigger ones for books and magazines. My mindset, like yours, is that if people know there's a place where they can find projects when they can't spend the money, maybe they'll think about me when they can.*

I've read on Twitter that you live in Amish country. How does being surrounded by a culture that so greatly values working with one's hands influence what you do as a designer?

MP: It's funny, because they don't look at it like we do. There's not as much ego or ownership associated with their craft, because it's a livelihood. They're very pragmatic and practical about everything. That perspective helps me keep it real in the sense that I may get too serious or self-important about something I'm doing, but then have to realize that I'm not saving the world. It's not nuclear physics. It's just crafting. There's a balance between becoming attached to the outcome and also being reverent about the fact that creativity is powerful. When you're creating, you're channeling something positive and bigger than you. I guess living in Amish country has given me a different perspective.

VH: *That's fascinating. You're juggling two concepts when you say, "Crafting is a big deal. Crafting has power. Crafting has value," but then say, "We're not curing cancer here." You're conveying that it's just crafting but also, dammit, it is crafting! It's a really remarkable balance.*

MP: Yes, it's a true dichotomy. I will say this: Something I've learned from the Amish (and that crafters should take to heart) is that they do not undervalue themselves *at all*. Their furniture, their quilts, and their crafts are not sold for nothing. They don't work all day on something and then charge a dollar for it. Their products are expensive because they value the work; they use good materials; and the craftsmanship is extraordinary. I think a lot of crafters forget to calculate their time and creativity when they're pricing things.

VH: *You're possibly most well known as the Impatient Beader, and I imagine it's self-explanatory, but will you explain the philosophy behind that name and the inspiration behind your book series of the same name?*

MP: I was sitting at home on the computer during that crazy year when I had to walk away from the QVC job, and we had to close the store. I went through a horrible phase where I just couldn't figure out what I was going to be when I grew up. I was trying everything I could—putting myself out there in so many different directions. Then, I had this epiphany, "I think I should write a book called *The Impatient Beader*. It should reflect my personal struggle between being really creative and wanting to make beautiful things, but also being somewhat lazy." There are two ways to look at it: either I'm lazy, or I'm a Zen master in training, because I'm always looking for the path of least resistance.

VH: *Or, you're a working mother and wife who's busy.*

MP: Right. I knew that's how most people felt; they had the impetus, but they didn't have the time, or they felt they were technically challenged. This will be a book for them. It'll be humorous and will make people comfortable. It will be a series of books that I can then expand outward in multiple directions. That was really how it started. I did a little research and found a publisher that I thought would welcome the idea. I sent them an e-mail, followed their protocol, and a week later, I'd sold my first book.

VH: *That doesn't happen very often.*

MP: No, it doesn't. I really feel like it happened because I was moving in the right direction.

VH: *Was jewelry making always your craft-fix of choice, or is it just what happened to take off for you?*

MP: It's just where I started in the industry, but I'm creative in every way. I've been thrift store shopping for 26 years. People who thrift are always bringing things home and repurposing them. It's just what we do—we're crafty kind of thinkers.

VH: *I don't know what your situation was, but for my family, a lot of it was financial. We just didn't have any money growing up. My mom stayed at home with the kids, and my dad worked for the airlines, so we had to make things. We made gifts; my mom made our clothes; that's just how it was then.*

MP: I grew up with a single mom who had three daughters, so she had to be very creative. We were surrounded by creativity, so I dabbled in everything because she did.

VH: *Do you still have time to do other crafts?*

MP: Yes. Well, I craft at work, so I don't like to craft on my time off. I work so much that I don't have a lot of time off, anyway. I do have a studio full of supplies, and right now, I'm really into inks and paper. I've re-branded myself into the Impatient Crafter, because I want to make sure that people get that if you're crafty, you're crafty.

VH: *What's your favorite thing about crafting, in general?*

MP: I love the freedom of being able to sit down, open my mind and just let it spill out onto whatever I'm doing—whether it's onto the page, into my beadwork, or whatever it is. I love that crafting has afforded me the luxury of being able to walk around the world and see everything as a possibility—like walking into a grocery store, seeing a logo, and thinking, "You know, I could recycle that into a pendant."

VH: *It's kind of a curse, too! What do you see as your role in the current craft movement?*

MP: I'm sometimes the jester, but I think my real role is to show all women (not that I'm dissing the menfolk) that we really can do anything. When you go in the right direction and open yourself up to potential, without filtering it or being too specific about how it has to be, then amazing things happen. We're not just creating crafts, we're creating our lives. That's big stuff. I like to think of myself, in some ways, as a self-help-through-creativity guru, but I do it with my tongue planted against my cheek, so it's not too smarmy.

VH: *What role, if any, has crafting played in your own sense of community?*

MP: It's created a network of incredible creative people in my life. I wouldn't know most of my current, very good friends without crafting. Viral marketing like corresponding on Facebook and Twitter have also been big. Community has changed my life.

VH: *As both an influential crafter and a mother, do you feel any sense of responsibility to make creativity accessible to everyone?*

MP: It's my mantra. It's my entire goal. I believe that everyone has the right to be creative. Everyone is an artist in his or her own way. I feel an absolute obligation

> I feel an absolute obligation to pay it forward by inspiring people to be creative. I'm not just selling people beading designs or paper crafting, I'm showing them how to embrace the power of the creative force.

Margot Potter

to pay it forward by inspiring people to be creative. I'm not just selling people beading designs or paper crafting, I'm showing them how to embrace the power of the creative force.

VH: *Is your daughter crafty?*

MP: She's incredibly crafty, but I cannot take any credit for that whatsoever. She's like the cobbler's kid who has no shoes.

VH: *I use that analogy all the time!*

MP: People always ask, "Do you craft with your kid?" I'm like, "Oh my God, no."

VH: *I craft with mine, but it's really rare that I actually make something for them.*

MP: That's what it is. We live in a two-story, former Amish schoolhouse. My studio is upstairs in a big room that opens up to my bedroom. My daughter's bedroom is up there, too. She'll come home from school and come up to grab supplies. She's really dimensional and makes incredible 3-D paper sculptures. She's smart and cool—I like my kid a lot.

For more information about Margot and her projects, go to: www.margotpotter.com

The Crafter's Studio

In the great tradition of *Inside the Actor's Studio* and James Lipton:

What craft sound or smell do you love?
I love and simultaneously hate the smell of Mod Podge.

What craft sound or smell do you hate?
See above.

What career, other than craft-world domination, would you like to try?
Well, I'm a performer, so my big goal is to get back to that—maybe open a cabaret club and do a cabaret show every night. I'm a person who reinvents myself every so often, so I have several more careers in me. Oh, and I'd like to write a novel.

When you burn yourself with a glue gun or pinch yourself with jewelry pliers, what is your favorite exclamation?
I have a terrible mouth, so bad that I had an older designer tell me that I had to stop using potty words on my blog. I like dropping the F-bomb.

Words to Craft by:

After college, I had no idea what to do with my art degree. It was harder than expected to discover my post-art school creativity. Without specific parameters set by a syllabus, it was really difficult to channel my ideas.

Name: Juliet Ames
Age: 28
Digs: Baltimore, MD
Daily Grind: plate breaker
Fave Crafts: creating jewelry out of recycled plates
More Info: craftherapy.blogspot.com

After a six-month hiatus, I just had to make something, anything! The result was a mosaic mailbox made of plates that I had collected from Goodwill. When the mailbox was complete, I was left with a pile of broken plate shards that were begging for a new purpose. I wrapped one in solder and made a pendant out of it. Instantly, I began getting orders for more.

I had no idea how much sentimental value is placed on broken plates. At craft shows, folks tell me stories about the broken plate pieces they have squirreled away because they couldn't bare to toss them. I've had the honor of making jewelry out of a customer's great grandmother's bowl that fell off a shelf, plates damaged in Katrina, and wedding china damaged in a move. Turning shards into heirlooms has been so rewarding. I am happy that I made something, even if it was just a mailbox.

Words to Craft by:

For my wedding, I knew I wanted to give my four bridesmaids a handcrafted gift, but I wasn't sure what to make them. Knitting would take too long. I'm a slow knitter and four projects at the same time was beyond me. My maid of honor's boyfriend contacted me wanting to know her ring size. He wouldn't share exactly why he wanted it, but it was pretty obvious. I didn't know her ring size, and I knew if I asked her, she'd get suspicious, and I'd crack under pressure.

Name: Jennifer Chen
Age: 29
Digs: West Hollywood, CA
Daily Grind: writer, playwright, and editor at a photography trade magazine
Fave Crafts: jewelry design, knitting, sewing, and bookbinding
More Info: www.mediabistro.com/jenniferchen

One of my favorite bead stores conveniently offered a ring-making class, so I decided to learn to make rings for each of my bridesmaids and nonchalantly ask them for their ring sizes. Perfect, except for the fact that my maid of honor waited to the last possible moment to tell me her ring size. Her boyfriend was frantic and so was I. But the e-mail came in time, and the next call I got from her, she announced she was engaged! I'm proud to say that my crafting skills helped a guy in need and provided the perfect gift to give to my best friend.

chapter twenty-five

Jenny Ryan

Jenny and I are what I call peripheral colleagues. We've worked with some of the same companies, know a lot of the same people, and attend similar events. Our paths had never directly crossed, though, before this interview. As with any two people who are truly passionate about the same things, conversation was as easy as if we'd been friends for years. Jenny's an author, designer, writer for the DIY site CRAFT (www.craftzine.com), founder of the handmade fair Felt Club, and co-owner of the Home Ec. workshop. She strives to get people creative and give Los Angeles a better, crafty rep!

VH

VH: *What's your first craft-related memory?*

JR: I think probably making Christmas ornaments with my dad. I kind of like that my first memory is with a male. I just feel like not enough guys are crafting these days, or if they are, they're not out of the closet about it. Part of what I like about crafting is trying to change that. Anyway, I remember making ornaments with my dad out of clothespins. We made little Buckingham Palace guards by painting them red, using a toothpick as the sword, and giving them little pipe cleaner arms.

VH: *Is your dad British?*

JR: No. He is a history buff, though. We also made clowns. I actually came across those ornaments on a visit a couple of years ago and brought them all back home with me.

VH: *Was your dad creative in other aspects?*

JR: I can remember him going through phases. He went through this whole period when he was all about making sourdough bread. I don't know that he'd even think of himself as a creative guy, but he totally is.

VH: *Is there a moment from your childhood connected to craft that really stands out for you—maybe something that helped shape who you are today?*

JR: I think maybe Girl Scouts. I remember one year we participated in the Toys for Tots drive with the Marines; we cleaned up toys to make them new again and made ornaments. I remember a lot of spray painting macaroni and making wreaths. I think that was the first time I realized how crafts could affect other people and how making stuff could make the world a better place.

VH: *Now as a professional designer/crafter, is there an equally important moment for you?*

JR: The first big holiday Felt Club craft fair that I threw. Seeing the droves of people that came out in L.A., a city that I think a lot of people have a bad impression of. If you're just driving through, it may seem like it's all just breast implants and strip malls. There's actually a lot more to it, though. What's cool about L.A. is something that people also bring up as a drawback: the sprawl. That translates into these cool pockets of creativity all over the city. You can spend a lifetime here and never finish discovering. Bringing a lot of those people together for Felt Club, showing them what they could do, and then seeing the response from all the visitors made me realize, "Wow, there's a really great scene happening here, and we're helping to perpetuate it."

VH: *Do you think that both of those memories aqually effected who you are as a designer today?*

JR: I think they're connected. I'm realizing more and more about the thread that connects all the different creative ventures I've done—I think it's wanting to reach out to others.

VH: *Who, if anyone, do you credit for opening the crafty doors for you?*

JR: My Aunt Jean. She was older, and I went to stay with her for a summer once. I'd always been crafty in that macaroni-and-glue way, but had never messed with a sewing machine or anything like that. I was probably in fifth or sixth grade when she got me quilting. I had been really intimidated by using a sewing machine before that. Working with her on this ugly, calico-print quilted pillow got me over that hump of being afraid of this piece of machinery. That fear seems so silly now, since my sewing machine is like an extension of me, but it was like learning to drive or something.

VH: *Tell me a bit about how you took your passion for being creative and turned it into a livelihood.*

> I remember one year we participated in the Toys for Tots drive with the Marines. I think that was the first time I realized how crafts could affect other people and how making stuff could make the world a better place.

JR: Sometime around 2000, I started a blog called Sew Darn Cute (sewdarncute. typepad.com). I was living in Seattle and working in the dot-com industry when it sort of imploded. All of these companies went out of business, owing me lots of money. I hadn't sewn since I was a kid but was still into crafts, especially visual arts and drawing. I had some free time all of a sudden and was overtaken by this urge to start making things again.

I was really into accessories and started making handbags, potholders, and different little household items for friends. They kept telling me, "These are really good; you should try to sell them." So, I created a website (that I built myself) and started selling things I'd made. It was just a hobby at that point. I didn't even get myself legal, the way I'd recommend people do now.

VH: *Well, it was different then. Not a lot of people had online shops, so it was harder knowing the protocol.*

JR: Oh, definitely! There was a lot less competition; there was no Etsy. You just had to figure things out as you went along.

VH: *There weren't a lot of craft sites period, which I think also gave us a big advantage over people. A lot of my strongest community came from those days of swapping links with other crafters, and e-mailing each other to figure out this whole Web thing.*

JR: Yes, it was a little bit more of a ghost town then. The way the community has grown leaps and bounds since the Web took off is fantastic.

I didn't know anything about running a business, but I kept it up, even though I wasn't making a living off of it. We moved to L.A. around that time. My husband's a cartoonist, so his living can be feast or famine. I always felt like one of us needed to have an office day job. I wasn't willing to give that up to pursue Sew Darn Cute full-time; I was scared, understandably. Eventually, I came to this realization that until I did allow myself the time and mental energy, I wasn't going to be able to take it to the next level and make more money. I finally just did it. My husband and I both stopped temping and went full-time with our creative pursuits. It was really rough for a while, especially since we'd just moved to L.A.

VH: *I don't even understand how you were able to make that work. I grew up there but came to Austin to raise my kids because L.A.'s so expensive.*

JR: Luckily, we got a really good deal on rent. Plus, we still kept temp jobs for a couple of years. It eventually got to the point where my husband had enough books in print that he was getting royalties, so we had a little bit of a cushion. We just went for it.

I started selling to more stores and participating in more shows like Renegade Craft Fair and Bizarre Bazaar. That's one of the reasons why I started Felt Club as an L.A.-based indie craft fair, because I didn't feel like there were enough

> I like being a dilettante crocheter—making freeform pieces and knitting really small pieces like baby items and skinny scarves. I'm really into instant gratification, which is what I like about sewing.

places for people like me to sell things—places where crafting wasn't just an afterthought, like a farmer's market where there might be one craft booth, but the rest of it is vegetables. I wanted something more focused on handmade and locally made goods. Felt Club has sort of overtaken my life and led to all these other things.

I became less interested in Sew Darn Cute as a business, simply because, for me, making stuff became a little less fun when it became my job. I couldn't make enough bags to keep up with the demand or make a profit, unless I was willing to hire someone else. Then there's that conundrum of, does it make it less special if someone's buying something that doesn't have your personal touch? There are some people who've done that very successfully; it just didn't feel right to me. I really liked having my hand on everything.

At the same time that I was weighing my options about Sew Darn Cute, I was approached by a book packager. They wanted to put together a proposal to do a Sew Darn Cute book. I started thinking about how great that would be. Rather than making the same tote bags over and over and then not having any time to develop new ideas, I could teach other people how to make these things. I could constantly develop new projects and wouldn't be stuck in the manufacturing mode. Eventually the book *Sew Darn Cute* got picked up and published by St. Martin's Press, and I stopped my retail business.

VH: *Is sewing the thing that speaks to you the most creatively out of all the crafty things you do?*

JR: I think so. It's what I enjoy doing most, and I can lose myself for hours in it; whereas, I like knitting and crocheting, but I sometimes get frustrated because I'm not that good and I'm too impatient. I like being a dilettante crocheter—making

> I'm just trying to be an enabler of craft.

freeform pieces and knitting really small pieces like baby items and skinny scarves. I'm really into instant gratification, which is what I like about sewing.

VH: *What's your favorite thing about crafting?*

JR: I think I'm a little bit OCD, but I like to say that I'm OCD-lightful! I like having control over things, but there's so little in life that you can actually control. You can, though, control the creation of something from start to finish. I think the empowerment aspect of that control and of being able to share with other people (like my aunt did with me) who think they can't sew or knit is also fantastic. Showing people they don't have to buy whatever crap is on the shelf at a big box store. They don't have to be satisfied with things the way they are; they can create their own environment.

For that reason, I opened a craft workshop called Home Ec. in Silverlake, CA. It's inside an existing shop, Reform School. We have a full roster of craft classes, and we sell fabric and kits and our own booklets. I'm really excited about it! I want to be able to show people not only the valuable time that goes into something handmade, but also that people can really make their own creations.

VH: *There's often an intimidation factor with crafting that I find really interesting. I think it's because, as a society, being creative was a luxury. We went through this weird thing when crafting was considered handicraft and women's work, so the only value was necessity. Then we went to, "Well isn't that nice—you get to be creative." There's this gap between value, livelihood, and frivolity.*

JR: I'm interested to see what effect the economic downturn has on people's view of crafting. It seems that people were already heading towards simple living with things like the slow food movement. I wonder if the recession will ultimately help people realize that they can be more self-sufficient.

VH: *I truly believe that hard times, be it social, personal, or economic, are made better through community. I wonder what effect our current state of unrest will have*

> One of the reasons I started Felt Club as an L.A.-based indie craft fair was because I didn't feel like there were enough places for people like me to sell things—places where crafting wasn't just an afterthought.

on the community aspect of crafting. *Since you perpetuate community through the work you do for CRAFT magazine online, for Felt Club, and (on a different level) through your blog and book, have you felt any boost in camaraderie during these times? Have you noticed a change in mood?*

JR: Definitely the latter, even in my own home. We were watching some Martha Stewart Christmas special where they cut away to shots of Christmas lights all over the world, and my husband said, "God, what a waste." Any other time in the past, he would've reacted differently, perhaps thinking it was cute. I think because of the whole doom and gloom thing that's happened economically, people are becoming more conscious of waste. The comments we get on the CRAFT blog lead me to believe that's true. People are even becoming more aware of the materials they craft with. Projects involving creative re-use are some of the most popular on our site. People are feeling the crunch but still wanting to be creative. It's just about finding different ways to do so.

VH: *It's about being creative about the way you're creative. What role do you feel you play in both the current craft movement and also the community?*

JR: Ah, I don't know! I'm just trying to be an enabler of craft.

For more information about Jenny and her projects, go to:
sewdarncute.typepad.com

The Crafter's Studio

In the great tradition of *Inside the Actor's Studio* and James Lipton:

What craft sound or smell do you love?
Remember those markers that smell like fruit? Those are pretty awesome in a really gross, chemical way.

What craft sound or smell do you hate?
I don't like the smell of E6000 industrial glue.

What career, other than craft-world domination, would you like to try?
Cupcake decorator.

When you burn yourself with a glue gun or spill that resin all over the floor, what is your favorite exclamation?
I say things like, "Oh my God, I hate my life!" In high school I was voted both class clown and most dramatic, so there you go.

Words to Craft by:

Creating things with my hands is as natural as breathing. When I am engrossed in a project, time flies out the window. Crafting takes me to a place where my hands and imagination work together without rules and wrong turns, and I go with the flow of what feels right. I recently relocated to Ireland, thousands of miles away from where I grew up, with cultural differences that are as vast as the east is from the west. But there is no time to feel like a strange cat in a strange house. I know crafting will keep me in touch with all things I have tucked in my heart—what a universal language crafting is!

Not knowing where to go or what to do in a new city, I stumbled across a crafting forum in Ireland. I could never have found a more helpful group of people. I feel an instant kinship with people who craft, whether I just lurk in their blogs, or appreciate a handmade product in a shop. It's the personal touch that never fails to make me feel warm and fuzzy, the same feeling I get when crafting. I feel like I wear my heart on my sleeve for the world to see. Knowing that other people appreciate my handmades, I come full circle.

Name: Odette Valentine Bron

Age: 29

Digs: Dublin, Ireland

Daily Grind: full-time housewife

Fave Crafts: sewing, card making (my own graphic designs), learning to crochet, and knitting

More Info: littlemsfirefly.blogspot.com

Words to Craft by:

My mom has a tiny sewing room in the basement that's our place of choice when we craft together. The time I've spent with her in that small room filled with fabric is uncountable. She works on her projects and hands out fabric and good advice when I want to sew a pair of pants, design a handbag, or learn how to quilt a pillowcase. Mom is an avid quilter with a passion for cutting thrifted fabrics apart and sewing them back together again in different shapes and patterns! It's like magic watching her design new totes, baby quilts, and large bed throws.

A couple of years ago, I started a small shop for our items and named it I Shop With Mom. I took photos of her finished items and priced them fairly but always too high for Mom, who does not know to appreciate the value of what she does. One of the proudest craft memories I have is hearing her squeal over the phone when I told her about her first online sale!

Name: Hanna Andersson, a.k.a. **iHanna**

Age: 32

Digs: Stockholm, Sweden

Daily Grind: personal assistant, web designer, and journalist

Fave Crafts: sewing, knitting, collage media art, painting, photography, book art, and more

More Info: www.ihanna.nu and ihanna.nu/blog

chapter twenty-six

Claudine Hellmuth

Claudine is one of the

many great people I've had the pleasure of meeting through my craft convention travels. Every time I see her, she's like a ray of sunshine, always with a positive attitude and a smiling face. Her artwork exudes happiness with its whimsical glory and playful application. She's made a name for herself spreading the collage gospel through workshops, books, DVDs, and her appearance on *The Martha Stewart Show*. She's an example of a child who loved paper, nurtured that love, and turned it into a successful business by following her passion. She chatted with me from her home in Washington, D.C., about finding her style, the challenges of being a professional artist, and what she loves most about crafting.

VH

VH: *What's your first craft-related memory?*

CH: I'm told that when I was really little, my mom used to spread around paper and finger paints and let me roll around in them—in my diaper! My first true memory, though, is when I was five or six. I decided I wanted to start a craft club for my neighborhood. I'd make up projects, and the neighborhood kids would come over to create them. I remember one project I organized: it was this pinecone Christmas tree thing that we glittered, decorated, and added little presents to go under it.

VH: *At that age, what made you think of organizing a craft club?*

CH: I have no idea! I had a name for the club and everything. It didn't last long, though. Mom said I lost enthusiasm once I realized how much work it took to organize and gather all of the supplies, which is kind of funny because those are the things I do when I teach my workshops now. Maybe that was my first workshop! My mom even helped me send out invitations, call all the moms, and plan the events.

VH: *You even had invitations? Did you make them?*

CH: Yes, they were all handmade from construction paper. I was way ambitious and wanted to have meetings every week but only ended up having two before they fizzled out.

That's my first real craft memory, although I was always making stuff. My mom wasn't into paper crafts but was very encouraging and helped me make things. She did teach me how to knit, which I really enjoyed.

VH: *Do you still knit?*

CH: No, I've forgotten how. She tried to teach me again over Thanksgiving, but I was all fingers and thumbs. I need to read a Vickie Howell book!

VH: *You know, I can help you with that. Was anybody else in your family crafty?*

CH: The German side of my family was full of artists and architects, but not really into crafting—more serious, academic-type stuff. I was really the only paper crafter in my immediate family. My grandma liked to crochet a lot.

VH: *Do you have a moment as a professional designer/crafter that stands out as much as the craft club memory from your childhood?*

CH: Oooh, that's deep! I have really fond memories of all of the private art classes I took when I was in high school. I have memories at all different stages, but I'm not sure if one stands out more than another.

VH: *Was there a moment when you realized, "Hey, I might be able to make a living at this," or "This is kind of a big deal that I'm a professional crafter"?*

CH: I think teaching my first workshop in Atlanta was pivotal. I hadn't taught professionally before, but people kept asking me to. At the time, I was working as a website designer. I finally gave in when this woman wouldn't take no for an answer. I taught a workshop and had a great time engaging with all the people and showing them my techniques. The whole experience of having a community that was created in the workshop was great. Then, when I got the check I was like, "Oh, wow. If I taught a bunch of these every year, maybe I could leave my day job." That really was a turning point, realizing that my workshops could help me segue from my day job to something else.

VH: *How did you come up with the content for these classes. Did you just wing it?*

CH: I just go through my way of working. As the way that I work changes, so do my workshops. For the first workshop, I simply made a list of a bunch of

> I think the most important thing is to just play and encourage people to experiment. I point out that it's just paint and paper, so paint over it, cut it up, or re-do it. Don't be afraid.

different techniques I love to work with: background techniques, transfer techniques, and things like that.

There aren't really any books out there about teaching these kinds of workshops. So, I read some business-y training-the-trainer books that contained some valuable information about engaging your audience, holding their attention, and breaking information into palatable bites. Then, I compiled all of that information and just taught the way I thought I would like to learn. It worked out, people liked it, and nobody booed me. I ended up getting laid off from my day job, but it was okay because after the success of the first class, I'd lined up a number of workshops that could tide me over for a while.

©claudine hellmuth

VH: *So, that's how your career really got started?*

CH: Yes. I mean, people in the art world already knew who I was because of some magazine articles that featured me. But after the workshops came the books, the product deals, and everything else.

VH: *Is there anyone in particular you credit for opening the crafty doors for you?*

CH: I would definitely say my mom and dad were very encouraging. As for getting known in my niche of the craft industry, I'd have to credit teaching at Art Fest. That was a big steppingstone for me, because people who hadn't heard of me before took my classes and got to know me. It spiraled out from there.

VH: *Did you go to art school?*

CH: Yes, I did. I graduated from the Corcoran College of Art and Design in D.C. I majored in fine art. Then, I had nothing to do to make money, so my mom suggested I take a class at George Washington University. There must've been some kind of divine intervention because I'd never even turned on a computer or used a mouse at that point (in 1997). We decided a Web development class would be a good thing. Once I finished, I had basic knowledge of PhotoShop and knew how to program a website. The Internet was so new that nobody else really knew what they were doing either, so I was able to get a job and learn as I worked.

VH: *Did you do a lot of collaging in school, then?*

> Crafters are really generous with their ideas and techniques; it's a really great community to be a part of for that reason.

243

©claudine hellmuth

CH: I did! Collage was part of my senior thesis at the Corcoran. They were really into mixed-media at the school and encouraged blending different things together. That was a great opportunity, because I was very traditional and thought I had to work only in oils, which is something I probably gained from the two years I spent at the Columbus College of Art and Design, a much more traditional school. I think if I'd stayed there, I'd be doing completely different stuff now, although I'm not sure how the Corcoran would feel about what I'm doing right now, either.

VH: *Wouldn't it be enough that you're able to make a living being an artist?*

CH: I don't know. I think there's some kind of stigma in the fine art world to have commercialized yourself.

VH: *This segues into what was going to be my next question. This is where the debate comes up about art* versus *craft and calling yourself an* artist *versus calling yourself a* crafter. *I'm curious because your medium, collage, can absolutely fit into both worlds. What's the difference, for you, between the two?*

CH: In a nutshell, for me, the difference between art and craft is this: It's art when you're making it your own, somehow. It's craft when you're copying someone else's pattern or design exactly, without veering away from it in any way, shape, or form.

VH: *That's interesting!*

CH: Yes, because even if you're making a scarf from a Vickie Howell pattern but changing up the colors and adding tassels, you're making it your own, so it's becoming art. If someone uses exactly the colors you chose in the pattern you chose, then I consider that crafting. There's nothing wrong with that—it's fun. I just always encourage people to make a slight twist so projects become uniquely theirs. That's what makes it exciting. Sometimes when you're first starting a craft, though, it's comforting to be able make something exactly as a template calls for.

VH: *Honestly, sometimes it's nice to be able to just follow a pattern. It's relaxing. Also (and this is different with knitting than with paper crafts), I like to see how other people write patterns and why they make the choices they do. It helps me continue learning.*

CH: Definitely. Especially when you're a professional at our level; it gets really tiring making so many decisions—sometimes the work can become un-fun. Sometimes it's nice to go back to something really simple and start from there, because it reminds you why you like to create. It kind of gets those juices flowing again, because I don't know about you, but sometimes I feel like I've got no ideas in my head.

VH: *Absolutely. What's your favorite thing about crafting?*

CH: My favorite thing is the making of stuff, and the feeling of raw materials. That even supersedes the end result of the project. It's the actual process of making something. The other thing I like about crafting is the community it creates, especially through the Internet. If we didn't have the Internet, I don't think we'd have what we have now.

VH: *I wouldn't have my career without the Internet.*

CH: Me either. Not at all. Being able to share pictures and tips with the community is really exciting. Crafters are really generous with their ideas and techniques; it's a really great community to be a part of for that reason.

VH: *Since collage is less of a mobile craft than others, how does the collage community manifest itself?*

CH: Really just through the Internet, for me. I meet with some fellow collage artists here in D.C., but it's mostly just to talk or do an art swap. That's usually how it works with paper crafters. It's not like knitting that you can take with you anywhere.

VH: *I've found that if people express themselves creatively in one way, they are likely interested in multiple forms of creativity. Do you find that to be true for yourself? Are there any non-handicraft, creative aspects to your life?*

CH: I wish I was one of those people. I'm always jealous of the creative types who are really balanced and diversified. I'm just really work-oriented. All other aspects of my life fall to the wayside.

VH: *What is the biggest challenge you've faced in trying to make a living through your craft?*

CH: Time management. I tend to fill my plate up so much, and then freak out and get migraines to get everything done.

> The other thing I like about crafting is the community it creates, especially through the Internet. If we didn't have the Internet, I don't think we'd have what we have now.

©claudine hellmuth

VH: *Do you, like me, get to the point where you fill your plate so much (partly because our industry doesn't pay very much, partly because we're driven) that you feel like you're letting everybody down later?*

CH: Yes! I'm kind of Type A. I always like to return e-mails on time and things like that. Now it's getting to where I might let e-mails sit for a couple of days or more, and I hate that about myself. I feel like I'm not able to do anything 100 percent. I'm juggling so many things at one time. It's hard to know what things you really have to say *yes* to, versus things that end up being time sucker-uppers. I'm struggling with that. I think I'll work on that theme next year—figuring out how many orders I can take and how many workshops I can teach while still making a living. Maybe that's just the nature of being a one-person business, thinking that each order may be your last. Instead of fitting things in when it's realistic, you just say, "Ok, I'll do it!"

VH: *You're probably best known for your Poppet images. What does your style and inspiration come from?*

CH: Those happened in about 2002. I had finished my first book, which focused more on Victorian-style collage that I'd been working on all through college. I was so burnt out. I didn't like my work. Everything just started looking pooh-y and ugly to me, so I started experimenting for at least a year, just making big messes. I remember I had these head photo images. When I was in college, I went through this phase where I made whimsical drawings. So, I started putting heads on top of those drawings and something just sort of clicked. I ended up spending another six to nine months messing around with them. I was doing this all on the side while I was doing my other work, until I was ready to show it to people.

My mom was concerned that I'd become known for a certain way of working, and that if I changed, people might not like it. Deciding what to do was a struggle. Some people got mad at me when I changed my style, but I was tired and something had to change.

VH: *Do you feel any sense of responsibility to spread a message among the craft community? If so, what is it?*

CH: I think the most important thing is to just play and encourage people to experiment. I point out that it's just paint and paper, so paint over it, cut it up, or re-do it. Don't be afraid. I think the reason more people aren't crafty is because there's some sort of inherent fear that it has to be perfect. I really encourage people to not worry about making the perfect piece for their living room, especially while they're learning new techniques. Really, if you're not playing or having a good time, then the work you're creating is not going to happen the way you want it to. You can't force it.

For more information about Claudine and her projects, go to:
www.collageartist.com

The Crafter's Studio

In the great tradition of *Inside the Actor's Studio* and James Lipton:

What craft sound or smell do you love?
The smell of gel medium.

What craft sound or smell do you hate?
I can't think of any. I love it all!

What career, other than craft-world domination, would you like to try?
Something with animals, but I don't know what.

When you cut yourself with a craft knife or ruin one of your designs, what is your favorite exclamation?
Sh@t! Sometimes I have the urge to hit Control V too, but then realize I'm not on the computer. It's really weird.

247

Words to Craft by:

I have always loved painting, drawing, and baking. This year I discovered a new medium that combines two of my favorite things: creating and eating cake! When I was in elementary school, my family always entered the school cake contest. My dad would plan an incredible cake sculpture to astound the masses. One year he made a castle, the next a grassy hill with a rainbow leading to a pot of gold. Our whole family would take part, adding our own special touches to his edible works of art.

Looking back, I realize that my inspiration comes from those moments with my family. Whether you create something out of your own passion or as a gift for someone else, creativity always stems from love. I do it because I enjoy seeing the excitement on someone's face when they see a cake I created especially for them—a bride beaming at her four-tier wedding cake with edible, hand-painted wildflowers, or a five-year-old with eyes widened as he sees a 3-D airplane cake. The joy I feel when creating is passed on to the recipient. For me, art and craft have always been wrapped up in love. Pass it on!

Name: Jaime Chapman

Age: 30

Digs: Austin, TX

Daily Grind: teacher and cake creator

Fave Crafts: painting and drawing on cakes

Words to Craft by:

I spent my career in antique malls and beauty salons. I loved designing business plans, decorating, and the excitement of putting it all together, but the monotonous routine always left me unfulfilled. At 50, I sold my last salon and wondered what to do with the rest of my life. I was not ready for the rocker! My friend and life coach Kathy Reed came to the rescue and said, "You should create something you love, not something that will burden you."

That was all I needed to hear. I dove in headfirst, made some really bad crafts, and did my first show where I met artists from the altered art world. A fellow artist showed me a copy of *Somerset Studio*, and I saw the light! For the next two years, I devoured every altered art zine and book I could buy, and thanks to artists like Claudine Hellmuth (see page 241), I found a rewarding way of life. I've even had the honor of being published. I'm a perfect example that you are never too old to find your passion and enjoy its blessings!

Name: Candyce Martens

Age: 53

Digs: Lake Villa, IL

Daily Grind: retired cosmetologist, salon owner, and antique dealer; currently a full-time artist

Fave Crafts: designer of altered art collages, assemblages, and window transfers

More Info: www.artisansball.com

chapter twenty-seven

Amanda Soule

Amanda, a.k.a. SouleMama, is a work-at-home mother and homeschooler to four children. She's a crafter in the most organic sense, using creativity to inspire, nurture, and enrich. As a writer, she's encapsulated that spirit with two family-oriented books and an inspirational blog that speaks almost as gospel to a community of mothers. She reaches out to a large community, rallying them to participate in causes that turn craft into service for other mothers in need. From her home in Portland, Maine, we spoke about parenting, *craftivism*, and finding one's own creative niche.

VH

VH: *What's your first craft-related memory?*

AS: My first craft-related memory is spending time with my grandmother, who was a professional seamstress. I would spend weekends with her during my childhood, and we would go to JoAnn Fabrics together on Friday nights to pick out a pattern and fabric. I'd go home with her and spend time in her sewing room, where we would sew all weekend, and talk and visit. At the end of the weekend, I would go home with something we made together. She sewed for people—she would quilt, make clothing, do mending, and things like that.

VH: *Is there a moment from your childhood connected to craft that really stands out for you?*

AS: Those weekends were super profound for me—the feeling of starting with nothing and having these materials that we would transform into something that was so useful and practical. The connection we had together was really important for me growing up. I grew up in a relatively large family where I was the oldest. It was just a powerful experience for me to make things.

VH: *Who, if anyone, do you credit for opening the crafty doors for you?*

AS: My grandmother was first person I would credit with opening my eyes to all the possibilities of crafting. I credit my thrifty nature to my other grandmother. Combined, they both influenced the work I do today.

VH: *Who inspires you professionally?*

AS: I'm hugely inspired by the blog world, for sure. It's sort of an ongoing motivation. I'm inspired by everyday crafters, in a way, more than professional or traditional art. I'm also inspired by people who just kind of make creativity work for their families, and find a way to carve it into their everyday lives.

VH: *We're at a unique place in time right now, when more and more mothers are able to work from home, so they can also be present in their kids' daily lives. Thanks to the Internet and Web stores, it's also becoming more common for moms to bring in extra family income via craft. You've done both. Please tell me about how you took your passion for being creative and turned it into a livelihood.*

AS: Interesting. We are definitely at a time when it's much more uncommon than it was for our parents' generation, or even before that, to have one parent working. It's more of a reality to have two parents in the workforce—it's helpful, but also necessary. For me, the passion for what I do sort of led the way. If I had to set out a plan, I would not have known how to go about that. Crafting was important for me because creating and making things were essential for my sanity and survival as a mom while I was at home with little ones. The career happened as a result—it was a case of following my heart. Hopefully the money will also follow.

VH: *Do you have an art school background?*

AS: No, I do not. I have a writing background.

VH: *What was your first professional crafting break?*

AS: I started knitting when my first son was born about nine years ago. My friends told me to sell my things—I would sell them to friends here and there, or at craft sales, but it just wasn't my speed. It was still pretty early on in the craft show world, before there were any Renegade Fairs and Bazaar Bizarres. The craft fairs I attended had totally different styles from what I was making. It just wasn't the right fit for me, so I started writing a blog, and from that, I started selling things here and there. I was approached by a publisher to write my first book. I would say that moment of being approached was my big step up.

VH: *You said you were making different things at craft fairs. What were you making?*

AS: I was mostly knitting funky, pixie-shaped hats, mittens, and scarves. The craft fairs were more about country chic décor. It was not my thing; it was a whole different craft vibe.

VH: *Is there one craft that speaks more to you creatively than others?*

AS: I consider myself a master of none of them. I love writing and consider it one of my crafty endeavors, because it's the thing that connects all the other crafts—so, I continue writing. I get super passionate about whatever it is I'm doing at the time. All winter, I spend time knitting. In the spring, I have a huge quilting urge. It changes with the seasons, with what I have available to me, and what I can make.

VH: *Is there any craft you're not interested in?*

AS: No, I don't think so.

VH: *What's your favorite thing about crafting?*

AS: The mindfulness that it brings to my day in the world of parenting and homeschooling four children that are home a lot. It is so helpful for me to have something tangible at the end of the day that I've made—not only to put my

> ❞
> I'm hugely inspired by the blog world, for sure. It's sort of an ongoing motivation. I'm inspired by everyday crafters, in a way, more than professional or traditional art.

mind, my spirit, and all my energy into something, but also to use my hands. It's really meditative, and to get something useful on the other end of it meets a lot of needs for me.

VH: *What role, if any, has crafting played in your own sense of community?*

AS: It's played an amazing role, particularly when I think of the online community. I would not be where I am if not for my online community. It gives me motivation, energy, and inspiration, just knowing readers are into the same things that I am. I've been able to make a career for myself, but beyond that, I also find community with a knitting group that I've been meeting with for eight years, every other week. It's a huge part of my social life and parenting life. Amazing friendships formed through this thread, and we're bound to each other through our love of crafts.

VH: *What are your favorite types of crafts to work on?*

AS: I do a lot of embroidery and sewing. I really like quick sewing projects. I need instant gratification, so I don't do any long-term quilting projects. I love projects that I can sit down and finish in one sewing session.

VH: *Something I haven't focused on much in this book, but would like to, concerns family as community. You nurture the crafty aspect of that on your blog and your book,* The Creative Family. *What does family as community mean to you, and how can crafting together as a family strengthen that union?*

AS: Crafting is definitely a foundation of our family and how we spend time together. When you create a space in which everybody is able to create together—in a way that is not overly structured, so that it's very open—I believe our true selves shine. It's not a task or a job; it's just who we are. It allows us to see each other in a unique way. Crafting together is pretty amazing because it nurtures our relationships.

VH: *Are any of your children not receptive to being creative?*

AS: They all have very specific, individual interests when it comes to what they want to do. One of them is very interested in traditional art—he likes to paint and draw. Another one is more tactile and engineer-like. He spends days playing with cardboard and duct tape. I think it's important to have many different choices for them in the home. They have free reign of some of the craft space, but there are some projects that require a little too much energy and clean up—I keep those on my top shelf.

VH: *Have you taught your children to knit?*

AS: I have. My eight-year-old is knitting a little bit. He knits scarves for all his stuffed animals. My six-year-old is way into the knitting tower (basically making

> When you create a space in which everybody is able to create together—in a way that is not overly structured, so that it's very open—I believe our true selves shine.

I-cords over, over, and over), which is fun for a child of that age. Finger-knitting is popular, too.

VH: *What do you hope your children gain from growing up in a creative home?*

AS: I think it gives them a sense that they can do whatever they want. They can have the imagination and energetic resources to make anything happen—to take the idea of crafting projects into a life they want for themselves.

VH: *Do you have any advice for parents who have a hard time juggling family and being creative?*

AS: My biggest advice is to start small and don't get wrapped up in the crazy expectation of spending days together making things. Just start by carving out little pockets of time where you can create together. That means turning off the computer, the television, the phone, and all that external stuff that can intrude. Families really need to make space for crafting, even if it's just an hour each week for a nature walk, drawing time, painting, or something like that.

VH: *Did the birth of your fourth child affect the time that you crafted with your other children?*

"

I love writing and consider it one of my crafty endeavors, because it's the thing that connects all the other crafts—so, I continue writing. I get super passionate about whatever it is I'm doing at the time.

AS: It did. Right now he is small enough that I can put him in the swing, but pretty soon, he'll be crawling; I think it's going to get harder before it gets easier. We have a pretty flexible work schedule, and we have some family days together, which are great, because two adults are a lot easier than one.

VH: *Is your husband creative in any way?*

AS: He is. He's got a really creative spirit. He isn't very creative in a crafty kind of way, but he's a very mindful guy. He's a great model for the kids.

VH: *You were talking about your background as a writer being connected to crafts. Do you find that writing or photography fill the same creative space as knitting or sewing?*

AS: I'm not sure that they do. I think that together they fill all the pieces, for whatever reason. That idea may be beyond what I can fully intellectualize or comprehend. There are times when I'm more drawn to one than the other; sometimes my need to paint is stronger than my need to take a picture. I don't know, I think I find a nice balance between writing, sewing, knitting, or handicraft. In writing my blog and book, it became obvious that when I go back and forth too much, I don't get anything written. It's better if I start with crafting and end up writing, or vice versa. They kind of work hand in hand; they feed each other.

VH: *You recently put global community in action by starting a project called Mama to Mama. Can you tell me about it?*

AS: I started it about a year ago, as an act of connecting mothers worldwide through *craftivism*. There are so many reasons why we craft: out of necessity, love, or for pleasure. And we craft, sometimes, to bring a little peace to our lives, our hearts, and our everyday moments. Taking that just a step further, we can—and do, like so many crafters before us—turn our crafting into peace for the world beyond our homes. The simple act of creating something with intention and heart for someone in need can have a beautiful effect on the lives of others. We can, indeed, do something to create a more just and peaceful world, all with the simple, mindful, and crafty work of our hands.

Mama to Mama's first project was a newborn hat and blanket set that went into safe birthing kits in Haiti. We collected over 5,000 caps, which was crazy, especially when they were all in my dining room!

VH: *Wow, that's really incredible. There's such strength in the craft community. I love that you've found a way to harness an aspect of it and funnel it where it's needed most. By the time this book comes out, you will have released another book based on the home. Can you tell me about the inspiration behind the book, and what you hope readers with families take from it?*

AS: *Handmade Home* features project for the family home, all based on repurposed

> Mama to Mama's first project was a newborn hat and blanket set that went into safe birthing kits in Haiti. We collected over 5,000 caps, which was crazy, especially when they were all in my dining room!

and vintage materials. A huge component of it is teaching people how to use what they have, and how to find thrifty, vintage materials. That idea was very important to me—it also inspired a chapter in *The Creative Family* called The Resourceful Family, which was about using what you have, and covered a different generation of DIY thinking—making things instead of buying them. That's where it started, and I incorporated useful things that I have in my house for my family and children.

A lot of the projects can actually be done with children, or involve making something for them. They are all pretty quick, because I had to be realistic in terms of family life and available time together. My hope is to bring inspiration to readers to think twice about buying something new. I want to help people make things for themselves for so many reasons: environmental, social, historical, and conservation. Making things doesn't have to involve spending a lot of money. We can fill our homes with things we value in so many other ways.

VH: *Is there anything else you'd like to say about what crafting means to you or has given you personally?*

AS: I think we've talked about the importance of crafting in my daily life—the meditative aspect is huge.

For more information about Amanda and her projects, go to:
www.soulemama.com

The Crafter's Studio

In the great tradition of *Inside the Actor's Studio* and James Lipton:

What craft sound or smell do you love?
I love the sound of a needle poking through the linen when embroidering.

What craft sound or smell do you hate?
Fusible interfacing.

What career, other than creative family-world domination, would you like to try?
I would love to be a singer.

When you spill paint or prick your finger with a pin, what is your favorite exclamation?
Dammit.

Words to Craft by:

I'm a late bloomer to the crafting scene (I didn't actually start until January 2008!), so my poor mother, all this time, has been lamenting that she's failed me. Well, better late than never, I say, and I seem to have arrived with a vengeance! It's almost as if I'm making up for lost time. I love to work on little pieces.

Most of the crafts I do are handiwork size, so I take 'em with me on the go. One of my favorite things about portable craft is that I *can* take it with me and share it with people around me. I drive public buses, so while I'm waiting at the station to go on a new trip, I'll whip out some embroidery, or a teddy arm that needs to be attached to a body, or a softie head that needs a nice big smile. A few people each day ask what I'm doing, and I explain my love of all things crafty. I'd like to consider, in some small way, that I'm helping to bring crafting back to the community—like a crafting ninja! One day, I hope to have a whole crafting bus full of crafting people, and we'll drive around and listen to music while we stitch, and bead, and knit, and sew.

Name: Holly McGuire

Age: 23

Digs: Melbourne, Australia

Daily Grind: University student and part-time bus driver. Unfortunately we don't have the cool yellow school buses down here!

Fave Crafts: Embroidery, and softie, bag making, patchwork (too scared to attempt a quilt!), material hoarding.

More Info: twocheeseplease@livejournal.com

Words to Craft by:

I have been knitting, crocheting, and sewing since childhood. When my daughter was born, I became engrossed in designing and knitting dresses for her and her Barbie Dolls. Then, when my son became of age, I made him a six-foot Dr. Who scarf that he so coveted. I took quilting lessons, combined quilting with knitting, and created wearable art. I experimented with freeform crochet and made a wall hanging.

Name: Elaine Frankonis

Age: 68

Digs: New Paltz, NY

Daily Grind: retired eight years ago from a position in the New York State Education Department; since then, full-time caregiver for my 92-year-old mother with dementia

Fave Crafts: knitting, crocheting, sewing, designing, and combining them all

More Info: www.kalilily.net

Now, as my mother's caregiver, I have less time and energy to be truly creative. I have at least five projects started that I've had to set aside because the patterns required a lot of attention to detail. So, I've started a lightweight crocheted afghan that's the same stitch over and over again. There is something about the rhythm of the half-double crochet that's mesmerizing and mentally relaxing. I can sit in the middle of a raging familial storm and rise above it on the rhythms of the repeating stitch mantra. I breathe in with the yarn-overs, breathe out with the pull-through loops. At this point in my stressed and frustrated life, crocheting is my link to stability and sanity.

chapter twenty-eight

Faythe Levine

I was introduced to Faythe at a Renegade Craft Fair in Brooklyn a few years back. She was there with her camera, working on the beginnings of what would become her successful documentary, *Handmade Nation*. I'm thrilled with the response that Faythe has gotten and the positive impact her work has had on the community as a whole. She's a creative spirit with the focused goal of offering a visual explanation of this wonderful DIY movement we're all a part of.

VH

VH: *Do you come from a crafty family?*

FL: I come from a very creatively supportive family. My mom has been in the natural food industry for my entire life, so for people who think of cooking as crafty, then yes. Neither of my parents ever said no to me if I wanted to try a new creative interest. They were so supportive of that! I think that had a huge, huge impact on who I became. Also, both of my parents are self-employed, so I came from a home where I saw how much work it takes to create your own business and the gratification that can come out of it. Above and beyond anything, my parents showed me what I could do with my life.

VH: *Which is such a unique gift. I think that because of the Internet, the next generation will have a lot more experience with self-employed parents, but for our generation, it was fairly rare. It was still very much the time of the 30-year gold watch, so a lot of us have had to learn how to be self-employed by fledging through.*

What's your first craft-related memory?

FL: Friendship bracelets and lanyards at Girl Scout camp.

VH: *Do you have a moment related to craft from your childhood that will always stick with you—something that had enough of impact that it led you towards a creative career?*

FL: I'm an only child, so I was in a lot of after-school programs and summer day camps. Camp programming had a huge influence on the time I spent working on projects. My aunt is an artist and art teacher, so I also have very specific memories of being at her house, watching her make a lot of papier-mâché projects. I think she was the first person I ever saw do big, sculptural work. I thought it was really cool and wanted to be like her. I think the combination of those two occasions set the tone for the crafty side of me. Then, when I was 10 years old, my parents enrolled me in a black-and-white photography class. That was my first exposure to working in a darkroom—it was awesome.

VH: *Is there a creative medium that speaks more to you than others?*

FL: I've moved through a lot of different media over the course of the last 15 years. I've done a lot of mixed media collage work and moved into working with textiles. Then I started working on the film *Handmade Nation* and didn't have time to do anything but that. Because that took up three years, I'm not really sure what speaks to me right now. I'm kind of waiting to see what I'll be into next.

VH: *I was actually going to ask you that. With the craziness of your current career, are you still able to make time for crafting?*

FL: Not so much. If there was ever time to work on something, I'd sew banners for craft fairs. I have a couple of really nice embroidered and appliquéd felt banners that I've made. Any downtime I had over the past few years, I spent making things applicable to *Handmade Nation*. Right before I started working on the film, I was doing a lot of stretched fabric pieces with hand-sewn sequins and appliqué. Sometimes when I'm flying, if I don't have to work on the plane, I'll do some embroidery or other needlework.

VH: *Did you go to art school or did you just come into all of this organically?*

FL: All organically. I actually haven't gone to any college. It's all self-motivated and self-taught.

VH: *I love hearing that because it's fairly similar to my path. Interviewing everyone for this book has shown how varied everyone's backgrounds are in terms of education, but they're not as varied in terms of family—as far as where their creative roots came from. Some people have master's degrees in fine art, while others went to community college like me. A lot of us, though, have the same types of memories of crafting with a relative or making something at camp. I think that's something really unique to this industry. The common thread among us is more about personal experiences, rather than paths of training.*

FL: Wow, that's interesting!

> My main motivation for making the documentary was that I felt like I was witnessing this amazing thing going on. I just wanted to capture the energy that all of us had, and that we were giving to each other and giving back to our community.

258

VH: *Did you always know that you'd make a living being creative?*

FL: I knew that I never wanted to be in the same place everyday. I knew there was no way I could sit in an office with a Monday through Friday routine. What I did was just create a lifestyle around what I was comfortable doing. When I'm home, I work at my store, and we have regular shop hours, but my travel schedule for tours and tutorials allows me to break up my schedule quite a bit.

VH: *Since I've never been able to make it out there, tell me a little bit about your store.*

FL: Paper Boat Boutique & Gallery opened in June of 2005, co-owned by me and my business partner, Kim Kisiolek. Kim and I had worked together at a coffee shop at one point, and then she worked for me when I had my company, Flying Fish Designs. We realized that we worked well together and that Milwaukee was missing a retail space where you could interact with all the goods you can find online. We had the idea to start a business, and within six months, we found a space and opened up the shop. Because I already had so many connections through the art fair I help coordinate (Art vs. Craft), my Flying Fish Designs company, and all of my online friends, it was fairly simple to get vendors involved. We work with about 250 vendors in the retail part of the store, and we have a small gallery space where I curate six to eight shows a year.

VH: *It sounds like you're doing exactly what you want to be doing.*

FL: Yes, it's good. So far, I'm really happy with what we've done.

VH: *Your documentary* Handmade Nation *focuses on the rise of the DIY movement. Making that film, what did you learn about why so many of us have gone back to making things ourselves?*

FL: A lot of what I learned reiterated what I was hoping to hear. There are people who want to have control over their own lives and feel empowered by making their lifestyle choices. Having the ability to shape their work around what works for them and their families is a big motivator.

VH: *Your film features independent crafters pretty exclusively. Why did you feel it was so important to place the focus there?*

FL: I think it was because that was the community I was immersed in. A question that people often ask me is how I picked the people that I wanted to interview for the film. It's the people I was working with; the people I was connected to; and the people I was excited about giving exposure to. My main motivation for making the documentary was that I felt like I was witnessing this amazing thing going on. I just wanted to capture the energy that all of us had, and that we were giving to each other and giving back to our community. I think it was really just as simple as featuring the people I was lucky enough to get to know when I first came into the whole scene.

VH: *So there wasn't any statement being made about this emerging group of people in the craft world?*

FL: There was and there is, but because it was the community I was looking to document, I felt like it explained itself. My intention was to show my audience that these crafters were doing this type of work on their own terms, and this is a way that you can lead your life if you so choose. My interest wasn't to explore outside of that.

VH: *Did you find a common bond among these crafters that maybe you wouldn't have if you'd stepped out of the indie world?*

FL: I was actually really surprised at some of the lifestyle differences that everyone had. I personally come from a pretty liberal, radical background. My gateway drug to DIY was the underground punk scene. I knew that not everyone was coming out of punk, but I was surprised at how conservative some people were. Not that it's an issue if someone's religious or whatever, I just didn't expect people to tell me that they craft with their church groups. What I realized was that the common bond between us is that we can't imagine a life without making something. That was really interesting for me. Although the indie community is very progressive and liberal as a whole, *indie* is just an umbrella term that fosters all different types of people who follow the movement.

> What I realized was that the common bond between us is that we can't imagine a life without making something.

VH: *I was recently talking to one of the bigwigs of the Crafts & Hobbies Association and was surprised to hear that even this many years into the current craft movement, the interpretation of indie style is still so varied. Did you have the same experience while making your movie? If so, do you hope that both the film and accompanying book will help clarify some misconceptions that may exist?*

FL: I think there is an aesthetic that is lumped into what *indie* means. I actually think it's starting to change a bit, as people grow into their style and process a little more. I also can't tell if I just think of a certain aesthetic because I'm removing myself from part of the community and looking for stuff that's different—I'm burnt out on seeing the same things all of the time.

A big part of why I wanted to make the film is because it's so difficult to explain, still, what indie craft is, or what the movement is about. I wanted the film, and, in turn, the book, to be for the community, but I also wanted them to be tools people could use as a way of explaining the scene to others outside of it—visual learning tools. It's been really exciting because a lot of museums and schools have responded to the film and are interested in showing it, so I feel like I accomplished that goal.

VH: *You're a curator and one of your creative media is photography, but your most recent projects focus on craft. For you, what's the difference between art and craft?*

FL: It's funny—I use the words totally interchangeably when I give lectures and do interviews. It throws people off, but I don't really care. I feel like there definitely is a time and place for the argument, and I understand it from an academic perspective. It's really frustrating to not be able to define something, especially when people are writing about it. My interest lies more with the fact that people are creatively motivated. That's what's important to me. It's so hard to get people to do anything anymore, and I'm so excited that people are making and creating work—setting a goal, reaching that point, and then sharing it with other people. That's really going to save us as a human race. The dialogue that happens around a creative community is so healthy, especially within the indie world. That's what's important to me, not the definition of what lies within a specific category.

VH: *The underlying theme of this book is community via craft. How do you see your role in the current craft movement and community?*

FL: I've always been someone who's had really good communication and networking skills. Really, over the last three years, I've honed in on that within the craft community—being able to connect a maker with a gallery, or a museum with a craft writer. I guess my role is just as a curator of information.

VH: *Do you feel any sense of responsibility as a feminist woman in a traditionally female community to use your voice as a forum for progression?*

FL: I do, but it's not my overt goal. I became exposed to the whole punk scene in the early '90s during the Riot Grrl movement. It was something I identified with as a woman. It was really exciting to know there were other women who were starting bands and supporting each other through a music community. So, when I stumbled across the DIY community, I was thrilled that it was a creative arts community comprised mostly of women, which isn't what the art world is. I'm hesitant to say I have a feminist agenda, but I like supporting the ladies. It's surprising how much women still get overlooked—without it being totally the point of what I'm doing, feminism is definitely part of it.

For more information about Faythe and her projects, go to:
www.handmadenationmovie.com

I'm so excited that people are making and creating work—setting a goal, reaching that point, and then sharing it with other people. That's really going to save us as a human race.

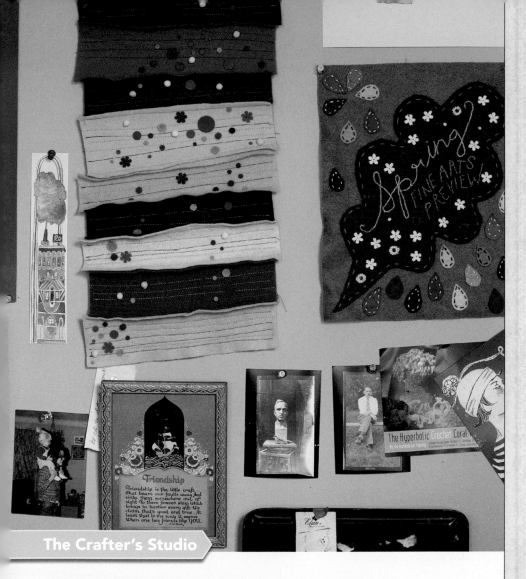

The Crafter's Studio

In the great tradition of *Inside the Actor's Studio* and James Lipton::

What craft sound or smell do you love?
I love the weird smell of Mod Podge.

What craft sound or smell do you hate?
Hmmm, I don't know if there is one.

What career, other than craft-world domination, would you like to try?
A job where I get paid.

When you burn yourself with a glue gun or cut yourself with with a craft knife, what is your favorite exclamation?
Oh, sh*t!

Words to Craft by:

I have been crafting since I can remember. I held my first exhibition at age five, when I hung a string across my doorway, pegged up a bunch of paintings, and bullied my family members into buying one. A few years ago, I discovered that puppet making is craft under another name. Foam, fur, and hot glue are the same no matter what you're building. This made me ridiculously happy, and through this discovery, I ended up working on the huge monster puppets in Spike Jonze's upcoming movie *Where The Wild Things Are*.

I am currently curating an exhibition called "Totem, Dolls with Souls" for the Fringe Festival in Melbourne. I'm asking artists to create self-portrait dolls depicting their inner feelings. I'm interested in showcasing the resurging craft movement, as well as finding out how people think about themselves. I am constantly knitting things—a new doll every couple of days. I've knitted robots, monsters (both mythical and movie), an anatomically correct heart, a camera and film, a book, and I'm currently knitting burlesque dancers, and saints. I am a photographer by degree, a prop maker by trade, and an art mercenary by choice.

Name: **Sayraphim Lothian**

Age: 31

Digs: Melbourne, Australia

Daily Grind: artist and curator

Fave Crafts: knitting (dolls!) and sewing

More Info: www.sayraphimlothian.com

Words to Craft by:

I was born an artist. One of my earliest memories was drawing in the pages of my parents' encyclopedia. I made bold, sweeping strokes with my crayons. My next childhood memory was the spanking that followed, which didn't deter me, because I later drew in the family Bible.

I recently built a shrine in my Spanish-style home. Dedicated to the Saint of Lower Electric Bills, the altar incorporates a thermostat and rests on cherry columns. I used delicately-shaped light bulbs for finials; a light socket became a candleholder; and Reddy Kilowatt and Thomas Edison memorabilia went into the mix. It makes me smile every time I see it, and there's been a marked difference in our electric bills.

Now I'm making fairy doors, which require woodworking, painting, sculpting, and (just as important) allowing my adult mind to think like a child. Now that I have been doing it for awhile, I sometimes marvel at a new memory of some forgotten innocence (or mischief) and view it as a blessing.

Name: **Elizabeth Mericas**

Age: 58

Digs: Austin, TX

Daily Grind: Doing art and selling it. Before that, I was a food critic, and a legal secretary. My worst job was working for a finance company. I once repossessed a TV while the family was watching it.

Fave Crafts: woodworking, found objects, and painting

chapter twenty-nine

Mary Engelbreit

Illustrator, entrepreneur, and founder of the award-winning magazine, *Mary Engelbreit's Home Companion*, Mary is a household name in the mainstream creative world. A veteran in the crafting industry, she's turned her recognizable drawing style into a billion-dollar licensing empire built on a house of cards—greeting cards, that is! I have great respect for Mary's professional journey, some of which we discussed from her studio in St. Louis, Missouri.

VH

VH: *Did you grow up in a crafty family?*

ME: No, I didn't. Although I don't really consider myself crafty now, I was the only one who liked to make stuff when I was growing up. My parents were very supportive and always had tons of craft supplies and drawing supplies around the house. A lady in the neighborhood was giving little painting lessons, so I participated. My parents were really, really supportive, but they didn't do crafts, and neither did either one of my sisters.

VH: *Did you just start doing things on your own, and they recognized that and were supportive?*

ME: Right, right!

VH: *What's your first craft-related memory?*

ME: Well, let's see. I remember making a book of all horse pictures. I drew all the horses, and I turned it into a book and made a cover out of cardboard. I thought it was absolutely beautiful.

VH: *Do you still have it?*

ME: You know, I don't. My sister and I were just talking about it. My mother never threw anything like that away—I know that it kicked around for a long time, but somewhere along the line, it got lost.

VH: *Have you done any more bookbinding in your career?*

ME: I did a book once; a while ago, I wrote a little poem called *Queen of the Cupcake*. I showed the original art at a show here in St. Louis, and then I printed and bound the books myself. I had all my friends over, and we bound them all ourselves with just ribbons. A couple of them were black and white. A few of them I hand-colored, and we tied the ribbons with all these cute little charms and things.

VH: *How can you say that you're not crafty?*

ME: I do make stuff, but not like all that cool stuff.

VH: *Don't you feel that you are a jumping-off point of inspiration for a lot of people?*

ME: Well, that could be true, which is very nice. A lot of people tell me that. So that's very nice to hear.

> **"**
>
> A little light bulb went off, and I realized how these things work—you sell things over and over.

VH: *Who, if anyone, do you credit for opening the professional creative doors for you?*

ME: Nobody. I mean, I didn't go to art school. I didn't like school. I don't really know what I read about getting into an art school, but they said you had to have a portfolio. I didn't even know what a portfolio was, and I had no idea how to put one together. Now, looking back, I realize I could have done it. I had tons of stuff, but I didn't really know, and neither did my parents. I just did not want to go to school.

I got a job at an art supply store here in town, because I lied and said that I would take a year off and then go to school. So, I met working artists at the store, and I learned how to use all these different supplies. It was like mini art school.

And then I got a job with a tiny advertising agency (and I mean tiny). It was the owner and me. He did the design work, and I did the illustration. I did that for a couple of years, which was great, because I learned all about the business of doing art. That was another great course in my non-existent schooling. And

then I just started freelancing. The owner left town, and I took over a lot of our clients. I started doing all these crazy little drawings on my own. I had a show in a local bookstore. Really, it just grew. I took advantage of every opportunity that came along.

VH: *Did you take any formal classes for illustration?*

ME: No.

VH: *How did you develop your style?*

ME: I taught myself to draw. I copied, and I had a lot of my mother's and grandmother's books from when they were little. My mother read to us all the time—every night, in fact. My family was big into reading. I had a lot of great old picture books from the '20s, '30s, and '40s. I copied those pictures, or I'd draw my own images for the stories she read to us. I was using the illustrations as a guide.

VH: *How would you describe that style?*

ME: Kind of vintage-cartoony. I tried to put a little humor in the drawings—they have an old fashioned look, but they say something funny. Another big influence came from old fairy tale books; they have illustrations with quotes underneath. When I started drawing, even when I was little, I would put some kind of quote or some words or something on the drawing. When I first started freelancing, doing greeting cards, I put quotes on my cards, which at the time, nobody was doing.

VH: *Do the same things inspire you now that did then, when you were flipping though those books?*

ME: Yes, actually, they do; arts-and-crafts style, art nouveau, and art deco. They're still my favorites to look at.

VH: *Is your main character—the little girl seen on most of your products—is she a version of you?*

ME: Well, yes, she is the only recurring character that I draw. I've drawn her since I was little, and yes, she does represent me.

VH: *How you were able to take your passion for drawing and turn it into a high-profile career?*

ME: I couldn't really imagine doing anything else. When I started having shows at the bookstore, I realized that people really loved the drawings. We had big crowds at these shows. I thought I'd like to illustrate children's books, and a friend of mine was in publishing, so he set up some interviews. I went up to New York with my little portfolio that I had now figured out how to set up. Book illustrations don't happen that way now—they don't take people off the street.

But the publishers saw me, and they were all so nice. One of them suggested that I do greeting cards, which was kind of funny because I was already doing greeting cards. I created handmade cards for a store in St. Louis that would order three dozen at a time, so I had already been doing that. I didn't realize that greeting card companies are always waiting for stuff to come in. They are always looking for the next new thing.

I sent some stuff to a company and right away, they started selling my work. I did that for two or three different companies. Then I decided (not realizing what I was getting into) that I could do more things the way I wanted to if I started my own greeting card company. I took my little array of cards up to the stationery show—I would just hear about these things, you know. You learn about things as you go, and I would take advantage of anything I heard about.

VH: *When you say that you started your own greeting card company, were you putting together a business plan and getting a loan, or was it just you and your cards?*

ME: No, I met somebody at a party—Bob Panke. He didn't know anything about art or greeting cards, but he had started a lot of businesses. I was talking to him about my idea at the party, and he thought it sounded fun. He came on as partner. Bob knew about borrowing money, which I did not, so he set up the company and got me going. He was very helpful. He and I took the cards up to the stationery show, and that's when somebody approached us to do a calendar. Then a little light bulb went off, and I realized how these things work—you sell things over and over. Bob went off to do other things, because he preferred starting businesses, not running them. So then my husband came on as a partner. He was in social work, but I talked him into leaving, and he came on. We started an art and licensing business, and it just took off.

VH: *At what point does the magazine come in?*

ME: We started the magazine 11 years ago. Some friends of mine were talking— we were all very much into home decorating. We all have cool houses, and we would buy decorating books that would come out. We would look at them and think about how we knew people with much cooler houses. We were not seeing what we wanted to see. They were way over-decorated—professionally decorated.

So we put out some books with Andrew McNeil, who does my calendars. When some of our decorating books did well, we thought, wouldn't it be fun to put out a magazine. Andrew McNeil was very receptive to the idea at that time. It was 15 years ago, or a little more. I don't think it would happen today, but it happened then, and it was fun. We started the magazine with only one issue. It was difficult to get advertising for just one issue when publishers like Hearst or Meredith can offer ads in seven or eight different publications. It was a very successful magazine; we're really sorry to see it go. The economy killed it along with many other decorating magazines.

VH: *Do you think you are going to find a buyer for it?*

ME: We did not find a buyer for it. The global list was sold to Martha Stewart, so anybody who had a subscription to our magazine is now getting *Martha Stewart* magazine. I own the name and the concept—I'm hoping to revive it when the economy recovers.

> "
>
> I could spend all day on Etsy looking at that stuff. I mean, it's like an addiction. There is such great stuff out there, and I love that.

VH: *What was your main goal with the magazine, when it came to how crafting and being creative was perceived by the public?*

ME: We were always making stuff for our homes: painting furniture, sewing curtains, and making cute things, and we just felt like a lot of other people were doing that as well. Our goal was to show the types of houses that real people lived in—houses that were actually decorated by the people who lived in them, and not places that called in a decorator and ordered expensive fabric. We wanted to show more handcrafted homes.

VH: *What's the biggest challenge in running a magazine?*

ME: Ads. If you don't have ads, you don't have a magazine. Ads were always a challenge. Of course, toward the end, what put everyone out of business is when the housing market failed. All those people who used to advertise in the shelter magazines stopped advertising. All the flooring, roofing, painting businesses— when all those people have a bad year, the first thing they drop is advertising. They all closed, but they'll come back.

VH: *Your list of licensed products is seemingly endless. Which of your lines has been the most fun to develop?*

ME: I like doing children's books. We have a beautiful series of dolls by Robert Tonner. He takes the designs right off the cards. The details are so beautiful. It's probably my favorite license. Then we have wonderful licenses with Leisure Arts and Plaid. They create these darling kits for making felt ornaments and centerpieces. The details are so beautiful. Most of them are a lot of fun to develop.

VH: *What's the most difficult part about working with outside companies, in terms of bringing your vision into fruition?*

ME: Every once in awhile there's somebody who we feel doesn't really get it. We feel they put the wrong designs on something. Usually it's a very collaborative effort, and everybody wants the best thing. We like the people we work with, and they like the designs. It's generally pretty fun.

VH: *What changes have you seen in the craft industry over the years?*

ME: I think it's including a lot more people. The Craft & Hobby Association trade show was the only show whose attendance was up. I think that's because they've made crafting so much more acceptable to everybody. Everybody is just so passionate about being there, and people are really into what they do. They are excited about new processes and supplies. It's just a really personal thing.

VH: *What do you think about the current DIY movement?*

> My family was big into reading. I had a lot of great old picture books from the '20s, '30s, and '40s. I copied those pictures, or I'd draw my own images for the stories my mother read to us.

ME: I think it's great. They have cute things out there. I could spend all day on Etsy looking at that stuff. I mean, it's like an addiction. There is such great stuff out there, and I love that.

VH: *You got your professional start in the '70s—how do you think the perception of women in the creative industries has changed over the past 30 years?*

ME: I never had a problem, so I don't know; it just never was an issue with me. There were never any problems, and I never noticed any discrimination or anything. I really can't speak to that.

VH: *Your background is as an illustrator, but is there another craft that speaks to you just as creatively?*

ME: There are a lot of things that I would like to try. I never learned to paint. I would like to paint, and I wish I knew how to sew. I bought a sewing machine; I thought I'd teach myself how to do it, but the sewing machine is still in the box. There are a lot of things that I would like to try, but I just haven't yet. I used to embroider all the time. When my husband and I were dating, I embroidered all his shirts and my blue jeans. I embroidered the kids' stuff when they were babies, but I haven't done that in awhile either.

VH: *The underlying theme of this book is community. What role, if any, has crafting played in your own sense of community? What outlet has enriched your own community the most?*

ME: The magazine was especially important. We were so lucky to be able to connect with all these people around the country. It is so funny, because you meet one person doing some cool thing, and they say, if you like this, you should meet so and so. It just grows and grows and grows. If we could put that magazine out from now to the end of time, we would have that many people. It just breaks my heart to not be able to showcase talented people that I meet. We are going to have seminar a year from now, a Home Companion seminar with instructors, classes, and speakers. We hope to jumpstart the magazine again.

VH: *Are you part of the online community?*

ME: No, I'm just figuring that out. I get on those blogs, and it's just a time sucker. I'm almost afraid to get on the computer. I get so involved in looking at all that great stuff that I can only do it when I have a certain amount of time.

VH: *As a crafty pioneer, I was wondering if you have any advice for artists who are hoping to build their own crafty empire?*

ME: Well, you have to surround yourself with people who support you. You can't have people around who discourage your efforts. I was fortunate to have nothing but support growing up and as an adult.

Then, you can't just blow off the business side, and act like you don't get it because you're an artist. I speak from miserable experience. You have to read every single word of every single contract. You have to really know what you are getting into. You have to spend some money on attorneys and copyright attorneys. You have to really research the business side of it. You can't just have a great product and hope that it's going to take off.

Even putting your stuff on Etsy or on the Internet—you have to protect yourself. I can tell you that there are people at major companies who do nothing but go on the Internet all day long and look at Etsy and all that stuff. They see what they like, then they either contact that person or get somebody they know to do it. You really have to be smart about the business side of crafting.

For more information about Mary and her work, go to:
www.maryengelbreit.com

The Crafter's Studio

In the great tradition of *Inside the Actor's Studio* and James Lipton:

What craft sound or smell do you love?
The smell of markers in the morning. I think it will eventually kill you.

What craft sound or smell do you hate?
I can't think of any.

What career, other than your own, would you like to try?
I wouldn't want to; I like this one.

When you burn yourself with a glue gun or poke yourself with a sewing needle, what is your favorite exclamation?
You don't want to know! I tend to swear like a sailor!

Words to Craft by:

I started out on a track to become a scientist. I got a B.S. in biology and went to graduate school to pursue a Ph.D. in environmental toxicology. When I nearly completed my Ph.D., I realized that I was being trained to do something I didn't want to do. I thought I would be working to save the environment, but really, I would be hiding away in a lab, working on new chemicals that could be potential drugs. Whoops!

Much to the surprise of my science friends and my family, I left school and started a craft business. I felt that using recycled material in my crafts and selling them was a way to 1) put a tiny dent in the amount of waste that ends up in landfills, and 2) educate and challenge people to think about what they do with their unwanted stuff, where it goes, and how it can still be useful if it stays in circulation. People are amazed at how I transform ugly old polyester pantsuits into durable, pretty, and functional rugs, and old plates into pretty mosaic frames. I love what I do, and I love telling people where my materials come from and what each creation once was.

Name: Emily Kircher

Age: 31

Digs: Madison, WI

Daily Grind: crafter; my business is Emily Kircher Recycling Artist (EKRA)

Fave Crafts: crocheting and mosaics

More Info: www.etchouse.com/ekra

Words to Craft by:

When I was a little girl, I had rheumatic fever and other illnesses. I was on strict bed rest for many months. There was no TV in my room, no radio, and no record player in the house. I read children's books and drew pictures, but in time I became so bored I was depressed. So, my grandmother sat by my bed and taught me to make a little doll quilt.

Then she taught me the only crochet stitch she knew—chain! I chained an entire skein of white yarn, and my grandmother had the patience to hand-stitch the entire chain into a set of little coasters. She knew I had to graduate into full crochet or she would be consumed with sewing endless circles of yarn. She got me a "teach yourself to crochet" book. I mastered that, and wanted more, so someone brought me a "teach yourself to knit" book. Then my mother stepped in and showed me embroidery.

The years confined in my bedroom were passed in the land of books and handcrafts. I eventually recovered, grew up, married, became a mother, and had a successful career in technology. Now, health issues have returned, and I am living a quiet, homebound life. Guess what I found waiting for me in my chair by the fire?

Name: Beth Jinkerson

Age: 55

Digs: Oak Ridge, TN

Daily Grind: former director of information systems for a U.S. Department of Energy contractor, now a fiber and bead artist

Fave Crafts: bead weaving, knitting, crocheting, embroidery, scrapbooking, painting

More Info: www.bethjinkerson.com

chapter thirty

Jay McCarroll

I have a confession. I didn't start watching *Project Runway* until its fifth season. I know, I know, what was I thinking? Fortunately though, my oversight didn't leave me completely clueless. It's true that I may not be able to tell you much else about the early episodes, but I do know all about the first season's winner, Jay McCarroll. You see, word travels fast in the crafty world, so when I heard that he included a bunch of knitwear in one of his collections, I immediatley tried to book an interview for my celebrity column in *Knit.1* magazine. Although that didn't work out, we did get to chat a few years later when Jay so graciously agreed to be part of *Craft Corps*. I talked to him from his New York apartment about fame, fabric, and his love/hate relationship with fashion.

VH

VH: *What's your first craft-related memory?*

JM: You know how they used to print those tins with patchwork fabric—it looked like patchwork calico fabric? My mom had a tin of buttons in the hall closet that I always used to play with. I remember always running my hands through it. She also had a closet full of yarn and fabric; I'd pull it all out and play with it.

VH: *When you say "play with," did you just kind of throw it around, or were you already constructing things in your mind?*

JM: I was dressing myself up in these things. I think I'd wrap myself in neat little dresses to wear around.

VH: *So, your mom was creative, obviously?*

JM: All my sisters were in the high school band, so my mom oversaw the uniforms and was always making flags and stuff. Because of that, there was always lamé,

China silk, and flaggy things around the house. I became a flag twirler for the color guard, so I would make flags and costumes for myself.

VH: *Is there a moment from childhood connected to craft that really stands out for you? Something that you have always carried with you, or that you think influenced your career?*

JM: They're all so intertwined—I can't remember exact ages when things happened, you know: seeing patchwork, seeing Amish quilts, thrift shopping where I'd look at how garments were constructed, different textiles, or amazing Lurex reds from the '50s to '70s. Nothing specific; just all of it.

VH: *Was it your mom who taught you how to sew and read a pattern?*

JM: Oh, yes. I was a fat kid; my waist was bigger than the length of my legs, so we'd shop in the husky department at Sears. She'd have to hem my pants, and eventually she got behind, so I kinda had to learn how to sew. Then I started making clothes, but I never ever used a pattern. I just laid down a shirt, traced its shape, and then made up my own pattern. That method still applies today, because I hate pattern making.

VH: *You still trace around garments?*

JM: No. I mean, I have slopers that I use to trace them, but I hate all that stuff—the technical side of everything. I like technical sewing, but I don't like technical drafting. I'd make a terrible architect.

VH: *Is there a moment since you've become a professional that will always stick with you? And it might just be a moment where you realized, "I kind of kick ass at this." Or, maybe it's when you realized you could make a living this way. Maybe it's just something inspiring that somebody once said to you?*

JM: I remember, maybe in fourth grade, I did a drawing of these three Asian women, and my teacher asked if she could buy it.

VH: *Really?*

JM: Yes, and she had it above her couch in her living room for years. Her housekeeper told me, "You know, I cleaned her house, and she had that painting in her house for fifteen years."

VH: *That's really lovely!*

JM: Anywhere I could draw and get it out of my system, I would. If there was a science fair—I didn't give a sh$t about science—but I drew a whole history of evolution. Anywhere I could draw, I implemented it. I had a gift for it, so I just kind of went with that.

VH: *Did you go to art school?*

JM: I went to Philadelphia College of Textiles and Science, which is now Philadelphia University, for a couple semesters. I was there when everyone was smoking a bunch of pot and you didn't really know who you were. Then I moved to London to study. That's where I got a good grasp on what I wanted to do, because I was being taught by really amazing professionals who were working with designers.

VH: *Were you just incredibly inspired by the fashion in London, or were you working directly with people who were in the industry?*

JM: Oh, no. I was still in school—I took a millinery class, then I took a corset class, and then we had an amazing history class where we'd go to the Victoria and Albert Museum one week and another museum the next. We were taught to see; whereas, in Philadelphia, it was more about technical learning: pattern making, drafting, draping, history of textiles and costumes. It was a great curriculum, but London seemed more hands-on.

My earliest memories of wanting to be a fashion designer were there. I just loved fabric; I think that's really all it ever was—and loving the tchotchke that goes along with making clothes. I love buttons and have millions of them. I love thread. I love adhesive things. I love the iron. I love spray starch. I love fabric. I love color. I love batik. I love all of those things. What got really confusing for me was that I was stuck in the fashion world around bitchy people, and I didn't really love making clothes. I feel like I should've been a textile designer. It's more earthy, and it's definitely more me, so I'm having kind of a mid-life crisis about my career path.

VH: *I was actually going to talk about that later, but let's do it now. You have the freakin' cutest fabric line ever! I actually just ordered some. What types of projects would you personally use your fabrics for?*

JM: I'm so over them; I don't use them. I think I'm going to revisit them in a couple of years, 'cause you get so caught up in the process that you're like, "Ugh." I use other people's fabric. I love Heather Ross's line. I make all sorts of things. Right now, I'm making beaded necklaces where I use her fabric in the background and bead on top of it. I make quilts or bags, or I make appliqué circles and put them on other things.

I've seen so many people make so many things out of my line, though—that's really the most exciting part of it for me. It's so cool that I can draw something on a piece of white paper and send it to a textile designer—her name is Emily Goodwin Wong—then it's on fabric, and then someone's wearing a shirt made out of it. It's so strange to me. I just think it's awesome. I'm really excited about that! We're going to do my prints on T-shirt knits, so people can make baby clothing or anything where you would apply a stretchy fabric.

VH: *I love jersey fabric; I'd live in it, if I could.*

JM: Me too. I'm wearing it right now. So, that's one new thing. After *Project Runway*, I was promised the world; I wanted the world; I didn't get the world, somehow. I

> It's so cool that I can draw something on a piece of white paper and send it to a textile designer, then it's on fabric, and then someone's wearing a shirt made out of it.

don't want to be disappointed anymore, so I focus on one little thing at a time. I'd love to apply my designs to everything, eventually.

VH: *Well, let's talk about* Project Runway *a little bit. As the Season One winner, you're totally the Kelly Clarkson of* Project Runway! *Can you tell me about your path from school, to reality TV star, to bonafide designer?*

JM: Well, I went to school, and then I studied abroad, and then I moved back to the States and finished my degree; actually, I'm three credits short of my college degree, which I think is hilarious.

VH: *You're still three credits short?*

JM: Yes. Even though I teach at the school, they will not give me a degree.

VH: *That is hilarious.*

JM: Very funny, so I just let it go. The other professors don't think it's so entertaining because they have masters, but, oh well. So then I almost finished my degree, and I moved back to London, and then I just made clothes. I applied for jobs at a bunch of places, but no one even got back to me because I was an American, and it's hard to get a job there. So, my mother sent my sewing machine over, and I made clothes and sold them at Camden Market for a couple of months. Then I was over London—I mean, it was gray and depressing, and I wasn't making any money, so I moved to Amsterdam.

Garden Friends by © Jay McCarroll for *Free Spirit*

I lived in an attic, was a performance artist for a couple of months, and then got homesick and moved back to Philadelphia. Actually, someone I met in Amsterdam was friends with Patricia Field in New York, and he brought her some of my stuff. She liked it, so I started selling at Patricia Field in New York. I'd do collections and put lines of clothes together in Philadelphia and show them. Then I'd ship them to New York, and they'd sell them there. After that, I started working in the adult industry; I managed a live sex website.

VH: *Oh, you weren't making the costumes and accoutrements—you were working on the website?*

JM: Oh, God no! Although I've been asked many times, I tried to keep those worlds separate.

VH: *You have your morals after all.*

JM: There were no morals left at the end of that. It was really a crazy experience, but I learned so much about humans, human nature, and the price of a human.

> I love the iron. I love spray starch. I love fabric. I love color. I love batik. I love all of those things.

277

How people are sex addicts, and that people can be bought and sold, was really, really interesting.

VH: *And so you thought, "Hey, I should go back to the fashion industry!"*

JM: Exactly. The industries are very similar, which I thought was funny. I was working so many hours there and making so much money that I stopped making anything. I was living in a beautiful apartment—I had a 1500 square-foot studio with a whole wall of just fabric, and it was the most amazing studio I ever could have asked for. But, I decided I didn't want to work in porn for the rest of my life. My entire family hated it, and I kinda had a nervous breakdown.

I moved home to my parents house at age 27 and set up a studio. I started making stuff and selling it at a little store near my parents' house. Soon after that, I opened a vintage store called Round Two, where I sold my work and other designers' stuff, and housewares and vintage clothes, and then the audition for *Project Runway* came up.

VH: *How did it come up?*

JM: I was involved with an organization called Gen Art that supports young film makers, fashion designers, and photographers. They have a film festival and lots of fashion programs, so I'd done international design contests with them before. They were casting the show, and they sent an e-mail to all of their past designers about it. I knew I would be perfect for this! So, I went to the audition and waited in line for six hours. It was like 95 degrees in New York, and I was in the sun the entire time. I was one of the last people of the day—thousands of people auditioned—and I got a call back. The rest is history.

VH: *I tried booking an interview with you a couple years ago for my celebrity column in Knit.1 magazine, and found out that even though you tend to incorporate knit and crochetwear into your collections, you aren't actually a knitter yourself.*

JM: I'm not. I'm so irritated by that.

VH: *Are you interested in learning at all?*

JM: Oh, I can't do it! I've tried so many times.

VH: *Knitting, crocheting, or both?*

JM: Either. It's terrible.

VH: *That doesn't make sense to me, since you're accomplished at so many other crafty things.*

JM: I'm heinous at it—I can't do it—I can't concentrate.

VH: *Have you tried drinking while you learn? That helps some people.*

JM: No. I can't do it. I tried. I can't do it.

VH: *Next time I'm in New York, I'm coming over with a bottle of wine and some needles. I'm going to teach you. I don't buy it for a second that you can't do it.*

JM: I honestly feel like I can't add it to my repertoire, because I'll get obsessive.

VH: *Well, what is it about knitwear that you dig, because you still incorporate it in your lines?*

JM: My mother's a crocheter, so it's probably because of her. We always had handmade crocheted afghans and things around the house, and I love the comfort of them—the stretchiness and being able to wrap them around your body. You know, so much of our world is knit. I love chunky, yummy knits, but T-shirts, underwear, socks—everything's knit. For me, they're so easy to work with; they're so moldable, and pliable, and forgiving.

VH: *Crafting and fashion have always arguably been influenced by each other. Do you see that as being true in the current trends?*

JM: I just hate fashion.

VH: *Well, that makes sense.*

JM: I hate it! I hate the people. I don't like the emphasis on luxury, sexuality, and women wanting to feel sexy all the time. I hate the outrageousness of pricing and the importance that we place on the length or width of a jean. It's like, oh my God, get a life! I also hate when something really amazing comes through in a trend, and it's something that we've all known about for years. You know, like "Oh, that's crochet," and then it's like, "Crochet's so amazing," and then five seconds later, "Crochet's disgusting."

VH: *So, they influence each other, but fashion would never claim crochet?*

JM: It's so funny, I went to the International Quilt Market this past season to launch my fabric line. It was so fun, and I left after three days not able to believe how welcoming, amazing, awesome, positive, and down-to-earth everybody was—because for the past years, I've been involved with the nastiest, meanest, most negative, bitchy, shallow people. Going through that and now coming back to my roots is what I really love.

VH: *Which is? What you really love is what?*

> I went to the International Quilt Market this past season to launch my fabric line. It was so fun, and I left after three days not able to believe how welcoming, amazing, awesome, positive, and down-to-earth everybody was.

JM: Just really playing with baubles and beads, and textures and fabrics, and colors. Right now I'm doing these little necklaces, and I don't even know what they're going to be. I'll probably put them on my website, but they're decorated with coconut shells, washers, and little seed beads. They're on batik fabric, and I hand stitched the outside and then put them on a knit lanyard. I can think of nothing better.

VH: *To switch gears, the underlying theme of this book is community. What role, if any, has crafting played in your own sense of community? Are you on the Web boards? Do you have some kind of group that you hang out with to be creative?*

JM: No, I stay away from the boards. I think if I were anonymous, I would go on them, but I don't want to give an opinion on anything. I don't want anyone to give me their opinion, so no, I don't do that. I wish I had a craft club. I had a friend that wanted to start one called Craftlete, like athlete. I'm a control freak, though, and a micromanager, so it probably wouldn't work. Just last night, my friend was over and we were watching *American Idol*, and she was like, "Show me how to bead," and I said "No, 'cause you'll steal my ideas, and then you'll get better at it than me." I'm a freak. She got mad because I made fun of what she made. Terrible, isn't it?

VH: *That sounds like all the qualities you said you hated about the fashion industry.*

JM: I know!

VH: *One thing that I haven't touched on as much as I'd like to in this book is charity. You support an organization called Alex's Lemonade Stand. Can you tell me about it, and why you felt it was important to be part of their message?*

JM: This little girl Alex Scott was diagnosed with cancer. She started a lemonade stand and eventually raised millions of dollars from it. Of course, people got involved, but it showed the determination of an eight-year-old, who is going out there and trying to raise money for childhood cancer and how inspiring that is. I love the whole idea of being pro-active about something. The organization's really nice, and they do a lot of really great things.

VH: *As a guy who grew up being creative, how important is it as a voice in the industry to encourage young boys to embrace their creativity?*

JM: Oh my God, I think it's great. It's so unbalanced. I teach at fashion school, and there are no boys in the program. It's strange. It's from years and years and years of societal roles: these are the women cooking food and sewing, and men are, you know, killing things.

VH: *Do you think there's still that bit of social stigma against boys crafting, like there was when we were kids?*

JM: Absolutely. Look on Etsy; there's one guy for every 900 girls! In fashion, there are lots of guys because it's accepted, but male knitters are few and far between.

> I'm a little bit scared about art programs getting cut in elementary school, because that time is such an important time. I mean, home ec class—I don't even know if they have it anymore.

VH: *It's rare, yes. I'm a mom to two boys, so I'm always trying to sing the creative gospel, but what would you tell young guys who still don't know that it's okay to be creative? Do you have any tips?*

JM: Hmmm. I just think people are who they are, and if they have it in them, and it's innate, it's going to come out in one way or another. I'm a little bit scared about art programs getting cut in elementary school, because that time is such an important time. I mean, home ec class—I don't even know if they have it anymore.

VH: *I don't know either. I don't think they do. I guess I'm hoping that these interviews with male designers like yourself will fall into the hands of a teenage boy who wants to be creative, but wasn't given the tools or doesn't know these crafty jobs exist. I don't know about your school, but at the business fairs we had, there were no recruiters for yarn companies or fabric design houses.*

JM: Well, that's why I was confused. Fashion was the closest thing to what I was interested in. I couldn't go to college for the love of fabric.

VH: *But the thing is, you could have. I just don't think the information is getting out there to boys.*

JM: I would agree. Socially, we are in the Dark Ages because of societal roles. Men are supposed to be men. Then you have fathers that don't get the crafty thing, but they're footing the bill for college education, so they're not gonna let kids go for it. Sissy isn't a college major. I don't know—I've never thought about it; I've always just done it.

For more information about Jay McCarroll and his work, go to:
www.jaymccarroll.com

The Crafter's Studio

In the great tradition of *Inside the Actor's Studio* and James Lipton::

What craft sound or smell do you love?
I love the sound of pouring beads out of a plastic bag into a plastic container.

What craft sound or smell do you hate?
When a vinyl that's been stashed away forever gets all sticky. You open it up and it smells cheesy. Like vinyl cheese.

What career, other than designer-world domination, would you like to try?
Geologist.

When you break a sewing needle or spill seed beads all over the floor, what is your favorite exclamation?
Aw, f@ck!

Words to Craft by:

Name: Stefanie Girard

Age: 38

Digs: Burbank, CA

Daily Grind: daily grindal craft designer, writer, and producer

Fave Crafts: crafting with a re-purpose, making new things with old or recycled materials, and upcycling

More Info: sweatersurgery.blogspot.com

I got a degree in industrial design from Pratt Institute. My first job was gluing Fruit Loops for a commercial, and I got hooked on production work. I moved to Hollywood and worked as a TV set decorator and prop master, often called upon to craft strange things such as alien spaceship stick shifts and torches. I also took a belly dancing class that led me to sew outfits, resulting in a belly dancing costume business. I love empowering women with spectacular costumes.

One day I was surfing the Internet, and I came upon a craft design job for a start-up website. I had a spiffy set-dressing portfolio, but my crafts? They were all over the house, but I photographed some of my home dec stuff and went to interview. I've been crafting for that boss ever since! My career took another turn when I interviewed for the HGTV show *Sew Much More*. I got my first production gig because I wrote great directions and knew how to sew, and I kept getting hired for other shows: *Simply Quilts*, *Jewelry Making*, and *Knitty Gritty*. My mother said, "I sent you to college to earn a living knitting and sewing?" She was kidding. Now here I am, author of *Sweater Surgery* and blogger for my publisher.

Words to Craft by:

Name: Michael Seales

Age: 37

Digs: Attleboro, MA (between Boston and Providence)

Daily Grind: rock star hairdresser

Fave Crafts: mostly crocheting and knitting, but I'm one crafty mofo!

My mum taught me needle arts when I was very young, and I've been hooked (no pun intended) ever since. My family has a long line of crafty women, but for me it was natural to be the only crafty lad—you could say my umbilical cord was made of yarn! My mim was a seamstress and crocheter, but it was my mother who proved to be my constant inspiration. I can remember her crocheting, knitting, painting, needlepointing, and sewing my whole life, with me by her side needing to know how it was done.

Now I crochet and knit everything I possibly can: bags, pillows, garments, toys, you name it. I'm sure it looks strange to most people to see a tattooed, bald man with a nose ring knitting in a cafe, but I'm comfortable enough with myself to put it right out there! I'm inspired by nature, animals, color, music, art, architecture, and my wonderfully talented mate, who is a fashion designer and hard-core crafter.

About the Author

Vickie Howell is a mother, designer, writer, and a voice for this generation's craft movement. She hosted the popular TV show *Knitty Gritty* for eight seasons, co-hosted DIY Network's *Stylelicious*, and appeared as the needle arts expert on Lifetime's Web series CRAFTED. Vickie writes a celebrity column for *Knit.1* magazine, a blog column for www.ilovetocreate.com, and is a contributor to publications worldwide. She is the author of several craft books including *Pop Goes Crochet!: 36 Projects Inspired by Icons of Popular Culture* (Lark Books, 2009) and *AwareKnits: Knit & Crochet Projects for the Eco-Conscious Stitcher* (Lark Books, 2009).

Her mission to perpetuate community via craft began in 2001 when she founded the original Los Angeles Stitch 'n Bitch group. Since then, she's continued to gather the crafty masses via collaborations, grass roots social networking, and speaking on national forums. In the fall of 2009, she teamed up with clothier Land's End to act as the spokesperson for their Feel Good Campaign, an effort to rally crafters to knit hats for the homeless with yarn provided by the campaign. Vickie truly believes that our collective creativity is a powerful force with unlimited, humanitarian possibilities. Craft.Rock.Love.

For more information about Vickie and her projects, go to:
www.vickiehowell.com

The Crafter's Studio

In the great tradition of *Inside the Actor's Studio* and James Lipton:

What craft sound or smell do you love?
The sound of metal knitting needles. If clanked together properly, they sound like swords.

What craft sound or smell do you hate?
The smell of wet wool.

What career other than yours would you like to try?
Late-night talk show host.

When you slice yourself with a rotary cutter or miscalculate a knitting chart, what's your favorite exclamation?
When the kids are around, I'm fond of "mother of purl!" When they're not, I go for straight-up "motherf*&^#r."

Crafter Bios

Alex Anderson is an instructor, lecturer, and founding partner of the world's first full-service, interactive online video/Web magazine created just for quilters. She hosted *Simply Quilts* on HGTV and is co-host of *The Quilt Show with Alex Anderson and Ricky Tims*. www.alexandersonquilts. com and www.thequiltshow.com

Christina Batch-Lee is the marketing and content coordinator for www. etsy.com, where she is happy to spread the word about the world's most vibrant handmade marketplace. She's a former art teacher and the founding editor in chief of *Adorn* magazine. www.artobject.etsy.com and www.twitter.com/missbatch

Traci Bautista is creative director and owner of treiC Designs. She is the author of *Collage Unleashed* and has been a regular guest artist on HGTV and DIY Network's *Craft Lab*. www.treicdesigns.com and kollaj.typepad.com

Susan Beal is the author of two publications, *Button It Up* and *Bead Simple*. She co-wrote *Super Crafty* with her craft collective, PDX Super Crafty. She also writes and designs projects for magazines, websites, and her craft blog, westcoastcrafty.com.

Amy Butler is inspired by her surroundings, friends, family, nature, and the rich textures of everyday life. She collects vintage fabrics from flea markets, shops, and her travels to use in her patterns and fabrics that are sold by national and international retailers. www.amybutlerdesign.com

Kathy Cano-Murillo is a writer, artist, and craft product designer who has sold her handmade Chicano Pop Art crafts to hundreds of retailers. She has authored seven books and is the founder of craftychica.com. She has a podcast series on iTunes, a Web series on LifetimeTV.com, and a Crafty Chica product line. www.craftychica.com

Natalie Zee Drieu is the senior editor for CRAFT, one of the largest crafting websites covering the modern craft movement. She has written three best-selling Web design books and one trade business book on broadband technology. Natalie is the founder of coquette.blogs.com.

Carol Duvall began her career in television as a writer, co-producer, and host. She hosted *Here's Carol Duvall*, a craft show that ran for 14 years, appeared as a guest on a variety of programs, and joined *The Home Show* as their craft expert in 1988. She also hosted *The Carol Duvall Show*, which ran for over 12 years on HGTV. www.diynetwork.com/carol-duvall-bio

Mary Engelbreit is known for her distinctive illustration style. Companies have licensed her artwork on calendars, T-shirts, mugs, gift books, and a list that's grown to 6,500 products, with more than one billion dollars in lifetime retail sales. Mary was also editor in chief of *Mary Engelbreit's Home Companion*. www.maryengelbreit.com.

Cathie Filian is an Emmy-nominated television host, book author, columnist, lifestyle expert, and designer. She created, produced, and co-hosted the HGTV and DIY lifestyle shows *Creative Juice* and *Witch Crafts*. www.cathiefilian.com

Jessica Marshall Forbes is a knitter who's been blogging since 2004. In 2007, she and her husband founded the knitting and crochet community, Ravelry. The site brings together people from around the world to share their projects, ideas, and inspiration. It has grown to over 465,000 users and 3.75 million page views per day. www.ravelry.com

Sandi Genovese brings innovation to new heights with scrapbooking and paper crafting. She hosted the DIY show *Scrapbooking*, appears on numerous television shows, and is author of multiple how-to books and DVDs. She has licensed collections with Mrs. Grossman's, C.R. Gibson, Imagine That Designs, and more. www.sandigenovese.com

Jackie Guerra is an Emmy Award-winning actress, author, and designer, who was the first Latina to star in a network sitcom, *First Time Out*. She was a DIY Network host, has produced and hosted hours of talk radio, and authored *Under Construction: How I've Gained and Lost Millions of Dollars and Hundreds of Pounds*. www.jackieguerra.com

Jenny Hart is the founder of Sublime Stitching. She introduced embroidery patterns with pinups, tattoos, and robots, and sparked a revolution in embroidery. She is an internationally published artist, illustrator, and author of multiple titles. www.sublimestitching.com and www.jennyhart.net

Claudine Hellmuth creates whimsical, retro collages called Poppets®. Her artwork has been featured on *The Martha Stewart Show*, in *The New York Times*, and on numerous television programs. She developed a product line with Ranger Ink, teaches collage workshops, and has published three books and DVDs. www.collageartist.com

Garth Johnson was born and raised on a farm in Nebraska, attended art school at the University of Nebraska, then got his M.F.A. in ceramics at Alfred University. He is a designer at Perkins+Will in Atlanta, and is an adjunct faculty member at Columbus State University. extremecraft.typepad.com

Leah Kramer is a computer programmer and crafter who founded the online community, www.craftster.org. She wrote *The Craftster Guide to Nifty, Thrifty and Kitschy Crafts* and plays a large role in the Boston craft scene. She was an owner of the store Magpie and organized the Boston Bazaar Bizarre craft fair for seven years. www.craftster.org

Faythe Levine is an artist, curator, author, and filmmaker. She is director and producer of the documentary film *Handmade Nation*, as well as co-author of a companion book of the same title. She co-owned Paper Boat Boutique & Gallery and produces the indie market Art vs. Craft. indiecraftdocumentary.blogspot.com

Jay McCarroll studied fashion design at the former Philadelphia College of Textiles and Science and the London College of Fashion. He owned a vintage shop before auditioning for the show *Project Runway* and winning the first season. He is on the advisory board for the fashion design department at Philadelphia University. www.jaymccarroll.com

Mark Montano earned an M.F.A. in costume history from the Fashion Institute of Technology and immediately began working with Oscar de la Renta. He started a fashion collection and showed during New York Fashion Week until 2004. He was a designer on TLC's *While You Were Out*, and has hosted several television programs. He is currently working on the third installment of *The Big-Ass Book of Crafts*. www.markmontano.com

Travis Nichols is an artist, writer, illustrator, and cartoonist. His comics have appeared in *Nickelodeon Magazine*, *Herbivore* magazine, various anthologies, and over a dozen self-published comic books. Travis was chosen as one of the "25 most fascinating vegetarians" by *VegNews* magazine in 2007. www.ilikeapplejuice.com

Shannon Okey has written numerous books on knitting, spinning, and felting. She was editor of *Yarn Forward* magazine, and has contributed to publications including *CRAFT*, *Spin Off*, and *Yarn Market News*. She runs a fiber arts learning space called Knitgrrl Studio, coordinates Cleveland, Ohio's Bazaar Bizarre, and founded Stitch Cooperative. knitgrrl.com and knitgrrlstudio.com

Jennifer Perkins combines pop culture and vintage goodies to create sassy jewelry. She has been featured in *Lucky Magazine*, *The Wall Street Journal*, and *The New York Times*, and has hosted multiple shows on the DIY Network. She is a founding member of the Austin Craft Mafia and author of *The Naughty Secretary Club: The Working Girl's Guide to Handmade Jewelry*. www.naughtysecretaryclub.com

Margot Potter is a designer, writer, public speaker, actor, vocalist, and host who creates innovative designs for major manufacturers and magazines. She has written six books and is a Ranger Ink instructor, an I Love to Create blogger, and an ambassador for Create Your Style with CRYSTALLIZED™-Swarovski Elements. www.margotpotter.com

Ed Roth founded Stencil1. He worked as senior designer for NBC's *Homicide: Life on the Street* website, for which he received an id Design Award, and he launched a Web and motion graphics design company called designTechnicians. Ed is currently developing new products for Stencil1, and is author of *Stencil 101* and *Stencil 101 Decor*. www.stencil1.com

Diana Rupp worked as a stylist and fashion editor before pursuing her passion—making stuff. In 2002, her Make Workshop craft school was born. Dubbed "the youthful doyenne" of needlework by *The New York Times*, Diana teaches, dreams of workshops, and writes books such as *Sew Everything Workshop*. www.makeworkshop.com

Wendy Russell is known as the host of HGTV's *She's Crafty*. She juggles styling, staging, and organizing homes and people. As a DIY expert, she has appeared on the television hit *Cityline* and has been a guest on numerous other shows. She has appeared in over 30 commercials, as well as in films and television series, including the Academy Award-winning film *Juno*. www.wendyrussell.com

Jenny Ryan is the creator of SewDarnCute, and has had her work featured in *BUST*, *knit.1*, and *Crochet Today* magazines. She has appeared on the needlecrafts show *Uncommon Threads*, as well as on KNBC's *Your LA* morning show. Jenny organizes the craft fair Felt Club and writes for *CRAFT*. Her book is called *SewDarnCute: 30 Sweet & Simple Projects to Sew & Embellish*. sewdarncute.typepad.com

Denyse Schmidt is firmly rooted in the techniques of American quilt making. Denyse reinterprets tradition to make modern, functional quilts that are fresh, lively, and offbeat. She authored *Denyse Schmidt Quilts: 30 Colorful Quilt and Patchwork Projects*, designed several fabric collections with FreeSpirit Fabrics, and teaches a series of improvisational patchwork piecing workshops. www.dsquilts.com

Amanda Soule is an author, crafter, and photographer who inspires her audience to find the simple beauty that exists all around them. Amanda is author of *The Creative Family: How to Encourage Imagination and Nurture Family Connections* and *Handmade Home: Simple Ways to Repurpose Old Materials Into New Family Treasures*. She writes daily on her craft blog, soulemama.typepad.com

Community Resources

Networking, Commerce & Inspiration

About.com: www.about.com
Great resource for craft information

Artfire: www.artfire.com
Online marketplace of handmade goods

Buy Olympia: www.buyolympia.com
Indie craft retailer

CRAFT: www.craftzine.com
Online craft magazine offering daily project ideas galore

Craft Corps: www.craftcorps.org
Community hub for crafters and their stories

Craft Mafia: www.craftmafia.com
Worldwide craft collective

Craftster: www.craftster.org
Crafty boards and networking site

Craft Stylish: www.craftstylish.com
Crafty inspiration hub and blog

Etsy: www.etsy.com
Online market for buying and selling crafty wares

Facebook: www.facebook.com
Social networking site

Flickr: www.flickr.com
Photo housing and community discussion website

Get Crafty: www.getcrafty.com
Crafty boards, articles, and inspiration

I Love to Create: www.ilovetocreate.com
Inspiration and community website

Knitty: www.knitty.com
Online knitting magazine

Meetup: www.meetup.com
Community resource for starting or joining a group

MySpace: www.myspace.com
Social networking site

Ravelry: www.ravelry.com
Needle arts networking site

Supernaturale: www.supernaturale.com
Do-it-yourself culture site

Twitter: www.twitter.com
Microblogging and communications site

Yahoo! Groups: groups.yahoo.com
Group communication boards

YouTube: www.youtube.com
Site to watch and upload craft-related videos

Conventions & Fairs

About: www.about.com
Photo, written, and video tutorials for pretty much any crafty topic out there

Bust Craftacular: www.bust.com/craftacular
Bust magazine's annual craft show based in Brooklyn, New York

CHA: www.craftsandhobbies.org
Industry trade and consumer show

Felt Club: www.feltclub.com
An annual Los Angeles, California, craft festival founded by Jenny Ryan (see page 234)

ICE: www.ice-atlanta.com
Indie craft experience and shopping spectacular in Atlanta, Georgia

Maker Faire: www.makerfaire.com
Techie and creative fair focused on inventions and unique uses for craft

Renegade Craft Fair: www.renegadecraft.com
Indie fair held in cities throughout the U.S.,with hundreds of exhibitors

The Switchboards: www.theswitchboards.com
A place for creative, independent business owners to talk shop

Trunkt: www.trunkt.org
Liaison for artisans and global buyers

Book Club Questions

Here are some topics to discuss at your next book or craft club meeting. Enjoy the read!

1. What's your first craft-related memory?

2. In her chapter, Kathy Cano-Murillo mentions how she was affected as a child by a teacher's lack of recognition of her artwork. What responsibility do you think that educators have to encourage children's creative attempts? With arts programs being cancelled in schools, does that increase our duty as adults to expose children to crafting (and other creative mediums) as a means of self-expression?

3. Filmmaker Fayeth Levine shares that she never went to college—jumping right on to her creative path after high school—whereas potter Garth Johnson mentions his master's degree in ceramics. What is it about art and/or craft as a profession that allows for such a huge variance in education levels? Discuss the creative roots of the members of your group. Are your crafty common threads based on educational background, profession, specific craft, or other personal experiences?

4. What role has crafting played in your own sense of community?

5. There's a common tag line associated with the "modern" crafting movement touting, "This is not your grandma's craft." Ironically, however, the interviews with younger craft leaders like Cathie Filian and Traci Bautista reveal that many of our creative paths were actually influenced greatly by our grandmothers. Discuss the reason for the disassociation with that generation of crafters. What relationship, if any, do you feel it has to do with how little value society places on what was formerly seen as "women's work"?

6. Which designers' stories could you most relate to? Which were you most inspired by?

7. What can we as individuals do to help elevate the value of craft?

8. Discuss how the increasing exposure of male crafters, such as Ed Roth and Mark Montano, is changing societal and/or gender stereotypes. Will crafting ever fully shake its stigma as a hobby and/or profession primarily for women?

9. Both in and out of the community, there's a big debate between the words "art" and "craft." In your opinion, what's the difference between being an artist and being a crafter?

10. What does crafting mean to you, or what has it given you?

11. Inside Your Crafter's Studio:

What craft sound or smell do you love?

What craft sound or smell do you hate?

What career other than your own would you like to try?

When craftastrophe occurs, what is your favorite exclamation?

Acknowledgments

First and foremost, I'd like to extend gobs of appreciation to the professional crafters who took time out of their extremely busy schedules to be a part of this project. You, along with the wonderful everyday crafters who so graciously submitted their profiles, made writing this book a wonderful experience. Thank you for constantly inspiring me—I'm humbled and honored to have you in *Craft Corps*.

I'd also like to thank Carol Taylor for coming up with the name of the book after hearing about my inspiration for it; Marcus Leaver for always making me feel like I'm not just another author; Paige Gilchrist for her infectious positivity and unwavering support; Valerie Shrader for being both an invaluable editor and crafty confidant; Gavin Young for her tireless crafter wrangling and text editing—I literally could not have finished this book without her; Kristi Pfeffer for lending her mad art skillz; Meaghan Finnerty for making this project a publicity priority; Jenny Medford for creating the M*A*S*H-inspired Craft Corps website; the transcribers (Noelle, Stephanie, Dawn, Erin, Janessa, and Sheila) who stepped in and helped me out for a pittance when I was under the deadline gun—I really appreciate it! Thanks also to all of my Facebook, Ravelry, and Twitter pals who've kept up with me every step of the way.

Finally, thank you to my own community of friends, both crafty and not. It really does take a village! I especially could not live la vida crafty without the support of my wonderful husband, Dave Campbell; my kiddos, Tanner, Tristan, and (my newest muse) baby Clover; my mom, Libby Bailey; my best friend, Tammy Izbicki; and my online knitting group, the MEOWers. I love you all very much!

Index